HEINEMANN MATHEMATICS 6

Textbook

These are the different types of pages and symbo... this book and associated workbook.

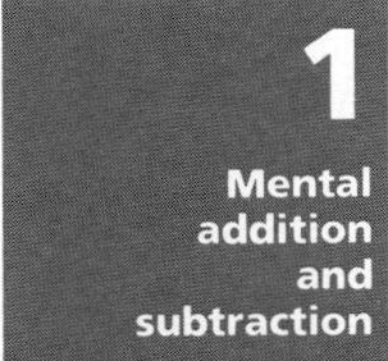

Most textbook and workbook pages are of this type. They deal with mathematical concepts, skills and applications in number, measure, shape and handling data.

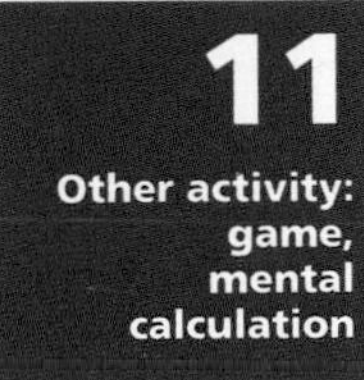

These pages provide self-contained activities which need not necessarily be tackled in the order in which they are presented. They are intended to give further opportunities for children to apply the mathematics they have learned or to extend their experience.

Problem solving

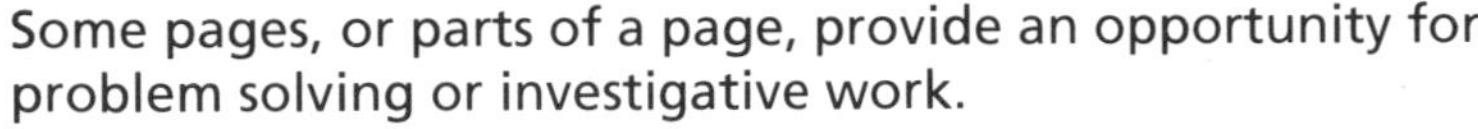

Some pages, or parts of a page, provide an opportunity for problem solving or investigative work.

Where a calculator would be useful this is indicated by a calculator symbol.

This symbol indicates that more work of this kind can be found on the numbered Reinforcement Sheet.

The work on this page is supported by the numbered Home Link-up activity.

Heinemann Educational,
a division of Heinemann Publishers (Oxford) Ltd,
Halley Court, Jordan Hill, Oxford OX2 8EJ

First Published 1995 ISBN 0 435 02226 1

Designed by Miller, Craig and Cocking
Produced by Oxprint
Printed in Spain by Edelvives, Zaragoza

99
10 9 8 7 6 5

Contents

** Homework activities for these pages are provided in Home Link-up.*

Measure

Measure		Textbook	Workbook	Reinf't Sheets	Extension Textbook
Length	Metres and cm, addition, subtraction, perimeter	69, 70*	17	22	
	Scale: finding true lengths	71, 72*			E17
	The kilometre, addition, subtraction	73, 74			
Weight	Kilograms and grams, addition, subtraction	75			
	Reading scales, to the nearest mark	76, 77*	24*	23	
	Multiplication, practical work	78			
Area	Irregular shapes		25		
	Rectangles	79	26		
	Composite shapes	80*	27*	24	E18
Volume	Millilitres, reading scales, to the nearest mark	81, 82*	28*	25	
	Cuboids, cm^3, 1 litre = 1000 cm^3	83, 84			E19
Measure	Imperial units: inches, feet, pounds, pints				E20, 21
Time	12-hour clock: am/pm, durations	85-8*		26, 27	
	24-hour clock: notation, durations	89, 90*	29*	28	E22, 23
	The second	91	30		
Other activities			92, 93		

Shape

Shape		Textbook	Workbook	Reinf't Sheets	Extension Textbook
Co-ordinates	Locating and plotting points, line symmetry	94*	31, 32*		E24
2D shape	Four-sided shapes, line symmetry, diagonals	95, 96*	18, 20		
	Equilateral triangle, isosceles triangle	97	20		
	Drawing shapes on co-ordinate grids		33	29	
	Congruent shapes, tangram, tiling	98*	18		E26
	Drawing circles using compasses, diameter	99, 100			
	Rotational symmetry	101, 102*			
3D shape	Cubes and cuboids: nets	104			
	Triangular prisms: nets, skeleton models	105			
	Pyramids: nets, skeleton models	106			
Angles	Degrees, turning, compass directions	108			
	Measuring in degrees, acute, right, obtuse angles	109, 110*	22	30	
Other activities		103, 107			E1, 12, 25, 27, 30

Handling data

Handling data		Textbook	Workbook	Reinf't Sheets	Extension Textbook
Handling data	Bar graphs, pictograms	111	34		
	Bar-line graphs and trend graphs	112–14*			
	Grouped tallies, mode, median, mean	115–17*			
	Class intervals	118	35, 36		
	Interpretation of data, database and tables	119–21			E28, 29
	Surveys	122*			
Probability	Likelihood, evens, listing outcomes	123–5*			
Record of Work grids			37–9		

1 Shipwrecked!

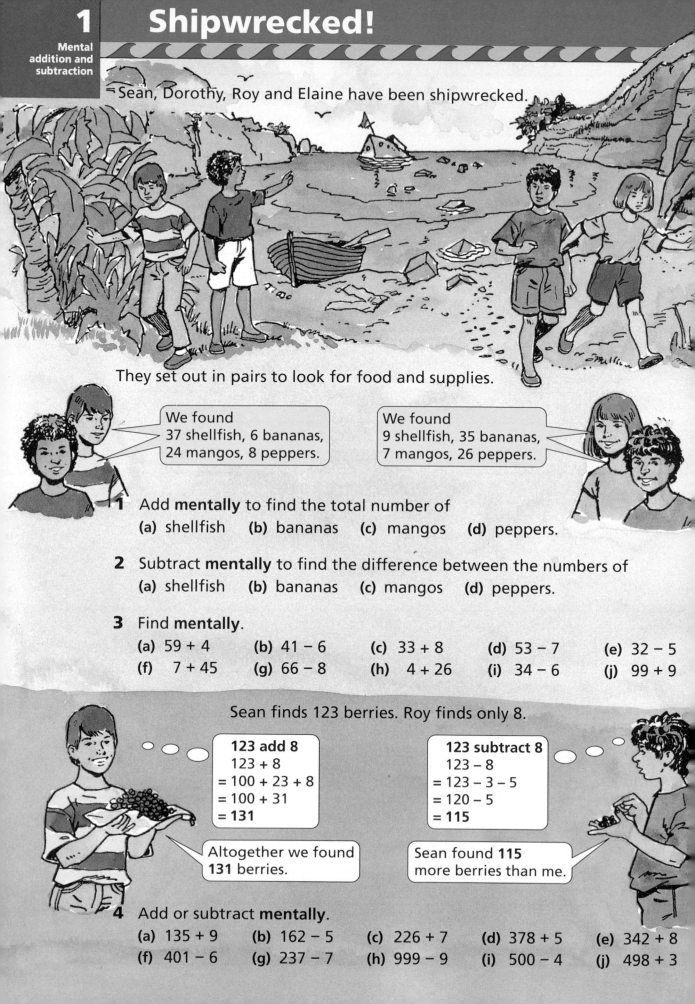

Mental addition and subtraction

Sean, Dorothy, Roy and Elaine have been shipwrecked.

They set out in pairs to look for food and supplies.

We found
37 shellfish, 6 bananas,
24 mangos, 8 peppers.

We found
9 shellfish, 35 bananas,
7 mangos, 26 peppers.

1 Add **mentally** to find the total number of
(a) shellfish **(b)** bananas **(c)** mangos **(d)** peppers.

2 Subtract **mentally** to find the difference between the numbers of
(a) shellfish **(b)** bananas **(c)** mangos **(d)** peppers.

3 Find **mentally**.

(a) 59 + 4 **(b)** 41 − 6 **(c)** 33 + 8 **(d)** 53 − 7 **(e)** 32 − 5
(f) 7 + 45 **(g)** 66 − 8 **(h)** 4 + 26 **(i)** 34 − 6 **(j)** 99 + 9

Sean finds 123 berries. Roy finds only 8.

123 add 8
123 + 8
= 100 + 23 + 8
= 100 + 31
= **131**

Altogether we found **131** berries.

123 subtract 8
123 − 8
= 123 − 3 − 5
= 120 − 5
= **115**

Sean found **115** more berries than me.

4 Add or subtract **mentally**.

(a) 135 + 9 **(b)** 162 − 5 **(c)** 226 + 7 **(d)** 378 + 5 **(e)** 342 + 8
(f) 401 − 6 **(g)** 237 − 7 **(h)** 999 − 9 **(i)** 500 − 4 **(j)** 498 + 3

Beachcombing 2

Mental addition and subtraction

Roy finds 35 flares.
Elaine finds 23.

35 add 23
Add the tens ⟶ 30 + 20 = 50
Add the units ⟶ 5 + 3 = 8
50 + 8 = **58**

Altogether we collected **58** flares.

1 Add **mentally**.

(a) 18 + 31 (b) 42 + 57 (c) 43 + 24 (d) 71 + 16 (e) 33 + 46
(f) 50 + 27 (g) 35 + 12 (h) 66 + 33 (i) 34 + 26 (j) 55 + 45

35 subtract 23
Subtract the tens ⟶ 30 − 20 = 10
Subtract the units ⟶ 5 − 3 = 2
10 + 2 = **12**

Roy found **12** flares more than me.

2 Subtract **mentally**.

(a) 48 − 22 (b) 57 − 34 (c) 96 − 25 (d) 62 − 51 (e) 79 − 42
(f) 84 − 43 (g) 38 − 18 (h) 49 − 16 (i) 85 − 71 (j) 99 − 44

Elaine finds 46 items of clothing.
Roy finds 30.

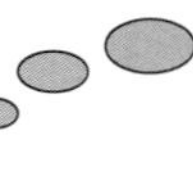

46 add 30
Add the tens.
46 + 30 = **76**

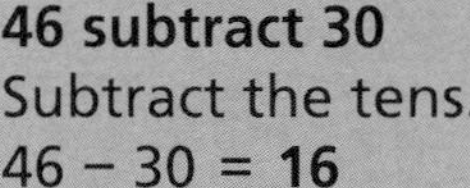
46 subtract 30
Subtract the tens.
46 − 30 = **16**

Altogether we found **76** items of clothing.

Elaine found **16** items more than me.

3 Add or subtract **mentally**.

(a) 28 + 20 (b) 37 + 40 (c) 52 − 30 (d) 19 + 30 (e) 41 − 20
(f) 34 + 30 (g) 66 − 50 (h) 85 − 40 (i) 23 + 50 (j) 87 − 60
(k) 68 + 30 (l) 59 + 40 (m) 99 − 80 (n) 14 + 40 (o) 32 + 50
(p) 25 + 60 (q) 84 − 20 (r) 76 − 70 (s) 13 + 80 (t) 30 + 70

Go to Workbook page 1.

The *Nemo*

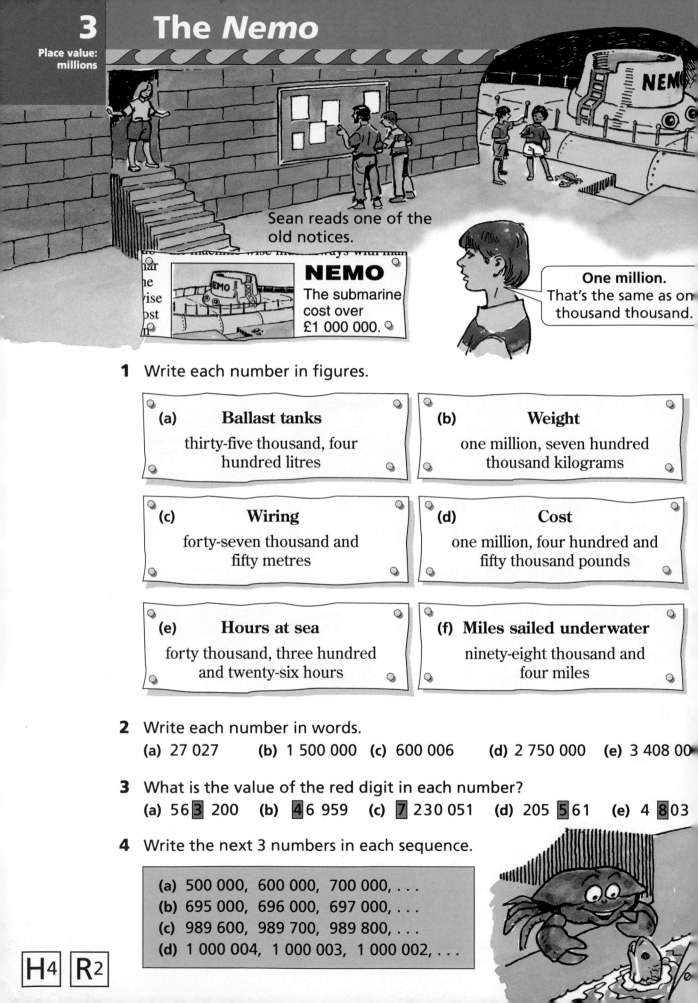

Sean reads one of the old notices.

NEMO
The submarine cost over £1 000 000.

One million.
That's the same as on
thousand thousand.

1 Write each number in figures.

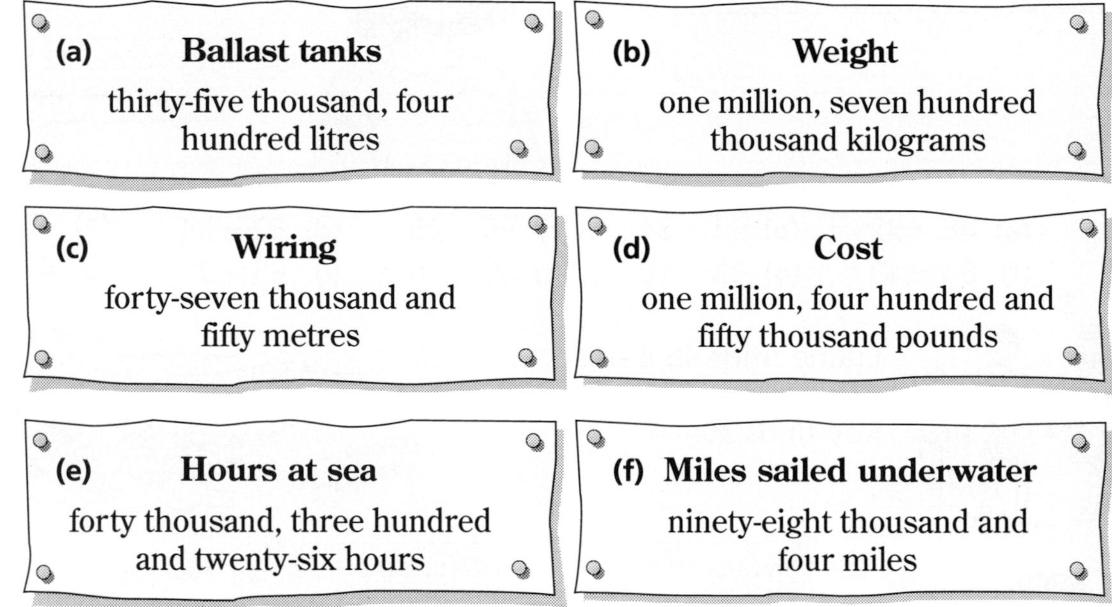

(a) **Ballast tanks**
thirty-five thousand, four hundred litres

(b) **Weight**
one million, seven hundred thousand kilograms

(c) **Wiring**
forty-seven thousand and fifty metres

(d) **Cost**
one million, four hundred and fifty thousand pounds

(e) **Hours at sea**
forty thousand, three hundred and twenty-six hours

(f) **Miles sailed underwater**
ninety-eight thousand and four miles

2 Write each number in words.
(a) 27 027 (b) 1 500 000 (c) 600 006 (d) 2 750 000 (e) 3 408 00

3 What is the value of the red digit in each number?
(a) 563 200 (b) 46 959 (c) 7 230 051 (d) 205 561 (e) 4 803

4 Write the next 3 numbers in each sequence.

(a) 500 000, 600 000, 700 000, . . .
(b) 695 000, 696 000, 697 000, . . .
(c) 989 600, 989 700, 989 800, . . .
(d) 1 000 004, 1 000 003, 1 000 002, . . .

Fish rescue

Please rescue us. This water is polluted.

1 Find the total number of each type of fish.

		In the Bay	In the Cavern
(a)	Jets	6371	2748
(b)	Gliders	6342	5196
(c)	Goldies	8256	3987
(d)	Zens	9384	6429

2 How many more of each type of fish are in the Bay than in the Cavern?

3 Copy and complete.

(a) 4732 − 2564 (b) 5284 − 2607 (c) 3116 − 2839 (d) 7306 − 6817 (e) 5041 − 1073

(f) 3620 − 2386 (g) 7300 − 5684 (h) 5008 − 3679 (i) 4000 − 1678 (j) 7000 − 3402

4 Find the number of crabs at each place.

(a) Bay: 2642 + 307 + 28

(b) Cavern: 4135 + 268 + 896 + 6041

(c) Reef: 5 + 343 + 1065 + 28

Problem solving

5 Altogether there are 6000 fish. Half of them are white. The rest are red or purple. There are 800 more red fish than purple fish. How many of each colour of fish are there?

5 Filling the tanks

Addition and subtraction of ThHTU

Dorothy has to fit all the *Bay* fish into these tanks.
Each tank shows the number of fish it can hold.

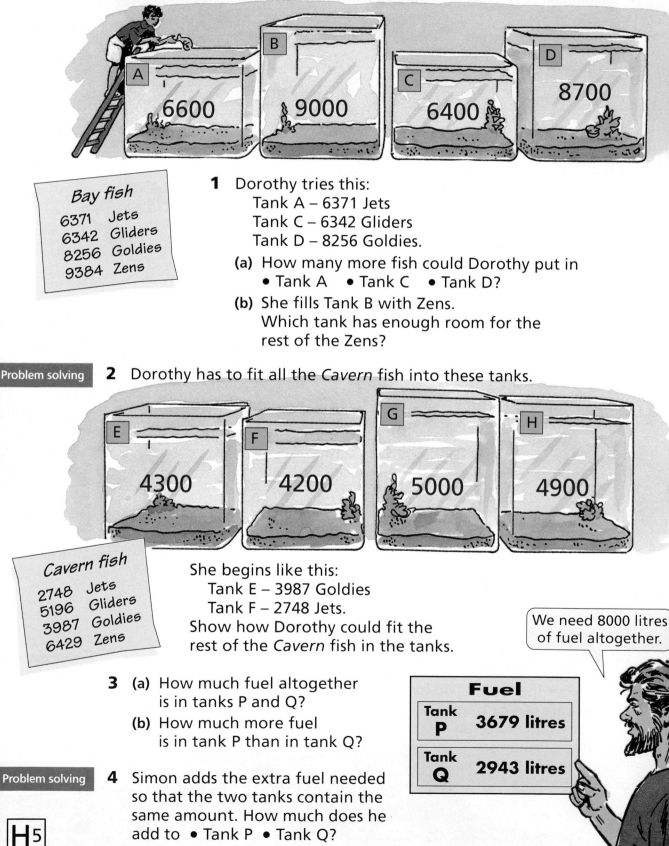

Bay fish
6371 Jets
6342 Gliders
8256 Goldies
9384 Zens

1 Dorothy tries this:
Tank A – 6371 Jets
Tank C – 6342 Gliders
Tank D – 8256 Goldies.

(a) How many more fish could Dorothy put in
• Tank A • Tank C • Tank D?

(b) She fills Tank B with Zens.
Which tank has enough room for the rest of the Zens?

Problem solving

2 Dorothy has to fit all the *Cavern* fish into these tanks.

Cavern fish
2748 Jets
5196 Gliders
3987 Goldies
6429 Zens

She begins like this:
Tank E – 3987 Goldies
Tank F – 2748 Jets.
Show how Dorothy could fit the rest of the *Cavern* fish in the tanks.

We need 8000 litres of fuel altogether.

Fuel	
Tank P	**3679 litres**
Tank Q	**2943 litres**

3 **(a)** How much fuel altogether is in tanks P and Q?

(b) How much more fuel is in tank P than in tank Q?

Problem solving

4 Simon adds the extra fuel needed so that the two tanks contain the same amount. How much does he add to • Tank P • Tank Q?

Mini-sub 6

Place value: rounding to the nearest 100, 10

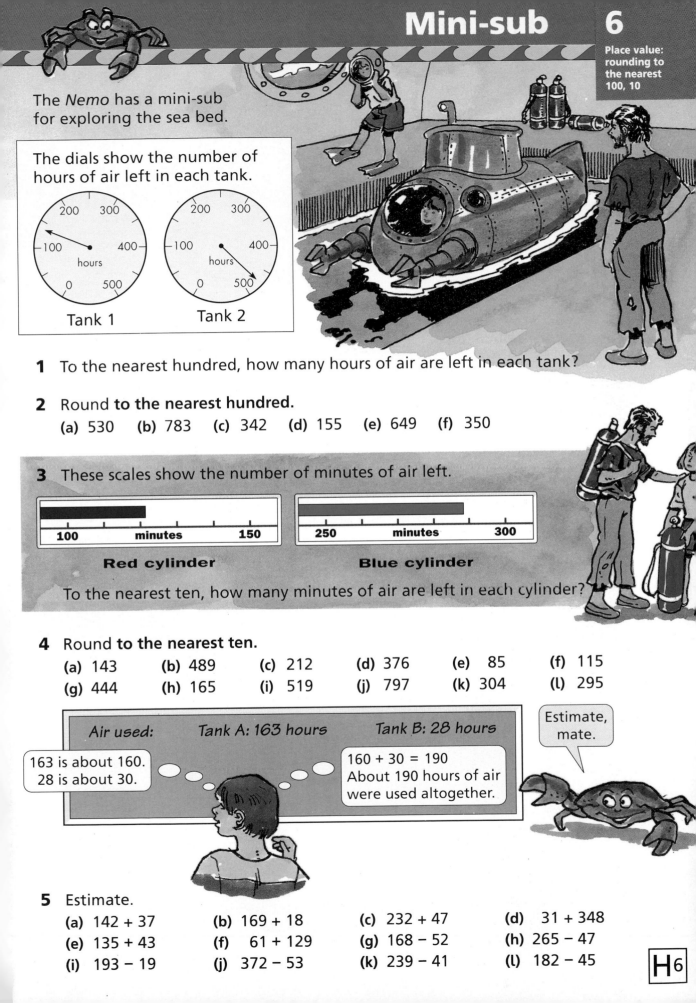

The *Nemo* has a mini-sub for exploring the sea bed.

The dials show the number of hours of air left in each tank.

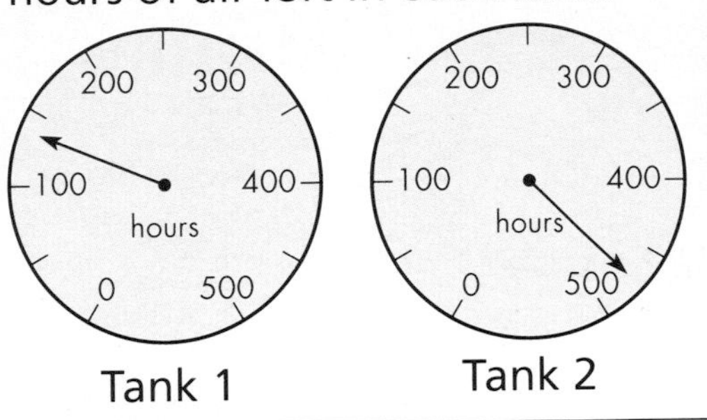

1 To the nearest hundred, how many hours of air are left in each tank?

2 Round **to the nearest hundred.**

(a) 530 **(b)** 783 **(c)** 342 **(d)** 155 **(e)** 649 **(f)** 350

3 These scales show the number of minutes of air left.

Red cylinder

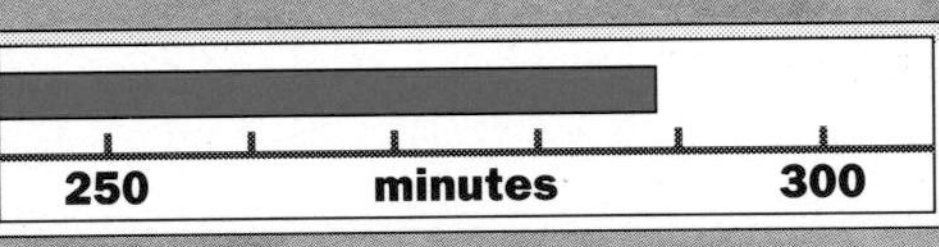

Blue cylinder

To the nearest ten, how many minutes of air are left in each cylinder?

4 Round **to the nearest ten.**

(a) 143 **(b)** 489 **(c)** 212 **(d)** 376 **(e)** 85 **(f)** 115
(g) 444 **(h)** 165 **(i)** 519 **(j)** 797 **(k)** 304 **(l)** 295

Air used: *Tank A: 163 hours* *Tank B: 28 hours*

163 is about 160.
28 is about 30.

160 + 30 = 190
About 190 hours of air were used altogether.

Estimate, mate.

5 Estimate.

(a) 142 + 37 **(b)** 169 + 18 **(c)** 232 + 47 **(d)** 31 + 348
(e) 135 + 43 **(f)** 61 + 129 **(g)** 168 − 52 **(h)** 265 − 47
(i) 193 − 19 **(j)** 372 − 53 **(k)** 239 − 41 **(l)** 182 − 45

The golden galleon

+, – of HTU: estimation

Simon and Elaine explore the store rooms of an old galleon.

There are 237 bottles in the first store and 486 bottles in the second store.

237 is about 200. 486 is about 500. Altogether there are **about 700** bottles.

1 In the same way find

(a) 215 + 370 **(b)** 125 + 283 **(c)** 492 + 317
(d) 392 + 130 **(e)** 176 + 319 **(f)** 521 + 106
(g) 265 + 692 **(h)** 450 + 177 **(i)** 124 + 850

There are 209 goblets in the first store and 776 goblets in the second.

776 is about 800. 209 is about 200. There are **about 600** more goblets in the second store.

2 In the same way find

(a) 842 – 325 **(b)** 793 – 587 **(c)** 609 – 192
(d) 715 – 483 **(e)** 941 – 138 **(f)** 555 – 269
(g) 750 – 215 **(h)** 643 – 250 **(i)** 950 – 707

3 There are **about 200** more hooks in one of these boxes than in another.

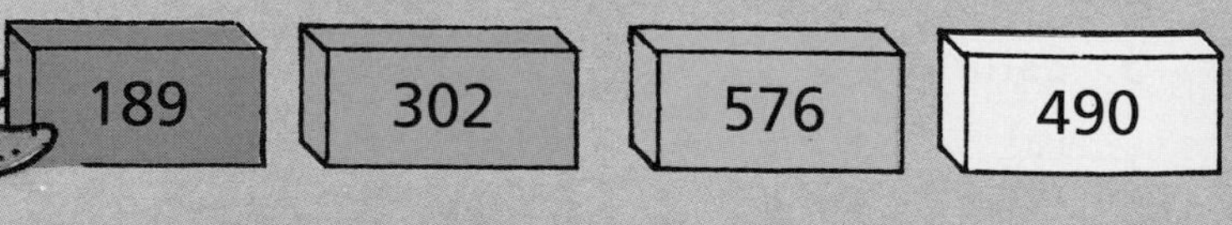
189
302
576
490

Which two boxes is Nipper talking about?

The treasure cabin

8

Place value: rounding to the nearest 1000, 100

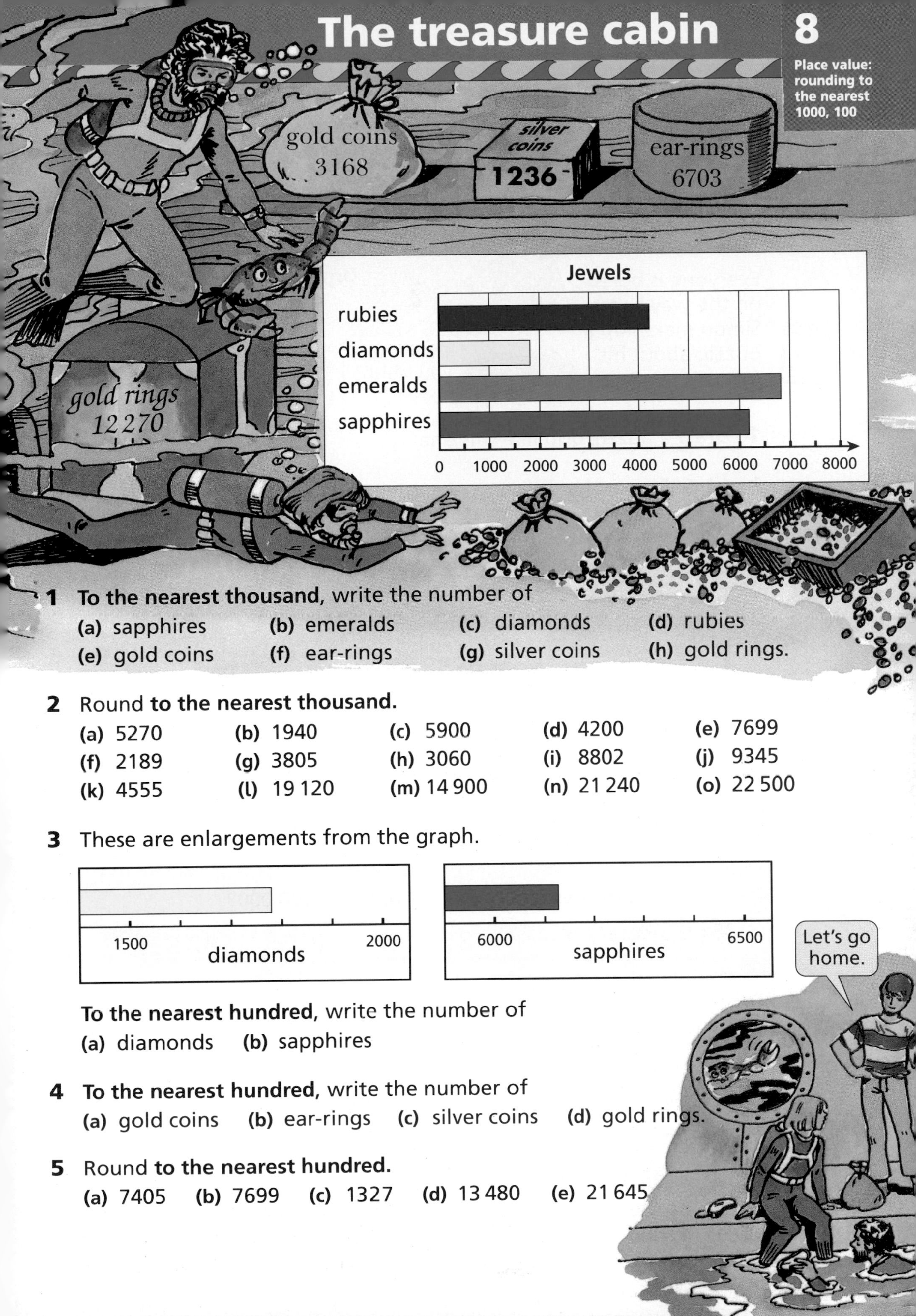

1 **To the nearest thousand**, write the number of

(a) sapphires (b) emeralds (c) diamonds (d) rubies
(e) gold coins (f) ear-rings (g) silver coins (h) gold rings.

2 Round **to the nearest thousand.**

(a) 5270 (b) 1940 (c) 5900 (d) 4200 (e) 7699
(f) 2189 (g) 3805 (h) 3060 (i) 8802 (j) 9345
(k) 4555 (l) 19 120 (m) 14 900 (n) 21 240 (o) 22 500

3 These are enlargements from the graph.

To the nearest hundred, write the number of

(a) diamonds (b) sapphires

4 **To the nearest hundred**, write the number of

(a) gold coins (b) ear-rings (c) silver coins (d) gold rings.

5 Round **to the nearest hundred.**

(a) 7405 (b) 7699 (c) 1327 (d) 13 480 (e) 21 645

9

Calculator: place value, + and –

NEMO

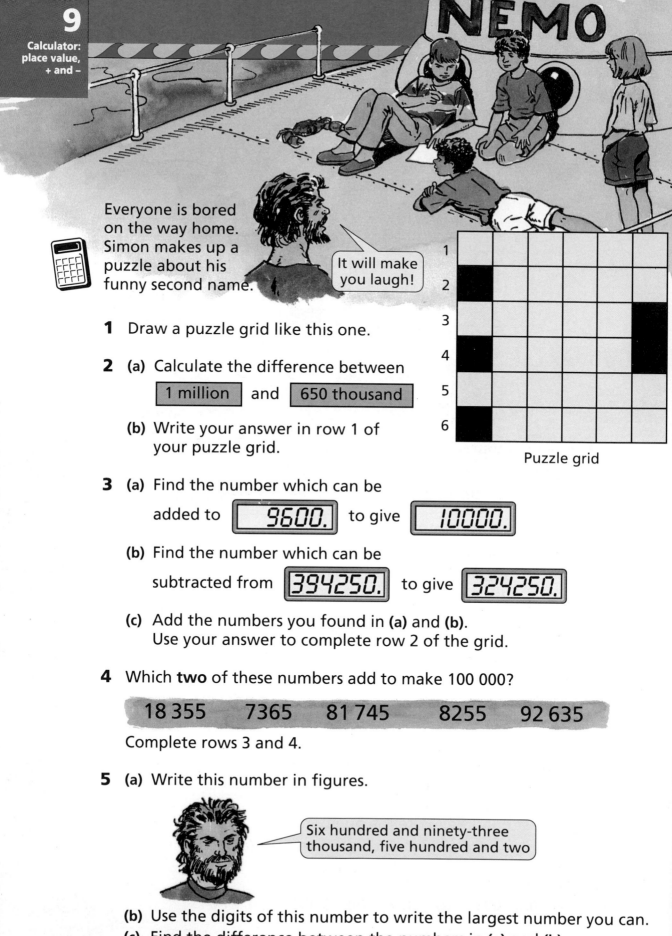

Everyone is bored on the way home. Simon makes up a puzzle about his funny second name.

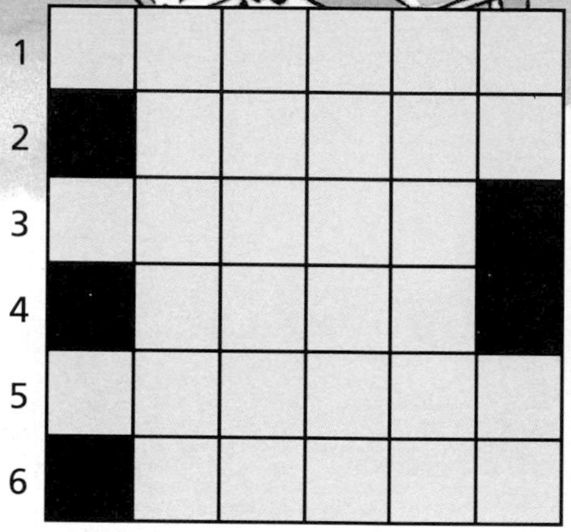

It will make you laugh!

1						
2						
3						
4						
5						
6						

Puzzle grid

1 Draw a puzzle grid like this one.

2 **(a)** Calculate the difference between

1 million and 650 thousand

(b) Write your answer in row 1 of your puzzle grid.

3 **(a)** Find the number which can be added to 9600. to give 10000.

(b) Find the number which can be subtracted from 394250. to give 324250.

(c) Add the numbers you found in **(a)** and **(b)**. Use your answer to complete row 2 of the grid.

4 Which **two** of these numbers add to make 100 000?

18 355   7365   81 745   8255   92 635

Complete rows 3 and 4.

5 **(a)** Write this number in figures.

Six hundred and ninety-three thousand, five hundred and two

(b) Use the digits of this number to write the largest number you can.

(c) Find the difference between the numbers in **(a)** and **(b)**. Write your answer in row 5.

6 Start with 126. . Keep adding on **50**.

Which **one** of these numbers should appear at some time in the display?

9216. 10676. 12600. 11756.

Write this number in row 6 of your grid.

7 Enter the digits from these squares in your calculator.
Turn the display upside down.
What is Simon's second name?

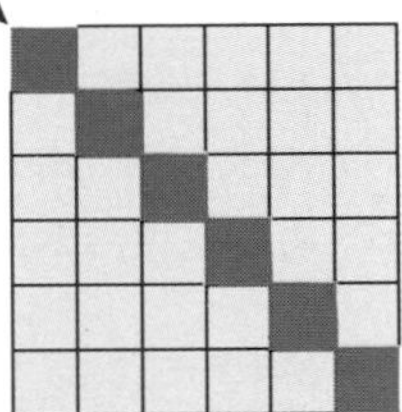

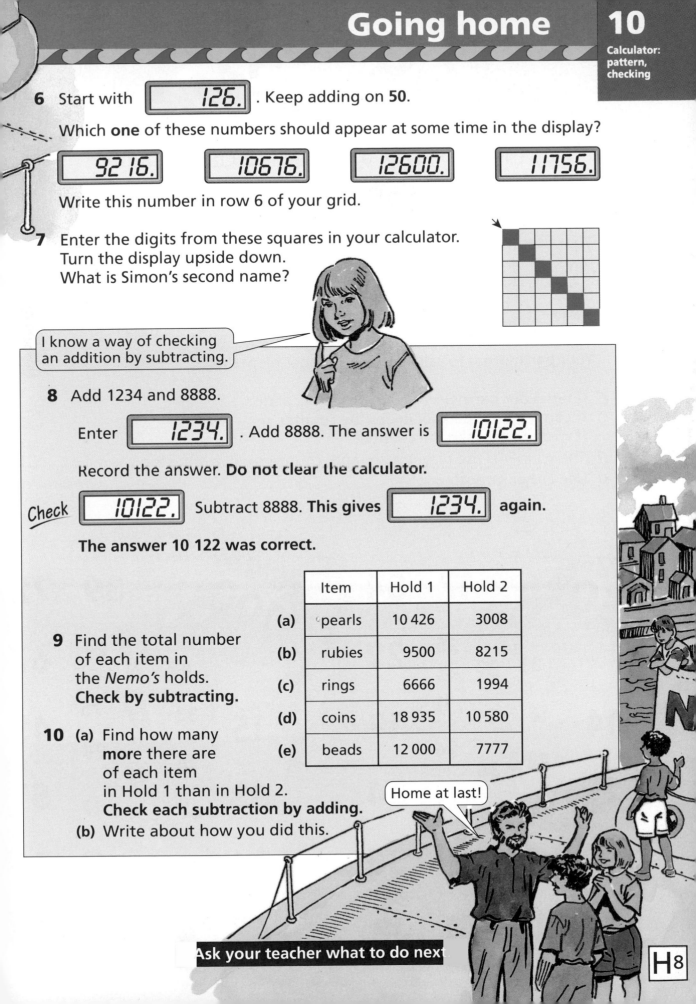

I know a way of checking an addition by subtracting.

8 Add 1234 and 8888.

Enter 1234. . Add 8888. The answer is 10122.

Record the answer. **Do not clear the calculator.**

Check 10122. Subtract 8888. **This gives** 1234. **again.**

The answer 10 122 was correct.

9 Find the total number of each item in the *Nemo's* holds.
Check by subtracting.

	Item	Hold 1	Hold 2
(a)	pearls	10 426	3008
(b)	rubies	9500	8215
(c)	rings	6666	1994
(d)	coins	18 935	10 580
(e)	beads	12 000	7777

10 (a) Find how many **more** there are of each item in Hold 1 than in Hold 2.
Check each subtraction by adding.
(b) Write about how you did this.

Home at last!

Ask your teacher what to do next

POOL GAME

Play this game with a partner. You need counters.

- Take turns to place a counter beside any one of the black numbers. For example, ⟶ 15
- **Your partner** has to say which number in the pool, added to the black number, gives the pool target. For example,

black number  + pool number  = pool target 

↑

Your partner has to calculate this number mentally.

- Check your partner's answer with a calculator. If correct, your partner keeps the counter. If wrong, you take the counter.
- The winner is the player with more counters when you stop.
- **Use either or both pools.**

Target 50

Black numbers: 17, 34, 22, 19, 24, 35, 12, 41, 13, 27, 39, 21, 14

Pool: 31, 23, 25, 16, 9, 11, 28, 36, 26, 38, 15, 37, 27, 33, 29

Target 100

Black numbers: 39, 72, 67, 43, 51, 86, 29, 47, 41, 62, 76, 33, 15

Pool: 49, 71, 24, 33, 57, 75, 14, 38, 28, 61, 59, 47, 67, 85, 53

DAILY NEWS
THURSDAY 15 MARCH

SUPERHERO RETURNS

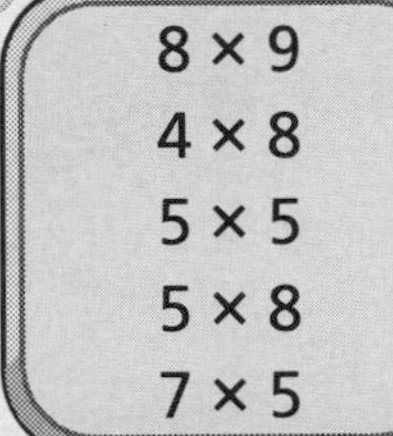

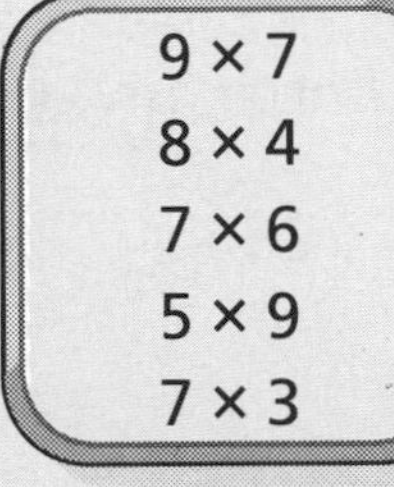

7 × 8
9 × 6
6 × 4
3 × 10
4 × 9

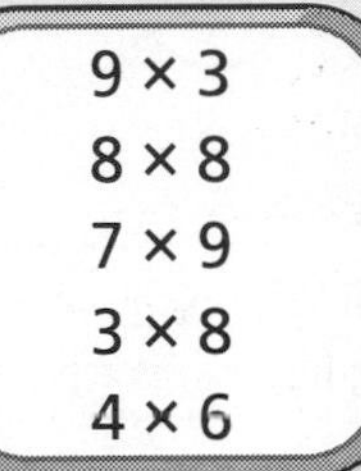

1 There are four security buttons on Superhero's door. To enter he must

- for each button, find the total of the products
- press the buttons in order, from highest to lowest total.

In what order should Superhero press the buttons?

2 Superhero crosses the security mat by stepping **only** on rectangles which have an even product. Which rectangles can he step on?

8 × 7	7 × 4	9 × 5	5 × 7
9 × 9	8 × 6	6 × 6	3 × 3
7 × 7	5 × 3	8 × 5	7 × 1
3 × 7	3 × 9	5 × 6	9 × 8

3

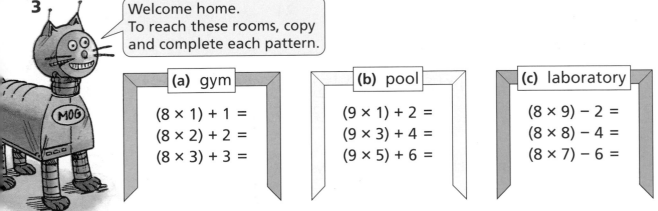

Welcome home.
To reach these rooms, copy and complete each pattern.

(a) gym

(8 × 1) + 1 =
(8 × 2) + 2 =
(8 × 3) + 3 =

(b) pool

(9 × 1) + 2 =
(9 × 3) + 4 =
(9 × 5) + 6 =

(c) laboratory

(8 × 9) − 2 =
(8 × 8) − 4 =
(8 × 7) − 6 =

(d) Write down what you **think** the next two lines in each pattern should be. Check.

Go to Workbook page 4.

13 Control panel

Multiplication: by 10, 100, associativity

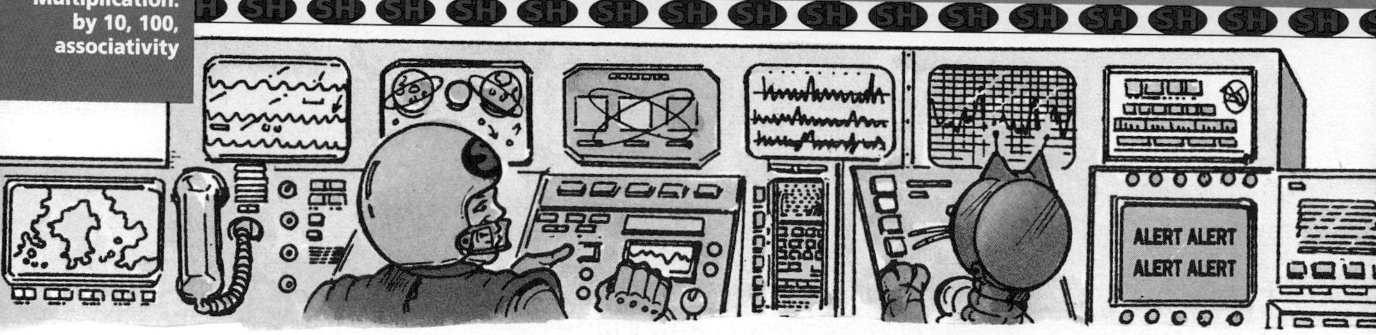

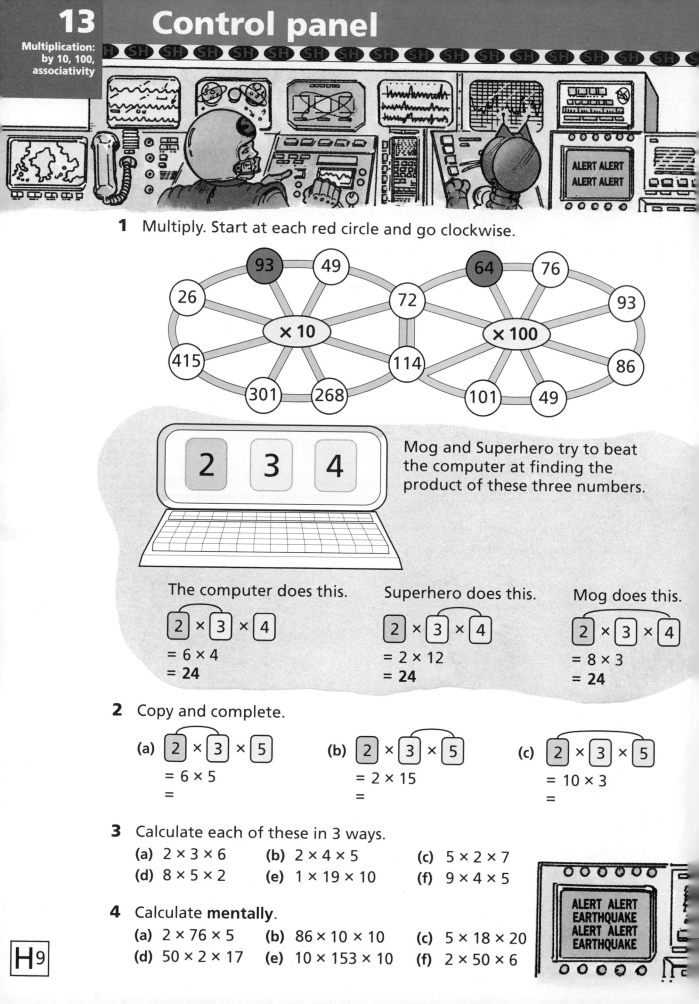

1 Multiply. Start at each red circle and go clockwise.

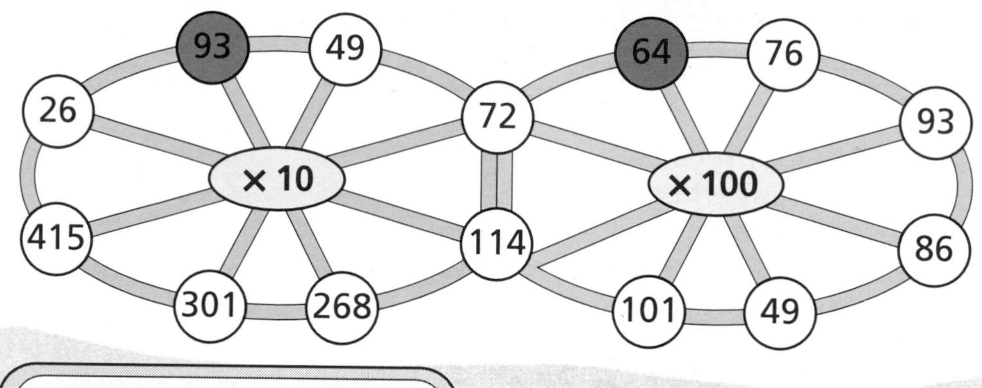

Mog and Superhero try to beat the computer at finding the product of these three numbers.

2 3 4

The computer does this.

2 × 3 × 4
= 6 × 4
= **24**

Superhero does this.

2 × 3 × 4
= 2 × 12
= **24**

Mog does this.

2 × 3 × 4
= 8 × 3
= **24**

2 Copy and complete.

(a) 2 × 3 × 5
= 6 × 5
=

(b) 2 × 3 × 5
= 2 × 15
=

(c) 2 × 3 × 5
= 10 × 3
=

3 Calculate each of these in 3 ways.

(a) 2 × 3 × 6 (b) 2 × 4 × 5 (c) 5 × 2 × 7
(d) 8 × 5 × 2 (e) 1 × 19 × 10 (f) 9 × 4 × 5

4 Calculate **mentally**.

(a) 2 × 76 × 5 (b) 86 × 10 × 10 (c) 5 × 18 × 20
(d) 50 × 2 × 17 (e) 10 × 153 × 10 (f) 2 × 50 × 6

Earthquake 14

Multiplication: ThHTU by 2 to 5

Superhero loads supplies on trucks, vans and planes.

1 Find the number of items Superhero loads on
- **(a)** 3 trucks – 2416 crates on each
- **(b)** 2 lorries – 4079 boxes on each
- **(c)** 5 planes – 989 packages on each
- **(d)** 4 vans – 2356 packs on each.

2 Find how many boxes of medicine Superhero loads on each convoy of trucks.

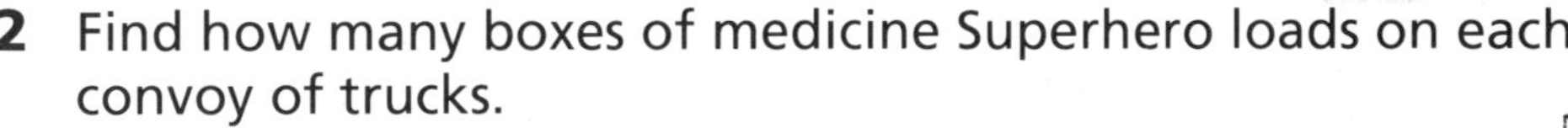

	Number of trucks in convoy	Medicine boxes on each truck
(a)	5	678
(b)	3	3209
(c)	2	4667
(d)	4	1790

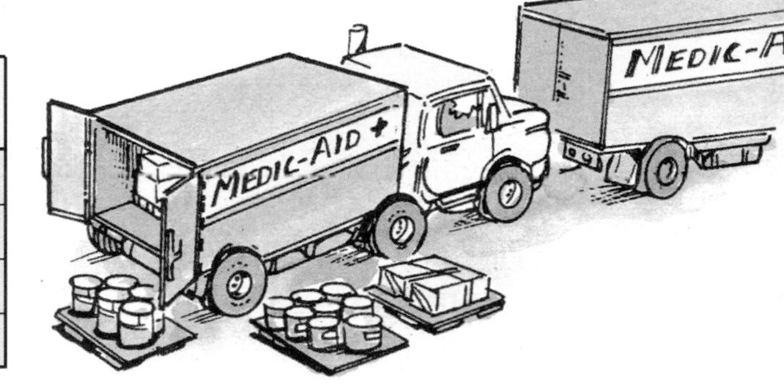

3
- **(a)** 3121 × 4
- **(b)** 5634 × 2
- **(c)** 3357 × 3
- **(d)** 2098 × 5
- **(e)** 4503 × 4

4

one village needs	one hospital needs	one camp needs
1650 crates of milk 867 tents 2009 blankets	2057 bottles of blood 1633 bandages 692 beds	845 tables 3096 stoves 4284 water tanks

How many of each item are needed by

(a) 4 villages **(b)** 5 hospitals **(c)** 3 camps?

5
- **(a)** 1554 × 3
- **(b)** 1670 × 5
- **(c)** 5909 × 2
- **(d)** 836 × 4
- **(e)** 4522 × 2
- **(f)** 2008 × 4
- **(g)** 509 × 3
- **(h)** 1757 × 5
- **(i)** 3069 × 4
- **(j)** 2374 × 5
- **(k)** 2 × 4883
- **(l)** 2718 × 3
- **(m)** 5 × 999
- **(n)** 3456 × 3

15 Fresh start

Multiplication: ThHTU by 6 to 9

Superhero helps to rebuild houses damaged in the earthquake.

1 Find how many of each item Superhero carries when he makes

(a) 6 trips – 1508 bags of cement each trip
(b) 8 trips – 975 planks of wood each trip
(c) 7 trips – 1425 boxes of nails each trip
(d) 9 trips – 872 pipes each trip.

2 Mog makes bolts, nuts, nails and screws from sheets of steel. Find the total for each.

	Number of sheets of steel	Number from one sheet
(a)	9	765 bolts
(b)	7	1427 nuts
(c)	6	1665 nails
(d)	8	948 screws

3 **(a)** 2134 × 6 **(b)** 3569 × 7 **(c)** 2807 × 8 **(d)** 1493 × 9 **(e)** 2678 × 7

4 Superhero uses 1958 bricks to build one new house.
How many bricks does he need to build

(a) 6 houses **(b)** 9 houses **(c)** 7 houses **(d)** 8 houses?

5 In the earthquake, 1274 people are made homeless.

Each person needs
6 kg of rice
9 litres of water
8 kg of beans

Superhero brings
7700 kg of rice
11 500 litres of water
10 100 kg of beans

Has Superhero brought enough food and water? Explain.

6 **(a)** 1404 × 9 **(b)** 6 × 718 **(c)** 1239 × 7 **(d)** 903 × 8 **(e)** 1570 × 8
(f) 9 × 1167 **(g)** 647 × 7 **(h)** 2096 × 6 **(i)** 7 × 876 **(j)** 1333 × 9

£ £ £ Earthquake Fund £ £ £

Help Superhero to raise money for the Earthquake Fund.

1

How much money is needed to repair

(a) 4 tractors **(b)** 3 lorries **(c)** 9 ploughs **(d)** 7 vans?

2 These are the costs of repairing buildings damaged in the earthquake.

A school £1907

A hospital £5290

A clinic £1648

A factory £1249

Find the cost of repairing

(a) 5 schools **(b)** 2 hospitals **(c)** 6 clinics **(d)** 8 factories.

3 Schools collected money with Mog's help.

West: 7 schools each collected £1430

South: 9 schools each collected £1178

North: 8 schools each collected £1056

East: 6 schools each collected £898

How much money was collected by schools in

(a) the West **(b)** the South **(c)** the North **(d)** the East?

4 Mog has made this **number search** to raise money.

- Copy it on squared paper.
- Multiply. Find the answers hidden in the number search.

R5

(a) 4768 × 2 **(b)** 1056 × 9
(c) 1257 × 4 **(d)** 1680 × 6
(e) 887 × 8 **(f)** 2789 × 3
(g) 1804 × 5 **(h)** 1468 × 7

Mog's number search

9	5	3	6	0	4	1
5	0	2	8	9	4	0
3	2	0	3	2	0	2
6	0	4	6	3	5	7
1	9	2	7	0	9	6

H11

R5

17 Superparty for a Superhero

Multiplication: ThHTU by 2 to 9 by calculator, money

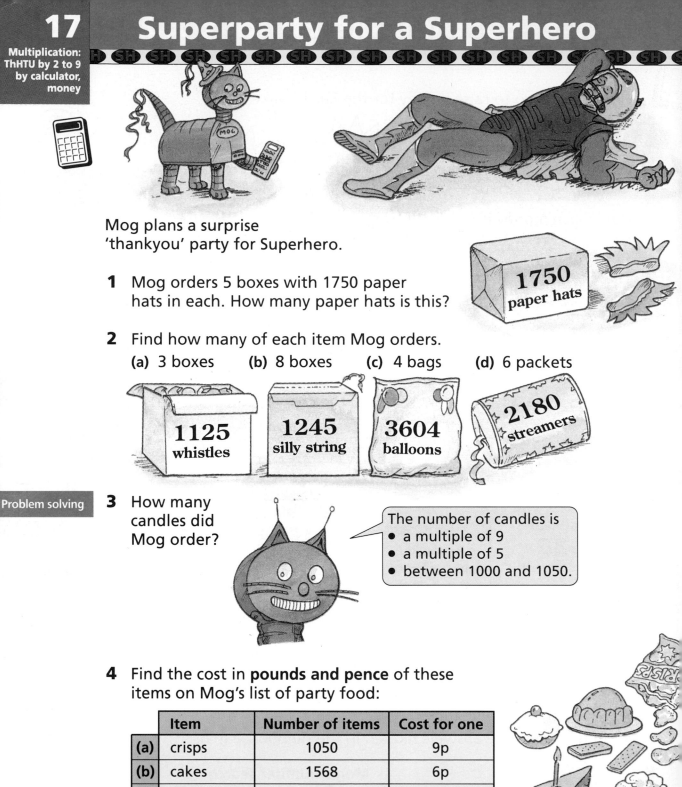

Mog plans a surprise 'thankyou' party for Superhero.

1 Mog orders 5 boxes with 1750 paper hats in each. How many paper hats is this?

1750 paper hats

2 Find how many of each item Mog orders.

(a) 3 boxes **(b)** 8 boxes **(c)** 4 bags **(d)** 6 packets

3604 balloons

Problem solving

3 How many candles did Mog order?

The number of candles is
- a multiple of 9
- a multiple of 5
- between 1000 and 1050.

4 Find the cost in **pounds and pence** of these items on Mog's list of party food:

	Item	Number of items	Cost for one
(a)	crisps	1050	9p
(b)	cakes	1568	6p
(c)	ice-creams	1350	8p
(d)	jellies	1524	7p
(e)	biscuits	1378	9p

Problem solving

5 Mog orders some large and some small boxes of party items at a total cost of £12. Large boxes cost £2·20 each and small boxes cost £1·08 each. How many large and how many small boxes does Mog order?

THANK YOU SUPER HERO!

1 The cost of hiring a pirate costume is £8·55.
At the party 11 people are dressed as pirates.
What is the total cost of hiring their costumes?

2 Find the cost of hiring these costumes.

(a) 13 clowns **(b)** 14 jesters **(c)** 25 Superheros **(d)** 22 Mogs

£7·49
each

£6·82
each

£3·24
each

£3·75
each
MOG

3 Mog is worried about the cost of the party!
Help Mog to find the cost of:

(a) 36 wigs at £2·70 each
(b) 79 hats at £1·09 each
(c) 85 tails at £1·36 each
(d) 55 masks at £3·79 each
(e) 72 cloaks at £1·86 each.

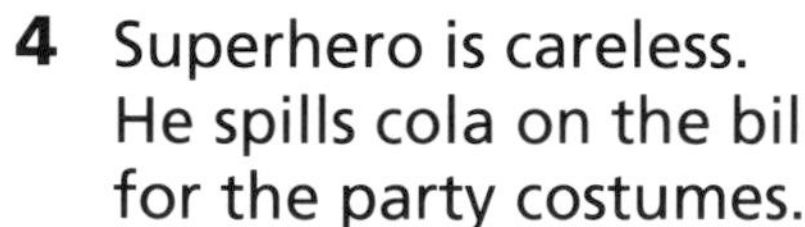

MOG

4 Superhero is careless.
He spills cola on the bill
for the party costumes.

Find the missing numbers.

Problem solving

Cosy Costumes
Charges for Superhero's party.

(a) 26 aliens at £ ■ each = £832
(b) ■ robots at £18 each = £666

5

Problem solving

The number of people dressed as dinosaurs times the number dressed as dragons is 493. There are 12 more dinosaurs than dragons.
How many people are dressed as dinosaurs and how many as dragons?

Ask your teacher what to do next

19 Chaos at Medic–Aid

Division: by 2, 3, 4, 5, factors

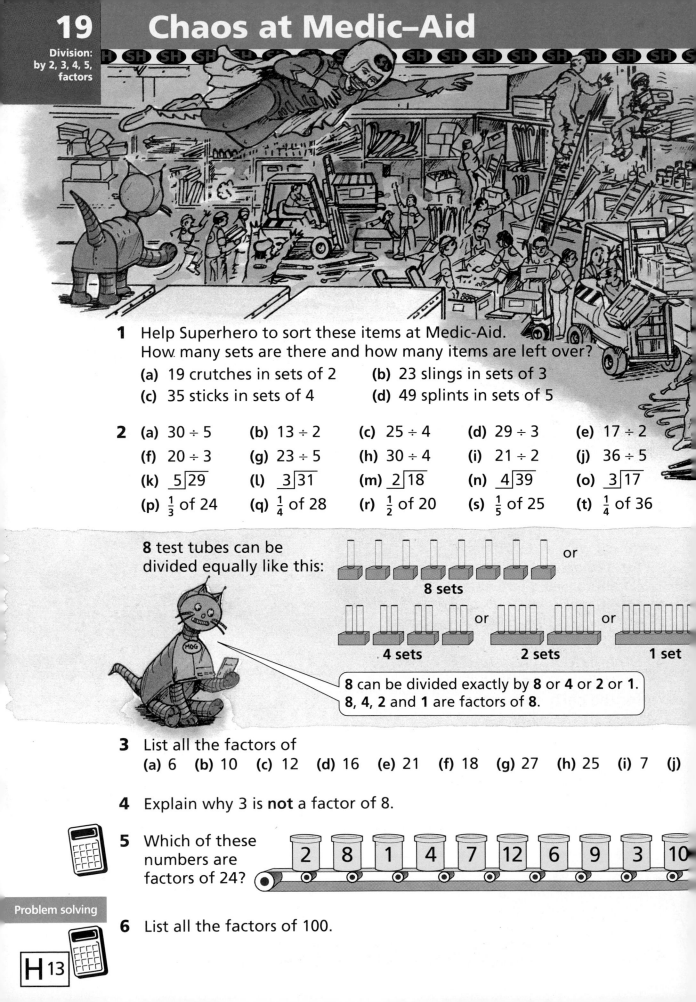

1 Help Superhero to sort these items at Medic-Aid.
How many sets are there and how many items are left over?

(a) 19 crutches in sets of 2 **(b)** 23 slings in sets of 3
(c) 35 sticks in sets of 4 **(d)** 49 splints in sets of 5

2

(a) $30 \div 5$	**(b)** $13 \div 2$	**(c)** $25 \div 4$	**(d)** $29 \div 3$	**(e)** $17 \div 2$
(f) $20 \div 3$	**(g)** $23 \div 5$	**(h)** $30 \div 4$	**(i)** $21 \div 2$	**(j)** $36 \div 5$
(k) $5\overline{)29}$	**(l)** $3\overline{)31}$	**(m)** $2\overline{)18}$	**(n)** $4\overline{)39}$	**(o)** $3\overline{)17}$
(p) $\frac{1}{3}$ of 24	**(q)** $\frac{1}{4}$ of 28	**(r)** $\frac{1}{2}$ of 20	**(s)** $\frac{1}{5}$ of 25	**(t)** $\frac{1}{4}$ of 36

8 test tubes can be divided equally like this:

8 sets or **4 sets** or **2 sets** or **1 set**

8 can be divided exactly by **8** or **4** or **2** or **1**.
8, 4, 2 and **1** are factors of **8**.

3 List all the factors of
(a) 6 **(b)** 10 **(c)** 12 **(d)** 16 **(e)** 21 **(f)** 18 **(g)** 27 **(h)** 25 **(i)** 7 **(j)**

4 Explain why 3 is **not** a factor of 8.

5 Which of these numbers are factors of 24?

2 8 1 4 7 12 6 9 3 10

Problem solving

6 List all the factors of 100.

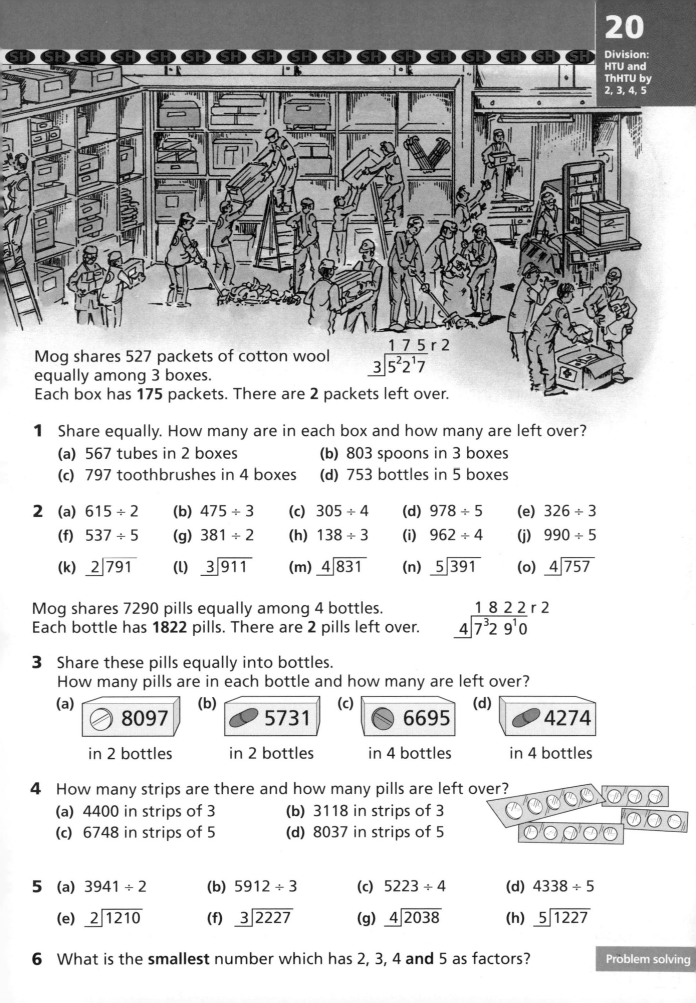

Mog shares 527 packets of cotton wool equally among 3 boxes.
Each box has **175** packets. There are **2** packets left over.

$$\begin{array}{r} 1\,7\,5 \text{ r } 2 \\ 3\overline{)5^{2}2^{1}7} \end{array}$$

1 Share equally. How many are in each box and how many are left over?

(a) 567 tubes in 2 boxes (b) 803 spoons in 3 boxes
(c) 797 toothbrushes in 4 boxes (d) 753 bottles in 5 boxes

2 (a) $615 \div 2$ (b) $475 \div 3$ (c) $305 \div 4$ (d) $978 \div 5$ (e) $326 \div 3$
(f) $537 \div 5$ (g) $381 \div 2$ (h) $138 \div 3$ (i) $962 \div 4$ (j) $990 \div 5$
(k) $2\overline{)791}$ (l) $3\overline{)911}$ (m) $4\overline{)831}$ (n) $5\overline{)391}$ (o) $4\overline{)757}$

Mog shares 7290 pills equally among 4 bottles.
Each bottle has **1822** pills. There are **2** pills left over.

$$\begin{array}{r} 1\,8\,2\,2 \text{ r } 2 \\ 4\overline{)7^{3}2\,9^{1}0} \end{array}$$

3 Share these pills equally into bottles.
How many pills are in each bottle and how many are left over?

(a)  8097 in 2 bottles
(b)  5731 in 2 bottles
(c) 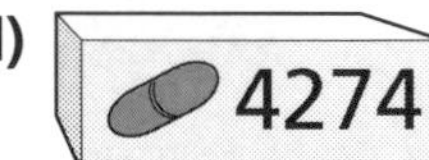 6695 in 4 bottles
(d) 4274 in 4 bottles

4 How many strips are there and how many pills are left over?

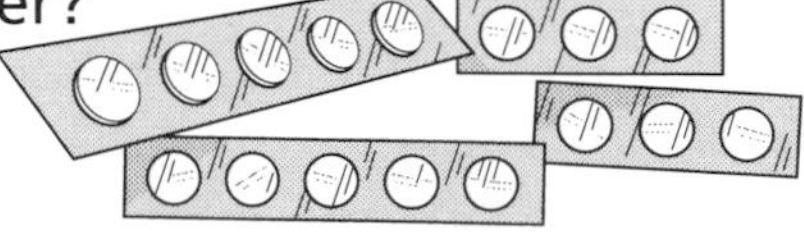

(a) 4400 in strips of 3 (b) 3118 in strips of 3
(c) 6748 in strips of 5 (d) 8037 in strips of 5

5 (a) $3941 \div 2$ (b) $5912 \div 3$ (c) $5223 \div 4$ (d) $4338 \div 5$
(e) $2\overline{)1210}$ (f) $3\overline{)2227}$ (g) $4\overline{)2038}$ (h) $5\overline{)1227}$

6 What is the **smallest** number which has 2, 3, 4 **and** 5 as factors?

Problem solving

21 Dispatching

Division: ThHTU by 2, 3, 4, 5

1 Superhero makes these labels.

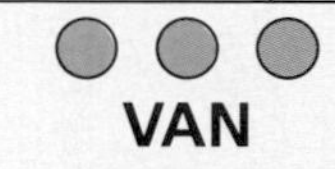

How many labels can be made from

(a) 7903 circles **(b)** 9296 triangles?

2 Find the number of each item to be sent to these towns.

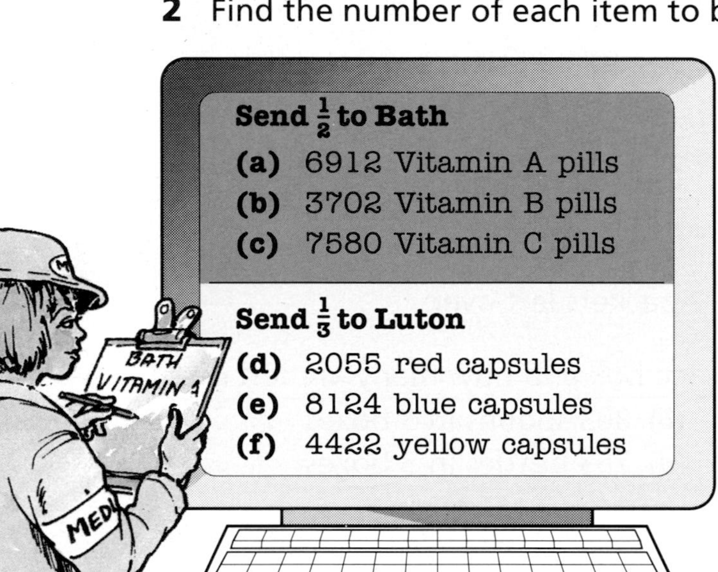

Send $\frac{1}{2}$ to Bath

(a) 6912 Vitamin A pills
(b) 3702 Vitamin B pills
(c) 7580 Vitamin C pills

Send $\frac{1}{3}$ to Luton

(d) 2055 red capsules
(e) 8124 blue capsules
(f) 4422 yellow capsules

Send $\frac{1}{4}$ to Oban

(g) 9304 round plasters
(h) 7396 square plasters
(i) 8312 oblong plasters

Send $\frac{1}{5}$ to Wick

(j) 9400 spoons
(k) 1865 spatulas
(l) 8670 swabs

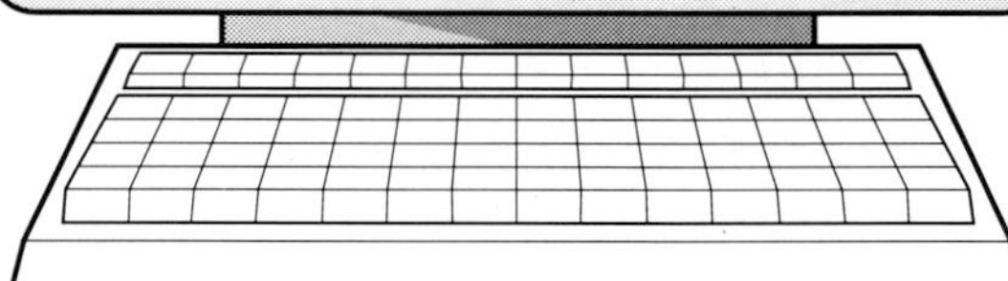

3 There are 8215 pills in a box.
They have to be divided equally among 3 shops.

(a) How many pills go to each shop?

(b) How many **more** pills should be added to the box so that each shop receives 2740 pills?

4 I can use only label numbers which have 3 **or** 4 **or** 5 as factors.

7946 9904 7617 8122 8555 6538 7149 6850 9874 3952 8371 6237

(a) Which of these labels can Mog use? Give a reason for each.

(b) Change the **units** digit in each of the **other** labels to make their numbers have **4** as a factor.
Write the new label numbers.

Problem solving

ewel thieves foiled by Superhero

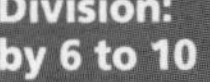
Division: by 6 to 10

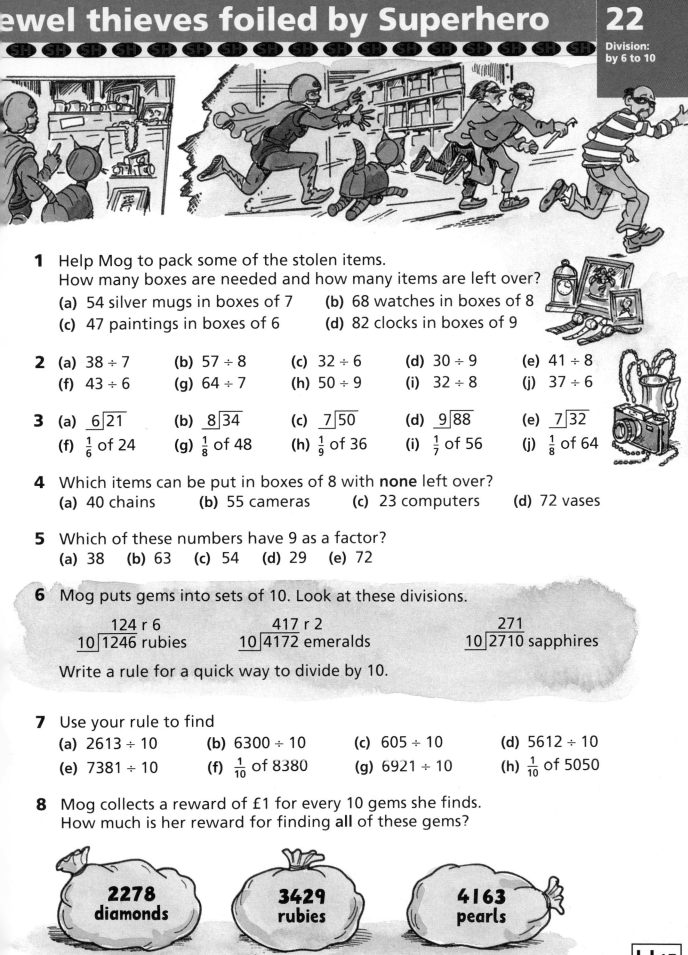

1 Help Mog to pack some of the stolen items.
How many boxes are needed and how many items are left over?

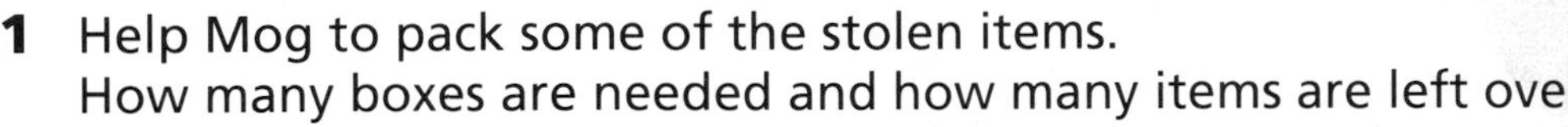

(a) 54 silver mugs in boxes of 7 (b) 68 watches in boxes of 8
(c) 47 paintings in boxes of 6 (d) 82 clocks in boxes of 9

2 (a) 38 ÷ 7 (b) 57 ÷ 8 (c) 32 ÷ 6 (d) 30 ÷ 9 (e) 41 ÷ 8
(f) 43 ÷ 6 (g) 64 ÷ 7 (h) 50 ÷ 9 (i) 32 ÷ 8 (j) 37 ÷ 6

3 (a) $6\overline{)21}$ (b) $8\overline{)34}$ (c) $7\overline{)50}$ (d) $9\overline{)88}$ (e) $7\overline{)32}$
(f) $\frac{1}{6}$ of 24 (g) $\frac{1}{8}$ of 48 (h) $\frac{1}{9}$ of 36 (i) $\frac{1}{7}$ of 56 (j) $\frac{1}{8}$ of 64

4 Which items can be put in boxes of 8 with **none** left over?
(a) 40 chains (b) 55 cameras (c) 23 computers (d) 72 vases

5 Which of these numbers have 9 as a factor?
(a) 38 (b) 63 (c) 54 (d) 29 (e) 72

6 Mog puts gems into sets of 10. Look at these divisions.

$\begin{array}{r} 124 \text{ r } 6 \\ 10\overline{)1246} \end{array}$ rubies $\begin{array}{r} 417 \text{ r } 2 \\ 10\overline{)4172} \end{array}$ emeralds $\begin{array}{r} 271 \\ 10\overline{)2710} \end{array}$ sapphires

Write a rule for a quick way to divide by 10.

7 Use your rule to find
(a) 2613 ÷ 10 (b) 6300 ÷ 10 (c) 605 ÷ 10 (d) 5612 ÷ 10
(e) 7381 ÷ 10 (f) $\frac{1}{10}$ of 8380 (g) 6921 ÷ 10 (h) $\frac{1}{10}$ of 5050

8 Mog collects a reward of £1 for every 10 gems she finds.
How much is her reward for finding **all** of these gems?

23

Division: HTU and ThHTU by 6, 7

Clearing up

1 In one of the crates there are 163 gold bars.
Superhero sorts them into sets of 6.
How many sets are there and how many bars are left over?

2 **(a)** 268 ÷ 6 **(b)** 514 ÷ 7 **(c)** 444 ÷ 7 **(d)** 605 ÷ 6 **(e)** 712 ÷ 7
(f) 300 ÷ 6 **(g)** 211 ÷ 7 **(h)** 810 ÷ 7 **(i)** 702 ÷ 6 **(j)** 978 ÷ 6

3 **(a)** $6\overline{)128}$ **(b)** $7\overline{)999}$ **(c)** $7\overline{)380}$ **(d)** $6\overline{)463}$ **(e)** $7\overline{)222}$
(f) $\frac{1}{6}$ of 558 **(g)** $\frac{1}{6}$ of 168 **(h)** $\frac{1}{7}$ of 539 **(i)** $\frac{1}{6}$ of 630 **(j)** $\frac{1}{7}$ of 462

Problem solving

4 Seven full trays of rings were stolen.
Superhero found 220 rings, filled 6 trays and had 28 rings left.

(a) How many rings does one full tray hold?
(b) How many rings are still missing?

5 **(a)** 6684 ÷ 6 **(b)** 7982 ÷ 7 **(c)** 9873 ÷ 7 **(d)** 7268 ÷ 6
(e) 2918 ÷ 7 **(f)** 3623 ÷ 6 **(g)** 4250 ÷ 6 **(h)** 1465 ÷ 7

6 **(a)** $6\overline{)1462}$ **(b)** $7\overline{)2168}$ **(c)** $7\overline{)9001}$ **(d)** $6\overline{)2102}$
(e) $\frac{1}{7}$ of 3451 **(f)** $\frac{1}{6}$ of 2946 **(g)** $\frac{1}{6}$ of 7152 **(h)** $\frac{1}{7}$ of 2674

7 Mog finds a box containing 1326 beads for bracelets.
How many bracelets can be made, each with 7 beads?

8 A set of 6 silver trays is worth £3486.
What is the value of each tray?

Problem solving

9 Mog finds that one gold chain weighs the same as two silver chains.
Three gold chains and one silver chain weigh 1162 grams.
What is the weight of each kind of chain?

Sharing the spoils

Colin Conman.

Clocks	Watches	Rings	Pens
247 ÷ 8	364 ÷ 9	276 ÷ 9	405 ÷ 8
= 37 each	= 44 each	= 36 each	=

I think the robbers have made mistakes.

Superhero found a note belonging to the robbers.
Help Superhero to find the mistakes.

1 (a) How many robbers were to share the clocks?
(b) How many clocks **should** be in each share?

2 (a) How many watches **should** be in each share?
(b) How many rings **should** be in each share?

Problem solving

3 What answer do you think the **robbers** had for the pens?

4
(a) 891 ÷ 8 (b) 994 ÷ 9 (c) 683 ÷ 9 (d) 229 ÷ 8 (e) 567 ÷ 9
(f) 399 ÷ 8 (g) 797 ÷ 9 (h) 796 ÷ 8 (i) 360 ÷ 8 (j) 871 ÷ 9
(k) $\frac{1}{8}$ of 704 (l) $\frac{1}{9}$ of 522 (m) $\frac{1}{9}$ of 225 (n) $\frac{1}{8}$ of 104 (o) $\frac{1}{9}$ of 396

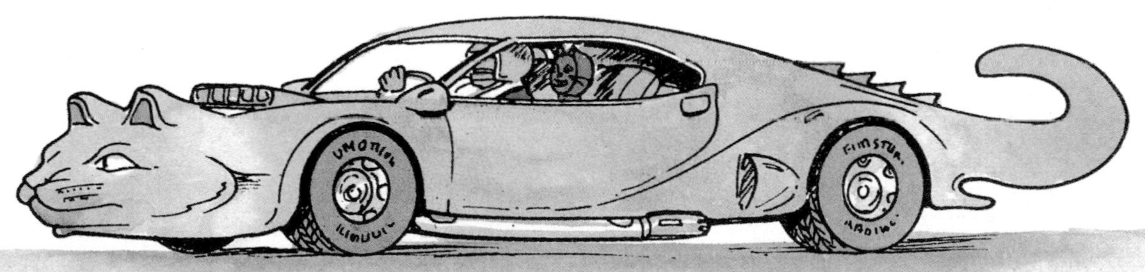

5 Superhero and Mog chase the robbers in the Mogmobile.

Time taken	Fuel used
8 hours	2168 litres

How many litres of fuel does the Mogmobile use each hour?

6
(a) 6343 ÷ 8 (b) 5891 ÷ 9 (c) 9810 ÷ 9 (d) 9652 ÷ 8
(e) 1144 ÷ 9 (f) 7315 ÷ 8 (g) 8200 ÷ 9 (h) 1500 ÷ 8
(i) 9)2254 (j) 8)6302 (k) 9)1807 (l) 8)6429

7 Superhero crashed the Mogmobile.
The repairs cost £1248.
Mog pays one eighth of the bill.
How much does Superhero pay?

On the run

1 Superhero sends Mog a secret message about the robbers.

3693 ÷ 3	4884 ÷ 4	6834 ÷ 2	3720 ÷ 3			
5965 ÷ 5	6054 ÷ 6	5580 ÷ 5	8928 ÷ 8	7440 ÷ 6	8351 ÷ 7	9128 ÷ 8
8547 ÷ 7	3706 ÷ 2		7812 ÷ 7	6309 ÷ 9	9544 ÷ 8	7412 ÷ 4

(a) Find the answer to each calculation in the message.
(b) Use the code to find where the robbers are hiding.

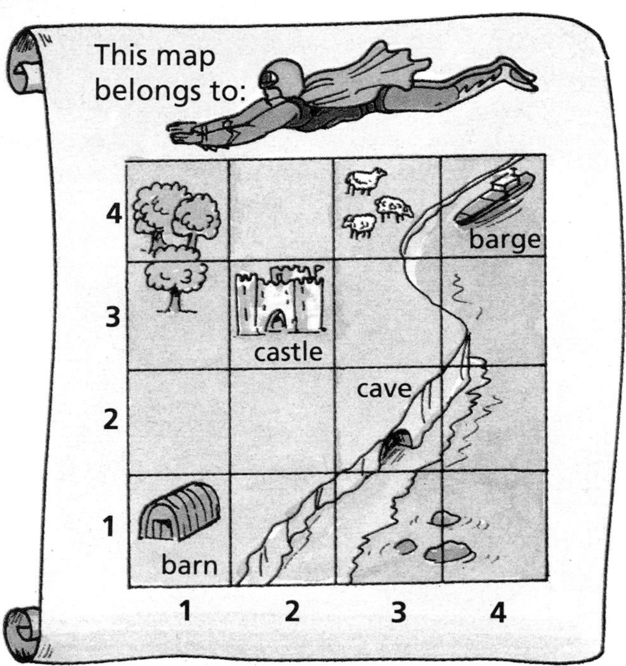

CODE

599 – **C**	1065 – **G**	1289 – **Y**
683 – **J**	1116 – **B**	1853 – **N**
701 – **A**	1123 – **X**	2476 – **M**
745 – **L**	1141 – **S**	2687 – **W**
754 – **T**	1193 – **R**	2807 – **U**
901 – **Q**	1211 – **Z**	3417 – **V**
1009 – **O**	1221 – **I**	3627 – **P**
1034 – **H**	1231 – **F**	3850 – **K**
	1240 – **E**	3999 – **D**

2 **(a)** What is Mog's reply to Superhero?

9585 ÷ 9	8680 ÷ 7	9904 ÷ 4	6846 ÷ 6	5608 ÷ 8	6786 ÷ 9
3770 ÷ 5	9306 ÷ 9	7158 ÷ 6	6200 ÷ 5	9920 ÷ 8	
5278 ÷ 7	8061 ÷ 3	9081 ÷ 9			

(b) Use Superhero's map. Where are the gems hidden?

Go to Workbook page 6.

1 Superhero and Mog are rewarded with a Superholiday. Their holiday costs £662 each week. Where do they go?

2 Use the code to find the name of the airline they use. Each letter is the **hundreds** digit of each answer.

Code

C = 1 U = 2 L = 3
H = 4 O = 5 A = 6
T = 7 E = 8 S = 9

9810 ÷ 2	9174 ÷ 6	9840 ÷ 8	6896 ÷ 4	9912 ÷ 7
9285 ÷ 5	7905 ÷ 3	8181 ÷ 9	8355 ÷ 3	Airlines

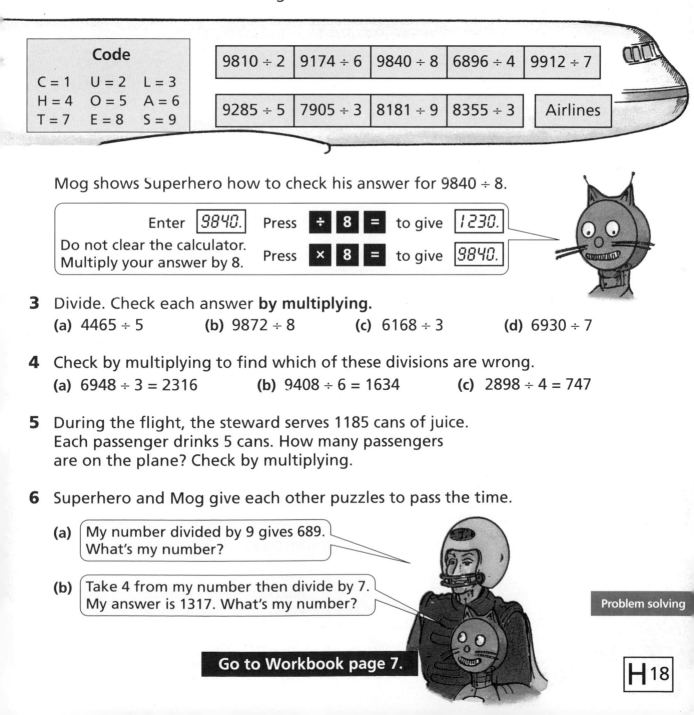

Mog shows Superhero how to check his answer for 9840 ÷ 8.

Enter 9840. Press ÷ 8 = to give 1230.

Do not clear the calculator. Multiply your answer by 8. Press × 8 = to give 9840.

3 Divide. Check each answer **by multiplying.**

(a) 4465 ÷ 5 **(b)** 9872 ÷ 8 **(c)** 6168 ÷ 3 **(d)** 6930 ÷ 7

4 Check by multiplying to find which of these divisions are wrong.

(a) 6948 ÷ 3 = 2316 **(b)** 9408 ÷ 6 = 1634 **(c)** 2898 ÷ 4 = 747

5 During the flight, the steward serves 1185 cans of juice. Each passenger drinks 5 cans. How many passengers are on the plane? Check by multiplying.

6 Superhero and Mog give each other puzzles to pass the time.

(a) My number divided by 9 gives 689. What's my number?

(b) Take 4 from my number then divide by 7. My answer is 1317. What's my number?

Problem solving

Go to Workbook page 7.

27

Division: interpretation of answers

Beach barbie

In Australia, Superhero and Mog help at a barbecue.
Mog makes up a division challenge. She asks three questions.

169 surfboards are shared equally among 9 teams. How many boards for each team?

How many groups of 9 surfers can be made from 169 surfers?

How many sand-buggie[s] each holding 9 surfers are needed to carry 169 surfers?

Oz divides 169 by 9 giving 18.777777

Oz has to decide whether the answer to each question is **18** or **19**.

18 boards for each team.

18 groups of surfers can be made.

19 buggies are needed.

1 Superhero stacks surfboards. How many stacks of 7 can he make from 458 boards?

2 Superhero marks out the sand-buggy course. With each stride he covers 8 metres. How many strides must he take to cover a distance of 714 met[res]?

3 At the Hungry Horace competition Mog shares this food equally among the 11 competitors.

150 onions	205 tomatoes	98 eggs
134 peppers	126 chillies	141 trifles

Make a list of what each person must try to eat.

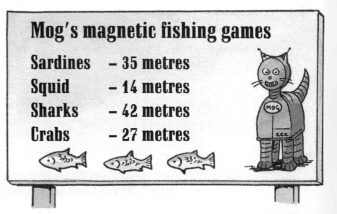

4 A jet boat can tow 13 skiers. How many jet boats are needed to tow 178 skiers?

5 Mog uses 1000 metres of fishing line for **each** of these games.

How many of each game can Mog make?

Mog's magnetic fishing games

Sardines – 35 metres
Squid – 14 metres
Sharks – 42 metres
Crabs – 27 metres

Homeward bound

1 Mog and Superhero spent £3654 during their six-week holiday.
What was the average amount spent

(a) each week **(b)** each day?

2 During two of their holiday weeks there were 167 hours of sunshine.

Use the graph.

In which of these cities do you think they spent the two weeks? Explain.

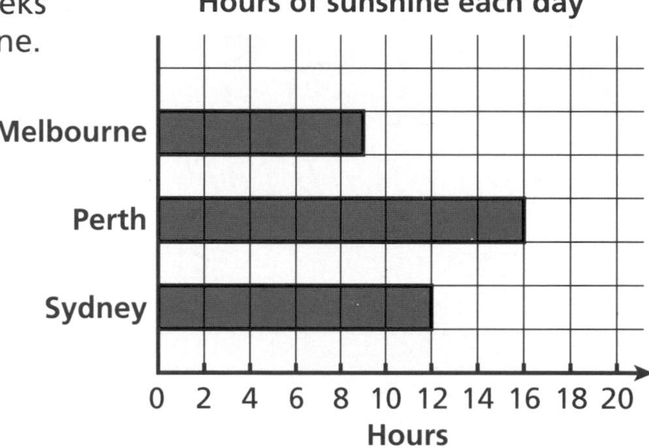

3 Superhero chooses presents for the children at home.
He wants 2000 of each of these cuddly toys.

(a)

(b)

(c)

How many **boxes** of each must he order?

4 Mog buys 4580 beads to make into necklaces each with 37 beads.
How many necklaces can she make?

5 Superhero collects 1624 cowrie shells and packs them in boxes of 85.
How many boxes does he need for all the shells?

6 **(a)** On the plane home there are seats for 284 people.
How many planes are needed to carry 5000 people?

(b) Superhero's plane took 24 hours to fly 11 400 miles from Australia.
What was the average distance the plane flew each hour?

Ask your teacher what to do next

Repeat it

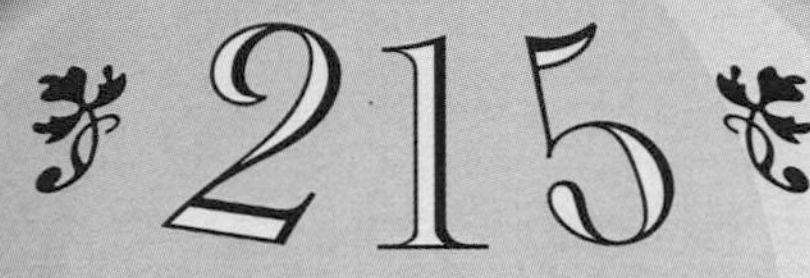

1 (a)
- Enter 215. `215.`
- Repeat 215 like this `215215.`
- Divide by 13, then by 11, and then by 7.

What do you notice?

(b) Try this for other **3-digit numbers**. Write about what you find.

2 (a)
- Enter 67. `67.`
- Enter a zero and then repeat 67. `67067.`
- Divide by 13, then by 11, and then by 7.

(b) Try this for other **2-digit numbers**. Write about what you find.

3 (a) Start with a **single-digit number**. Write the instructions you need this time. (*Hint: you need zeros.*)

(b) Check that your instructions work for other **single-digit numbers**.

4 (a) Multiply 13 by 11 and then multiply by 7.

(b) Multiply the answer to $13 \times 11 \times 7$ by
- 215
- 67
- 9

(c) Discuss with your teacher why the instructions in questions 1, 2 and 3 work.

Merlin Castle

1 For each shield, write the fraction coloured

- yellow • green • orange.

(a) (b) (c) (d)

2 For each design, write the fraction

- coloured blue • not coloured blue.

(a) (b) (c) (d)

In this window 4 of the 100 panes are red.

$\frac{4}{100}$ of the window is red.

3 What fraction of the window is

(a) green **(b)** blue

(c) yellow **(d)** orange?

Go to Workbook page 8.

31 The Great Hall

Fractions: equivalence

1 Write equal fractions for each pair of designs.

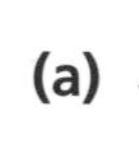
(a) 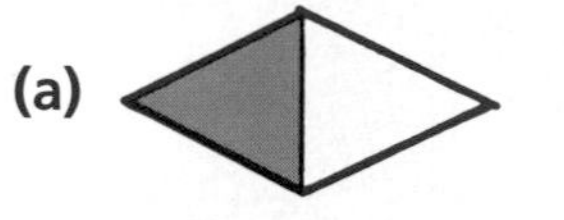 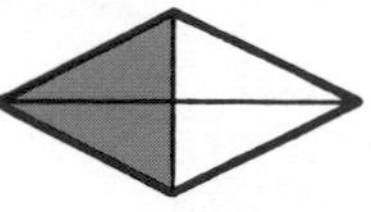

(b) 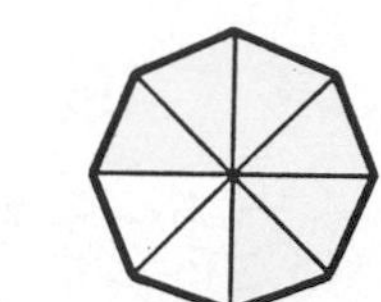

(c) 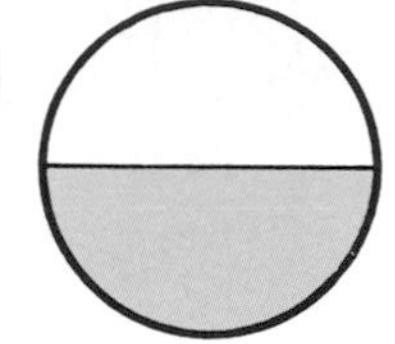 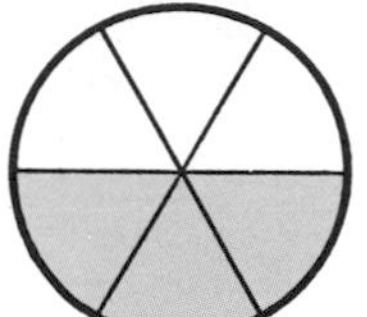

(d)  

(e)  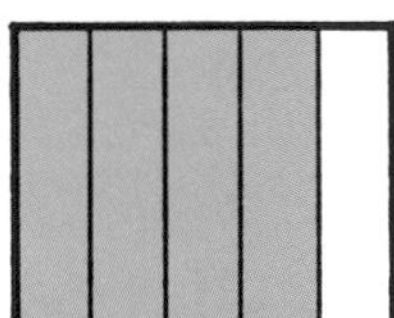 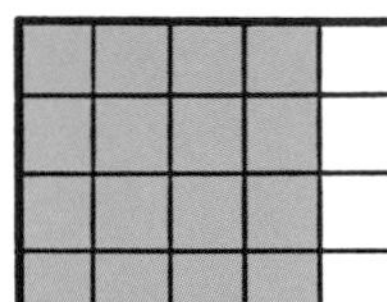

(f)  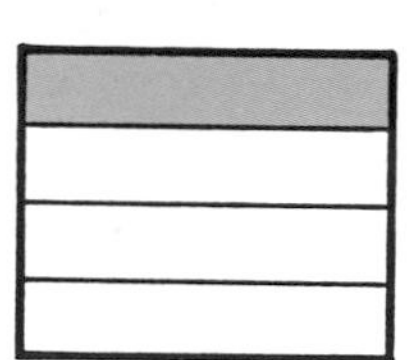 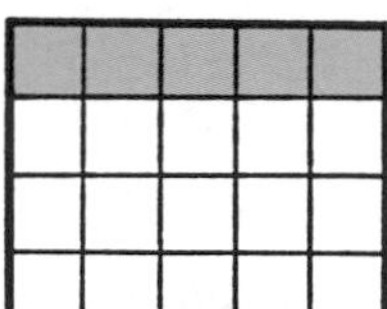

To make an equal fraction **multiply** the top **and** bottom by the same number.

$\frac{1}{2} \xrightarrow{\times 4} \frac{4}{8}$: $\frac{1}{2} = \frac{4}{8}$ (× 4 top and bottom)

$\frac{2}{3} \xrightarrow{\times 3} \frac{6}{9}$: $\frac{2}{3} = \frac{6}{9}$ (× 3 top and bottom)

2 Find the missing numbers.

(a) $\frac{1}{2} = \frac{3}{6}$ (× □ top and bottom)

(b) $\frac{3}{5} = \frac{6}{10}$ (× □ top and bottom)

(c) $\frac{3}{4} = \frac{15}{20}$ (× □ top and bottom)

3 Copy and complete.

(a) $\frac{1}{2} = \frac{}{10}$ (b) $\frac{1}{3} = \frac{}{6}$ (c) $\frac{1}{4} = \frac{}{12}$ (d) $\frac{1}{10} = \frac{}{100}$

(e) $\frac{2}{3} = \frac{}{12}$ (f) $\frac{3}{4} = \frac{}{8}$ (g) $\frac{1}{10} = \frac{}{20}$ (h) $\frac{7}{10} = \frac{}{100}$

4 Change (a) $\frac{1}{2}$ to eighths (b) $\frac{4}{5}$ to tenths (c) $\frac{2}{5}$ to twentieths.

5 Find **two** other fractions equal to

(a) $\frac{1}{4}$ (b) $\frac{3}{5}$ (c) $\frac{9}{10}$ (d) $\frac{2}{2}$

Go to Workbook page 9.

1 Write equal fractions for each pair of designs.

(a) 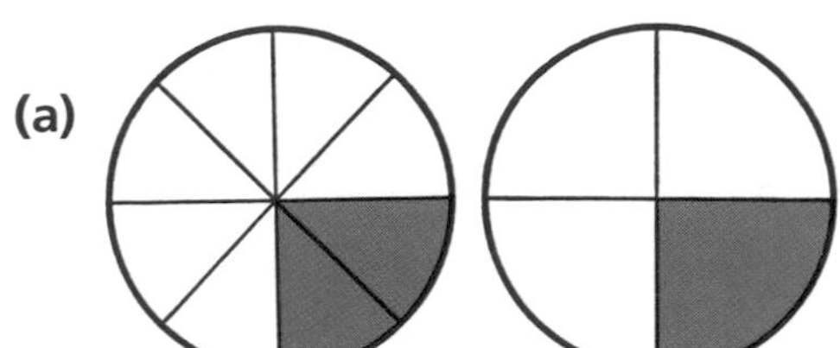

(b)

(c) 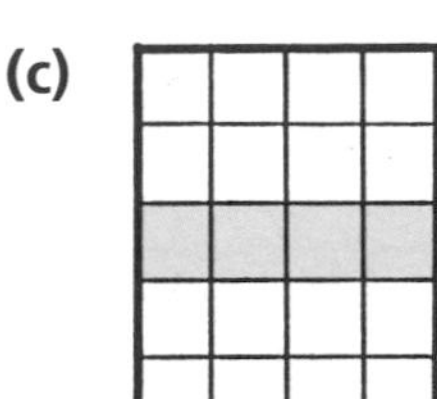 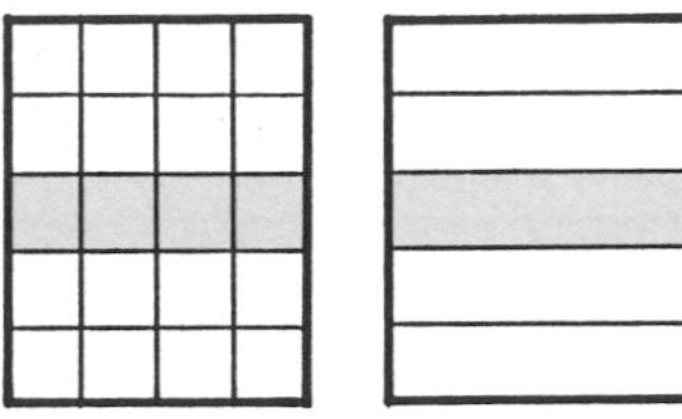

(d)  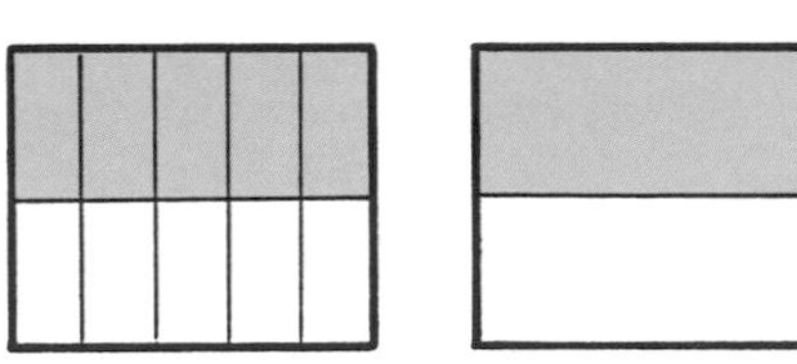

(e)  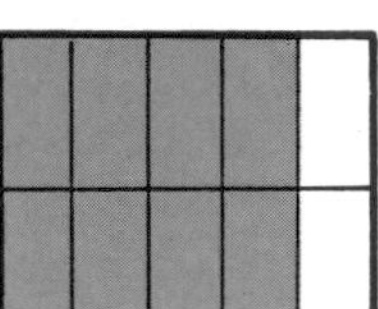 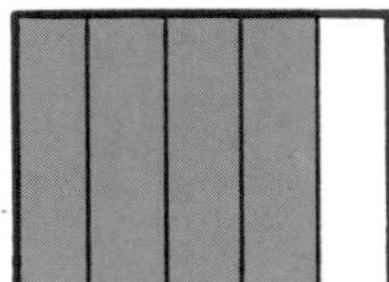

(f) 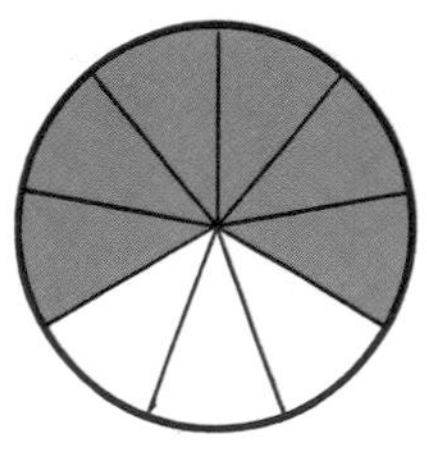 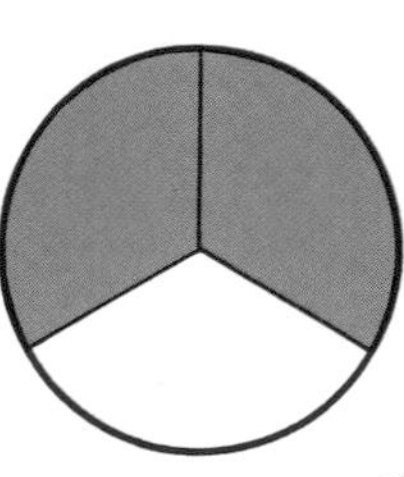

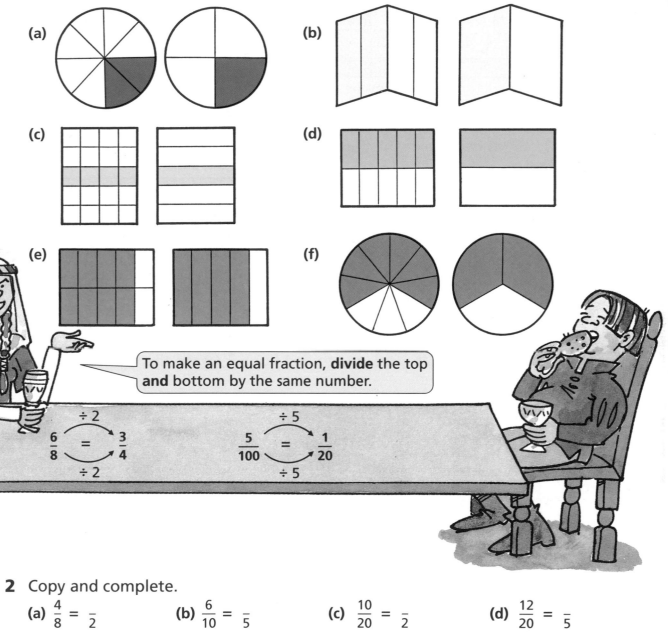

To make an equal fraction, **divide** the top **and** bottom by the same number.

$$\frac{6}{8} = \frac{3}{4} \quad (\div 2)$$

$$\frac{5}{100} = \frac{1}{20} \quad (\div 5)$$

2 Copy and complete.

(a) $\frac{4}{8} = \frac{\ }{2}$ (b) $\frac{6}{10} = \frac{\ }{5}$ (c) $\frac{10}{20} = \frac{\ }{2}$ (d) $\frac{12}{20} = \frac{\ }{5}$

(e) $\frac{3}{9} = \frac{\ }{3}$ (f) $\frac{9}{12} = \frac{\ }{4}$ (g) $\frac{90}{100} = \frac{\ }{10}$ (h) $\frac{50}{100} = \frac{\ }{2}$

3 Change

(a) $\frac{30}{100}$ to tenths (b) $\frac{15}{20}$ to quarters (c) $\frac{8}{20}$ to fifths.

4 Simplify.

(a) $\frac{4}{10}$ (b) $\frac{10}{20}$ (c) $\frac{4}{12}$ (d) $\frac{10}{100}$ (e) $\frac{3}{12}$

(f) $\frac{16}{20}$ (g) $\frac{6}{9}$ (h) $\frac{8}{10}$ (i) $\frac{25}{100}$ (j) $\frac{20}{100}$

33 The tower

Fractions: equivalence

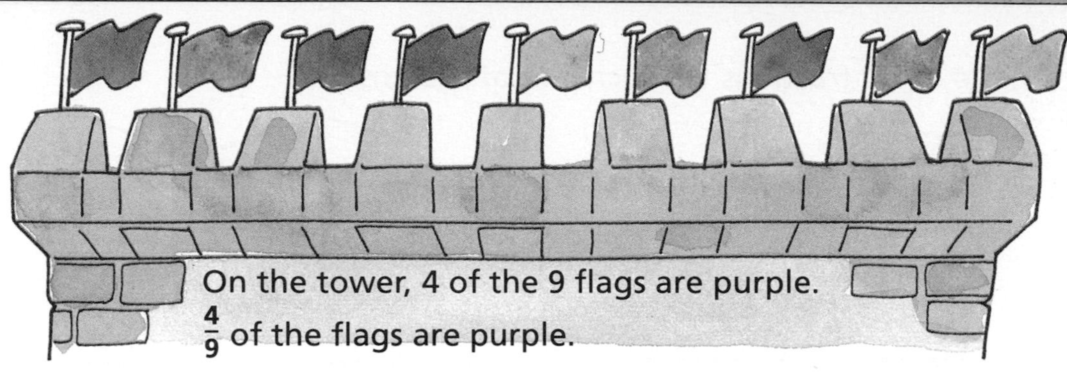

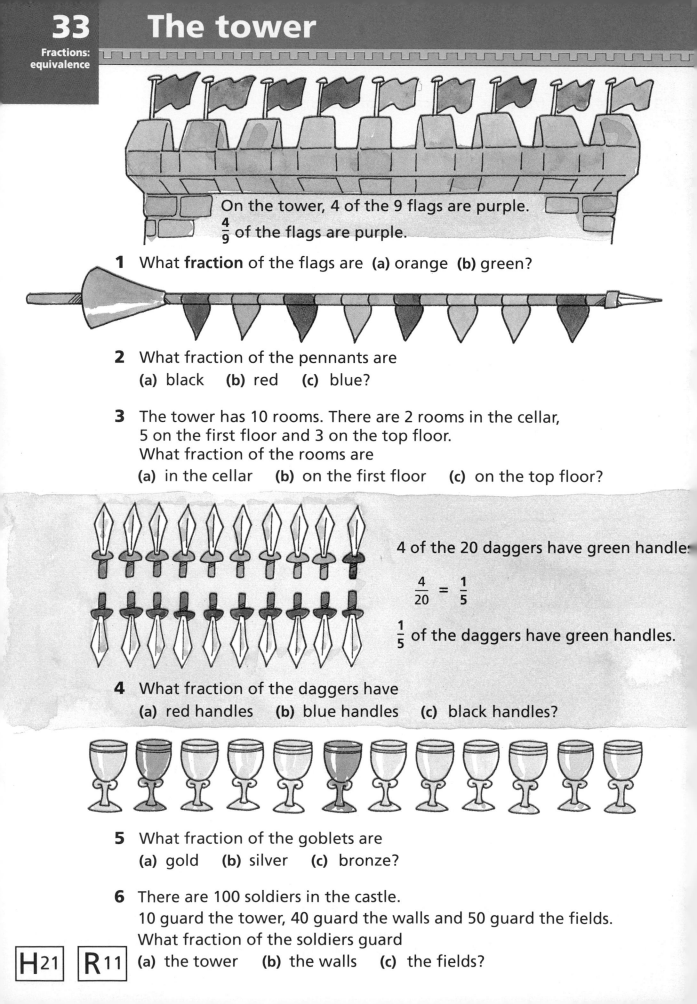

On the tower, 4 of the 9 flags are purple.

$\frac{4}{9}$ of the flags are purple.

1 What **fraction** of the flags are **(a)** orange **(b)** green?

2 What fraction of the pennants are
(a) black **(b)** red **(c)** blue?

3 The tower has 10 rooms. There are 2 rooms in the cellar, 5 on the first floor and 3 on the top floor.
What fraction of the rooms are
(a) in the cellar **(b)** on the first floor **(c)** on the top floor?

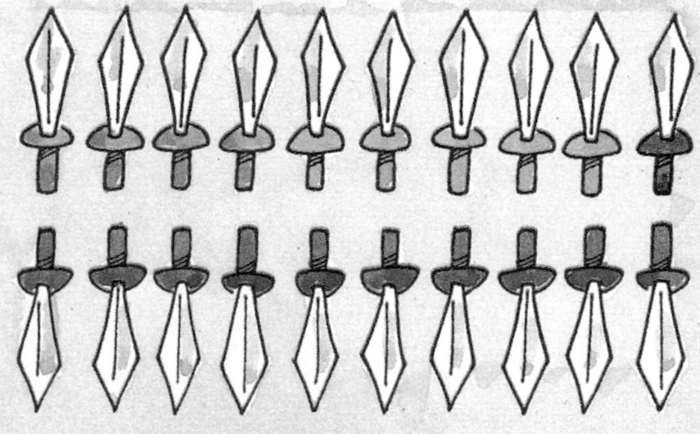

4 of the 20 daggers have green handles.

$$\frac{4}{20} = \frac{1}{5}$$

$\frac{1}{5}$ of the daggers have green handles.

4 What fraction of the daggers have
(a) red handles **(b)** blue handles **(c)** black handles?

5 What fraction of the goblets are
(a) gold **(b)** silver **(c)** bronze?

6 There are 100 soldiers in the castle.
10 guard the tower, 40 guard the walls and 50 guard the fields.
What fraction of the soldiers guard
(a) the tower **(b)** the walls **(c)** the fields?

H21 R11

The villagers

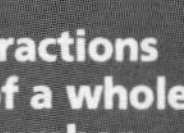

34

Fractions of a whole number

ye Olde Inn
To find $\frac{1}{10}$, divide by 10.

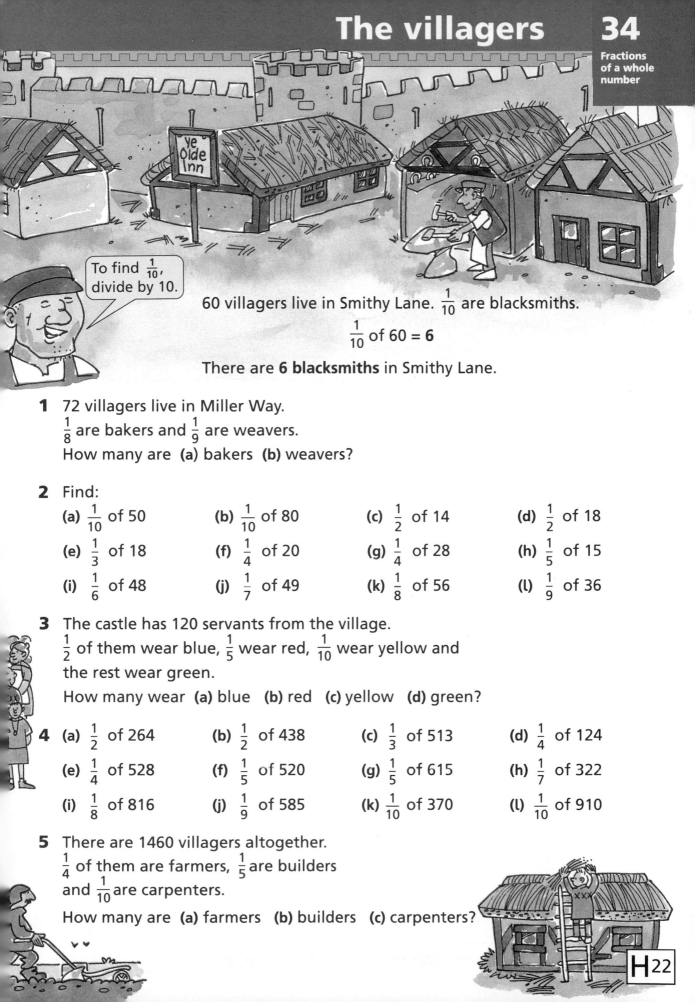

60 villagers live in Smithy Lane. $\frac{1}{10}$ are blacksmiths.

$\frac{1}{10}$ of 60 = **6**

There are **6 blacksmiths** in Smithy Lane.

1 72 villagers live in Miller Way.
$\frac{1}{8}$ are bakers and $\frac{1}{9}$ are weavers.
How many are **(a)** bakers **(b)** weavers?

2 Find:

(a) $\frac{1}{10}$ of 50 **(b)** $\frac{1}{10}$ of 80 **(c)** $\frac{1}{2}$ of 14 **(d)** $\frac{1}{2}$ of 18

(e) $\frac{1}{3}$ of 18 **(f)** $\frac{1}{4}$ of 20 **(g)** $\frac{1}{4}$ of 28 **(h)** $\frac{1}{5}$ of 15

(i) $\frac{1}{6}$ of 48 **(j)** $\frac{1}{7}$ of 49 **(k)** $\frac{1}{8}$ of 56 **(l)** $\frac{1}{9}$ of 36

3 The castle has 120 servants from the village.
$\frac{1}{2}$ of them wear blue, $\frac{1}{5}$ wear red, $\frac{1}{10}$ wear yellow and the rest wear green.
How many wear **(a)** blue **(b)** red **(c)** yellow **(d)** green?

4 **(a)** $\frac{1}{2}$ of 264 **(b)** $\frac{1}{2}$ of 438 **(c)** $\frac{1}{3}$ of 513 **(d)** $\frac{1}{4}$ of 124

(e) $\frac{1}{4}$ of 528 **(f)** $\frac{1}{5}$ of 520 **(g)** $\frac{1}{5}$ of 615 **(h)** $\frac{1}{7}$ of 322

(i) $\frac{1}{8}$ of 816 **(j)** $\frac{1}{9}$ of 585 **(k)** $\frac{1}{10}$ of 370 **(l)** $\frac{1}{10}$ of 910

5 There are 1460 villagers altogether.
$\frac{1}{4}$ of them are farmers, $\frac{1}{5}$ are builders and $\frac{1}{10}$ are carpenters.
How many are **(a)** farmers **(b)** builders **(c)** carpenters?

35 Castle kitchen

Fractions: mixed numbers, halves and quarters

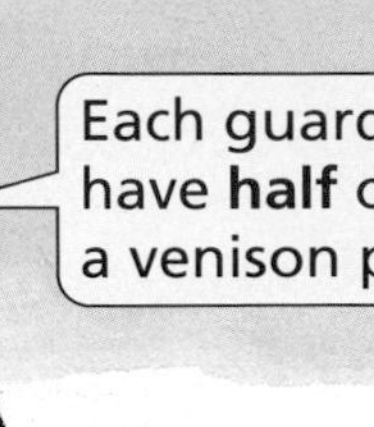

Each guard is to have **half** of a venison pie.

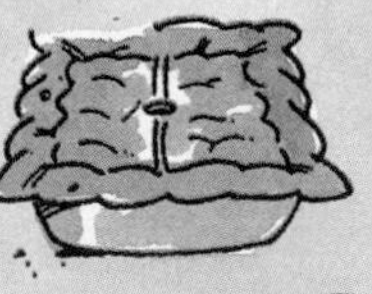

$3\frac{1}{2}$ = 7 halves = $\frac{7}{2}$

Cook can feed **7 guards**.

1 How many guards can Cook feed with

(a) $6\frac{1}{2}$ pies **(b)** 2 pies **(c)** $8\frac{1}{2}$ pies **(d)** 5 pies **(e)** $9\frac{1}{2}$ pies?

2 Copy and complete:

(a) $4\frac{1}{2} = \frac{}{2}$ **(b)** $1\frac{1}{2} = \frac{}{2}$ **(c)** $6 = \frac{}{2}$ **(d)** $5\frac{1}{2} = \frac{}{2}$ **(e)** $7 = \frac{}{2}$

I need 5 halves for 5 guards.

5 halves = $\frac{5}{2}$ = $2\frac{1}{2}$

Cook needs **$2\frac{1}{2}$ pies.**

3 How many pies are needed to feed

(a) 3 guards **(b)** 8 guards **(c)** 13 guards **(d)** 17 guards?

4 Write in another way: **(a)** $\frac{7}{2}$ **(b)** $\frac{3}{2}$ **(c)** $\frac{10}{2}$ **(d)** $\frac{15}{2}$

Each guard is to have a **quarter** of a berry tart.

5 How many guards can Cook feed with

(a) 1 tart **(b)** 3 tarts **(c)** $3\frac{1}{4}$ tarts **(d)** $3\frac{3}{4}$ tarts

(e) $2\frac{1}{4}$ tarts **(f)** $4\frac{3}{4}$ tarts **(g)** $1\frac{1}{2}$ tarts **(h)** $5\frac{1}{2}$ tarts?

6 How many tarts are needed for

(a) 4 **(b)** 5 **(c)** 8 **(d)** 11 **(e)** 7 **(f)** 9 **(g)** 10 guards?

7 Write in another way:

(a) $1\frac{1}{4}$ **(b)** $1\frac{3}{4}$ **(c)** $2\frac{3}{4}$ **(d)** $4\frac{1}{4}$ **(e)** $\frac{12}{4}$ **(f)** $\frac{19}{4}$ **(g)** $\frac{13}{4}$ **(h)** $\frac{14}{4}$

Ask your teacher what to do next

Alltmouth

36

Decimals: first decimal place, notation

Allton
Quarry View
Blind Towers
berallt
Hedge House
Bridge Hotel
Suspension Bridge
Point of Allt
Alltmouth Garage
Carrow Farm
Allt Sands
Home Farm
Springfield Farm
New Allt

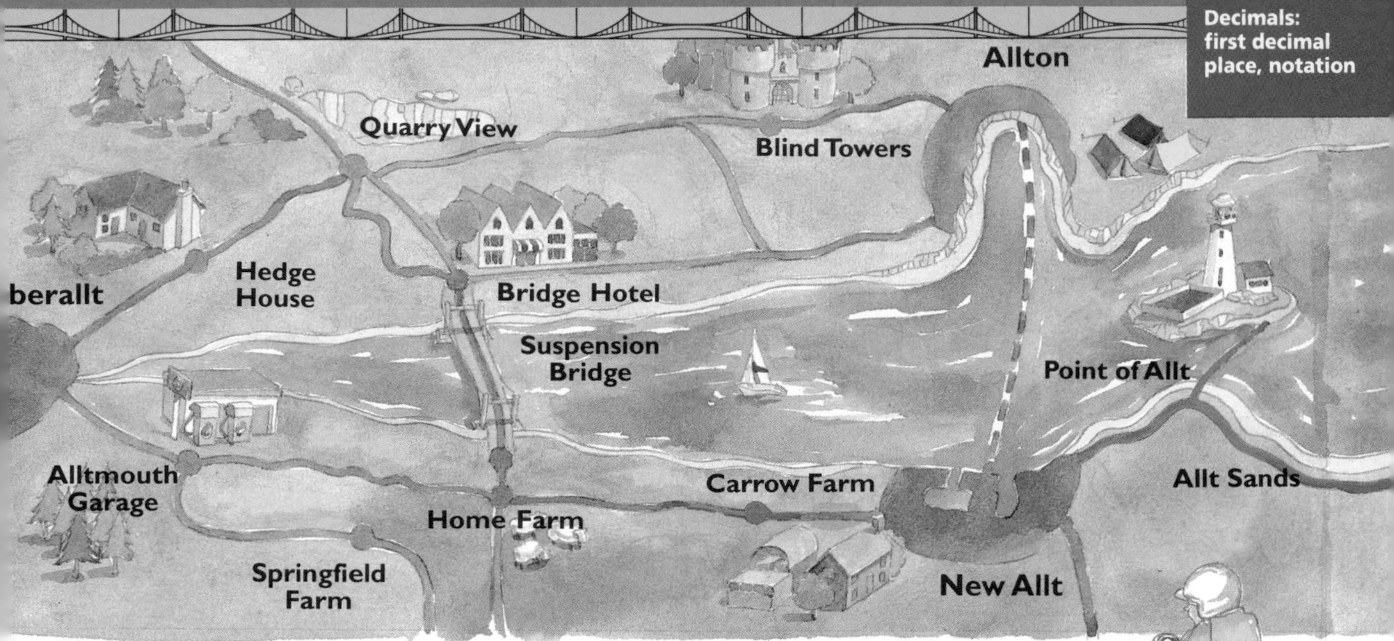

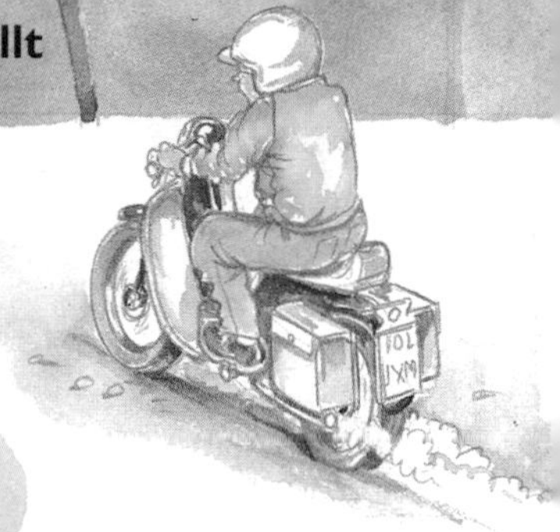

Stan delivers parcels around Alltmouth.

0
1
2

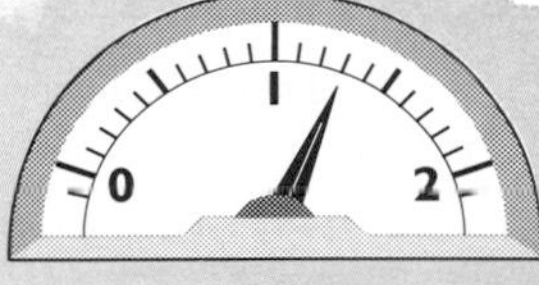

This fuel gauge shows that there are 1·3 litres of fuel in the tank.

1·3 = 1 unit and 3 tenths = 10 tenths and 3 tenths = 13 tenths

1 Write these readings in tenths.

(a)

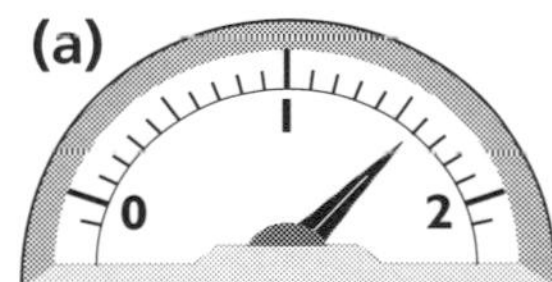

0
1
2

(b)

1
2
3

(c)

2
3
4

(d)

2
3
4

0
10
20
tenths

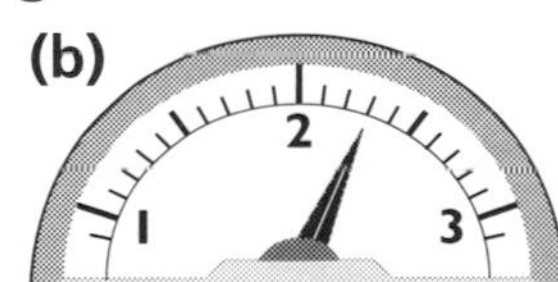

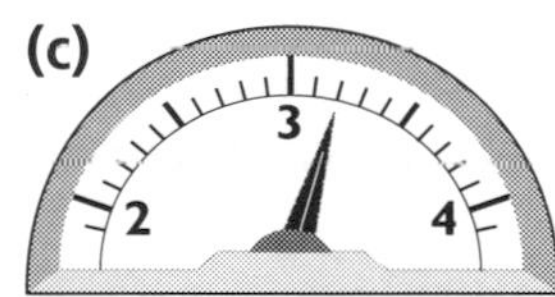

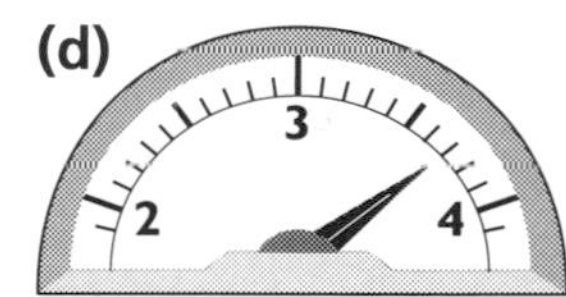

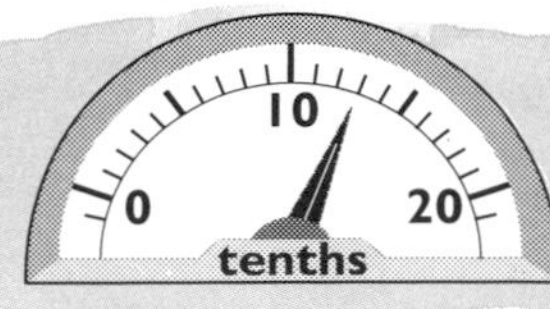

This gauge shows 13 tenths.

13 tenths = 1 unit and 3 tenths = 1·3

2 Write these readings in the same way.

(a) 41 tenths **(b)** 35 tenths **(c)** 20 tenths **(d)** 19 tenths

3 Write in decimal form.

(a) seven tenths **(b)** two tenths **(c)** one unit and five tenths

(d) three units and nine tenths **(e)** nineteen and one tenth

(f) thirty and eight tenths **(g)** twenty-five and six tenths

4 The table shows volumes of fuel used by Stan.

Mon	Tue	Wed	Thu	Fri	Sat
13·2 l	12·3 l	13·8 l	12·6 l	13·0 l	12·5 l

Write the volumes in order, starting with the smallest.

37 Alltmouth Moped Deliveries

Decimals: first decimal place, addition

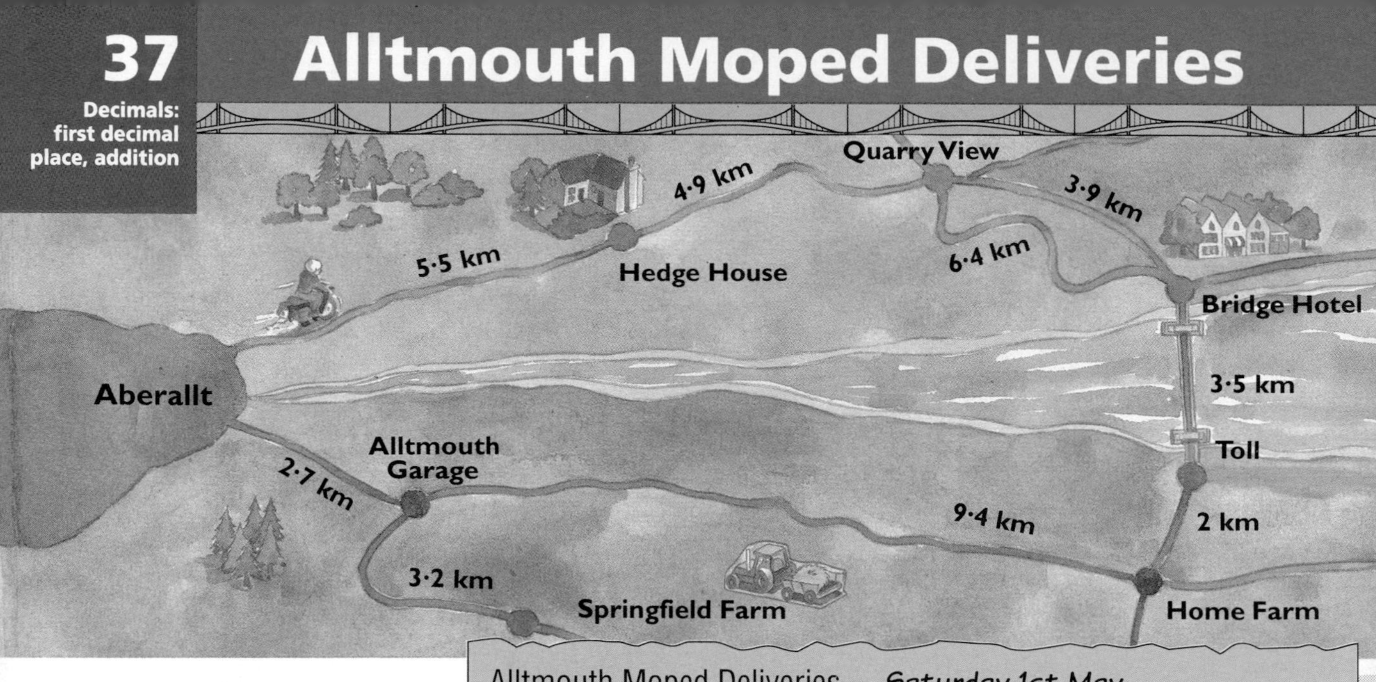

Alltmouth Moped Deliveries – *Saturday 1st May*

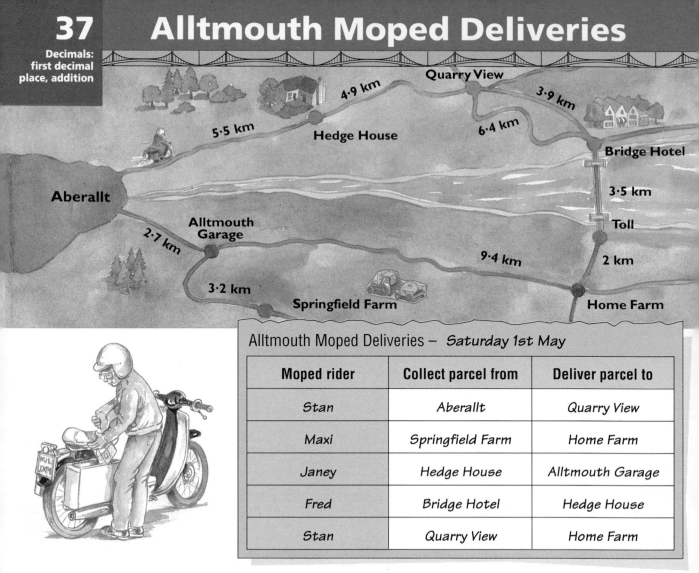

Moped rider	Collect parcel from	Deliver parcel to
Stan	*Aberallt*	*Quarry View*
Maxi	*Springfield Farm*	*Home Farm*
Janey	*Hedge House*	*Alltmouth Garage*
Fred	*Bridge Hotel*	*Hedge House*
Stan	*Quarry View*	*Home Farm*

1 Find the total distance for each delivery.

2 What was the total distance travelled by Stan?

3 What is the total weight of the parcels delivered to
- **(a)** Springfield Farm and Quarry View
- **(b)** Alltmouth Garage and Hedge House
- **(c)** Bridge Hotel and Home Farm?

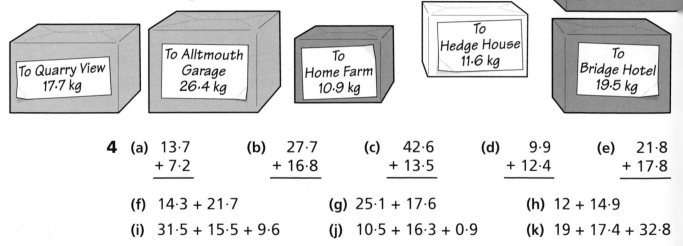

To Quarry View 17·7 kg

To Alltmouth Garage 26·4 kg

To Home Farm 10·9 kg

To Hedge House 11·6 kg

To Bridge Hotel 19·5 kg

4
- **(a)** 13·7 + 7·2
- **(b)** 27·7 + 16·8
- **(c)** 42·6 + 13·5
- **(d)** 9·9 + 12·4
- **(e)** 21·8 + 17·8
- **(f)** 14·3 + 21·7
- **(g)** 25·1 + 17·6
- **(h)** 12 + 14·9
- **(i)** 31·5 + 15·5 + 9·6
- **(j)** 10·5 + 16·3 + 0·9
- **(k)** 19 + 17·4 + 32·8

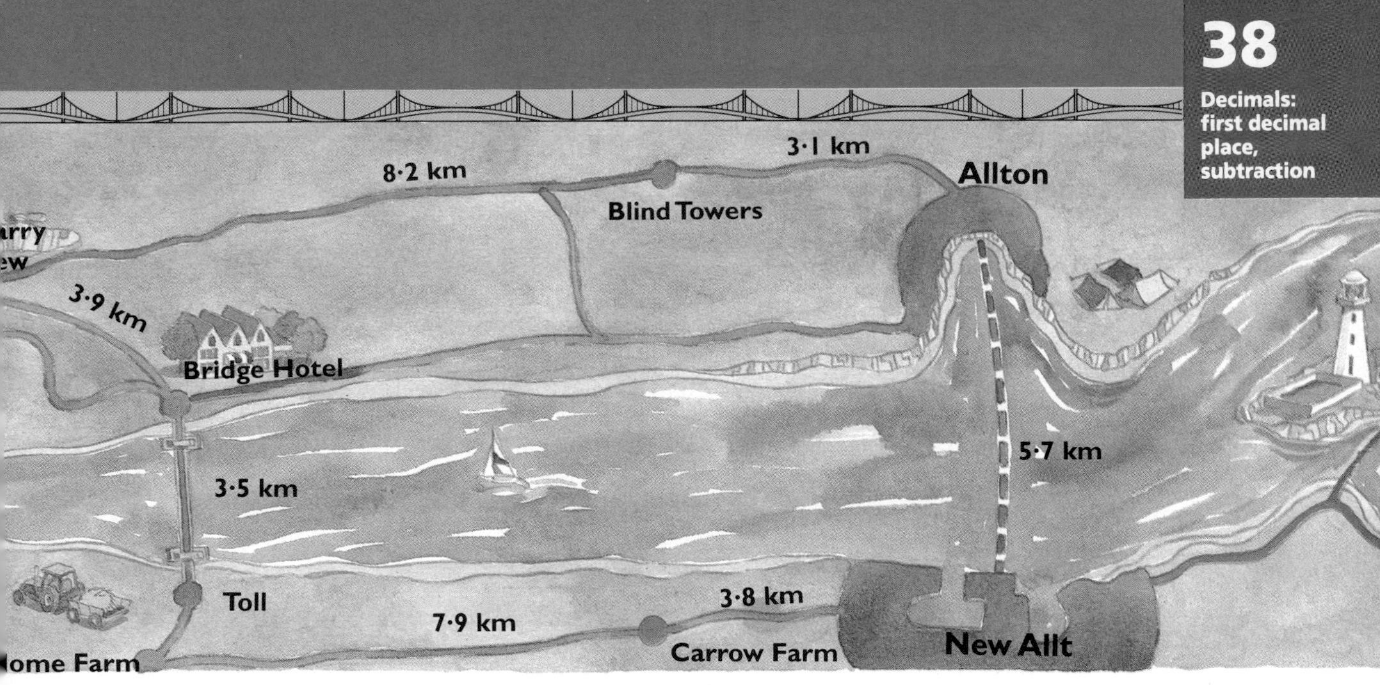

1 Which distance is longer and by how much:

(a) Bridge Hotel to Quarry View **or** Bridge Hotel to the Toll

(b) Allton to Blind Towers **or** Allton to New Allt

(c) Carrow Farm to Home Farm **or** Carrow Farm to New Allt?

2

(a)	(b)	(c)	(d)	(e)	(f)
4·9 − 2·4	8·4 − 2·6	3·1 − 0·5	7·2 − 3·8	9·6 − 4·7	5·0 − 3·3

3 From the road sign, how much further is it to Rumness than to:

(a) Ogton

(b) Breckford

(c) Linton

(d) Blaybury?

Linton	17·3 km
Ogton	19·6 km
Blaybury	20·5 km
Breckford	34·8 km
Rumness	41·3 km

4

(a)	(b)	(c)	(d)	(e)	(f)
46·4 − 21·7	50·1 − 17·7	26·6 − 18·9	36·8 − 15·9	47·2 − 20·6	30·0 − 9·8

5 Stan has to deliver all these parcels to Allton.

Problem solving

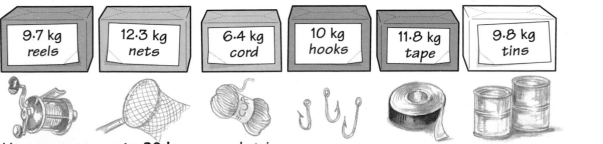

9.7 kg reels | 12.3 kg nets | 6.4 kg cord | 10 kg hooks | 11.8 kg tape | 9.8 kg tins

He can carry **up to 20 kg** on each trip.
What is the smallest number of trips he needs to make?

39 Setting sail

Decimals: first decimal place, multiplication

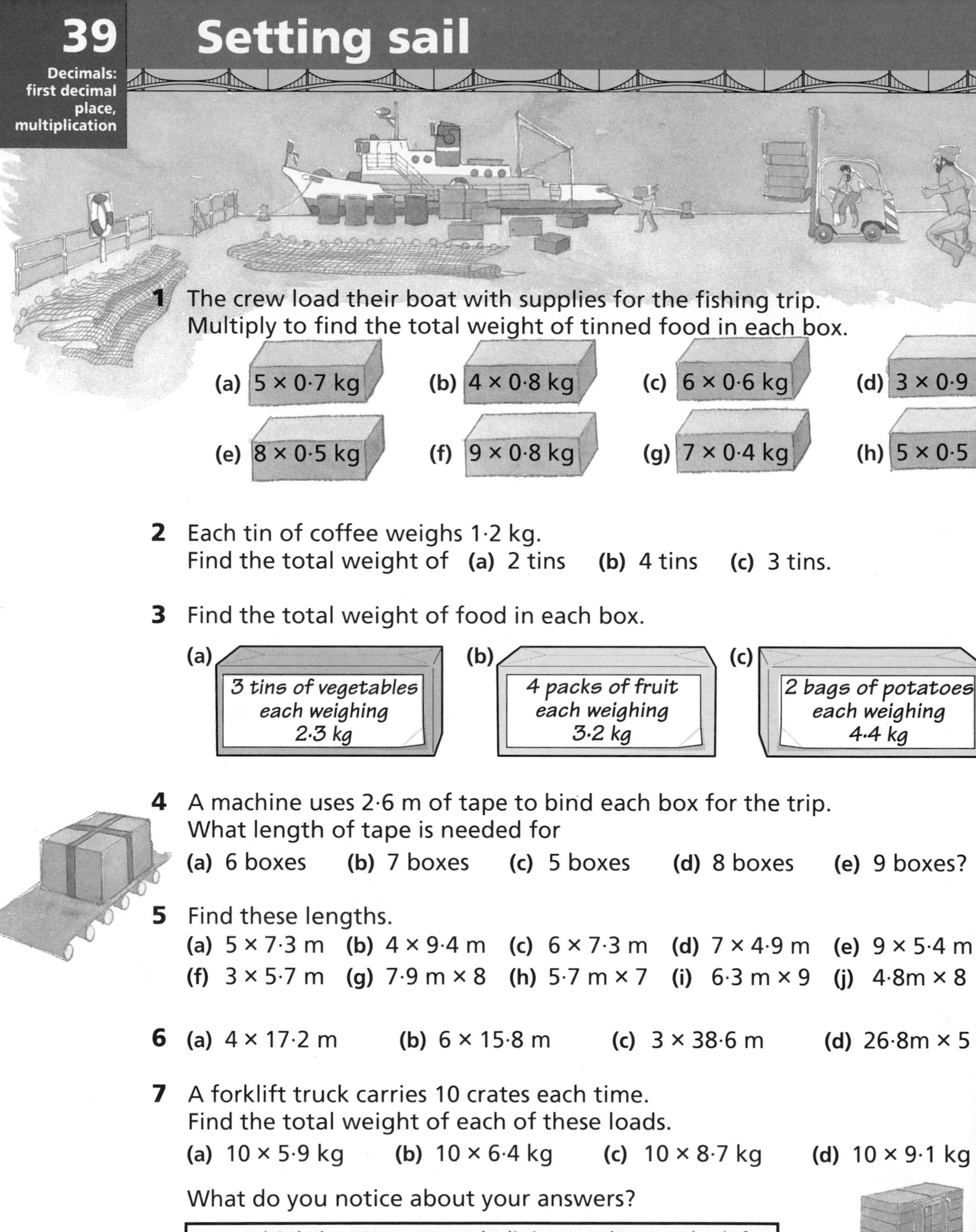

1 The crew load their boat with supplies for the fishing trip.
Multiply to find the total weight of tinned food in each box.

(a) 5 × 0·7 kg **(b)** 4 × 0·8 kg **(c)** 6 × 0·6 kg **(d)** 3 × 0·9 k

(e) 8 × 0·5 kg **(f)** 9 × 0·8 kg **(g)** 7 × 0·4 kg **(h)** 5 × 0·5 k

2 Each tin of coffee weighs 1·2 kg.
Find the total weight of **(a)** 2 tins **(b)** 4 tins **(c)** 3 tins.

3 Find the total weight of food in each box.

(a) *3 tins of vegetables each weighing 2·3 kg*

(b) *4 packs of fruit each weighing 3·2 kg*

(c) *2 bags of potatoes each weighing 4·4 kg*

4 A machine uses 2·6 m of tape to bind each box for the trip.
What length of tape is needed for

(a) 6 boxes **(b)** 7 boxes **(c)** 5 boxes **(d)** 8 boxes **(e)** 9 boxes?

5 Find these lengths.

(a) 5 × 7·3 m **(b)** 4 × 9·4 m **(c)** 6 × 7·3 m **(d)** 7 × 4·9 m **(e)** 9 × 5·4 m

(f) 3 × 5·7 m **(g)** 7·9 m × 8 **(h)** 5·7 m × 7 **(i)** 6·3 m × 9 **(j)** 4·8m × 8

6 **(a)** 4 × 17·2 m **(b)** 6 × 15·8 m **(c)** 3 × 38·6 m **(d)** 26·8m × 5

7 A forklift truck carries 10 crates each time.
Find the total weight of each of these loads.

(a) 10 × 5·9 kg **(b)** 10 × 6·4 kg **(c)** 10 × 8·7 kg **(d)** 10 × 9·1 kg

What do you notice about your answers?

> To multiply by 10, move each digit one place to the left.

8 Find **mentally**.

(a) 10 × 6·3 **(b)** 10 × 4·8 **(c)** 10 × 9·5

(d) 10 × 12·1 **(e)** 10 × 26·6 **(f)** 10 × 30·3

(g) 41·7 × 10 **(h)** 57·6 × 10 **(i)** 68·8 × 10

1 Sam uses cord to repair the fishing nets.
Find mentally each length of cord when he cuts

(a) 0·6 m into 3 equal lengths **(b)** 0·8 m into 4 equal lengths.

2 Find these lengths of cord for net repairs.

(a) 6·8 m into 2 equal lengths **(b)** 10·5 m into 5 equal lengths
(c) 13·3 m into 7 equal lengths **(d)** 20·7 m into 9 equal lengths

3 **(a)** $3\overline{)8{\cdot}7}$ **(b)** $4\overline{)9{\cdot}6}$ **(c)** $8\overline{)17{\cdot}6}$ **(d)** $9\overline{)30{\cdot}6}$ **(e)** $6\overline{)40{\cdot}8}$
(f) 49·5 ÷ 5 **(g)** 56·4 ÷ 6 **(h)** 60·2 ÷ 7 **(i)** 71·2 ÷ 8 **(j)** 83·7 ÷ 9

4 Ice is shared equally among fish boxes.
Find the weight of ice in each box.

(a) 27·6 kg among 4 boxes **(b)** 41·4 kg among 6 boxes
(c) 60·8 kg among 8 boxes **(d)** 69·3 kg among 7 boxes

5 Jack shares rope equally among the fishing boats.
Share these lengths of rope equally.

(a) 16 m among 5 boats **(b)** 22 m among 4 boats
(c) 37 m among 2 boats **(d)** 33 m among 6 boats

6 **(a)** 38 ÷ 4 **(b)** 53 ÷ 5 **(c)** 34·8 ÷ 6 **(d)** 53·1 ÷ 9 **(e)** 46·9 ÷ 7
(f) 89 ÷ 2 **(g)** 70·2 ÷ 3 **(h)** 74 ÷ 5 **(i)** 86·4 ÷ 8 **(j)** 93·8 ÷ 7

7 **(a)** 33 ÷ 10 **(b)** 46 ÷ 10 **(c)** 99 ÷ 10 **(d)** 167 ÷ 10 **(e)** 203 ÷ 10

Sam sees a pattern when dividing by 10.

To divide by 10, move each digit one place to the right.

8 Use Sam's method to find

(a) 66 ÷ 10 **(b)** 78 ÷ 10 **(c)** 299 ÷ 10 **(d)** 360 ÷ 10 **(e)** 7 ÷ 10

9 Use Sam's method to find which of these answers are wrong.

(a) 266 ÷ 10 = 26·6 **(b)** 103 ÷ 10 = 13·3 **(c)** 417 ÷ 10 = 41·7

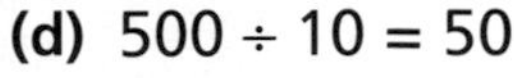

(d) 500 ÷ 10 = 50 **(e)** 516 ÷ 10 = 56·1 **(f)** 323 ÷ 10 = 33·2

41 Back from the sea

Decimals: first decimal place, +, −, ×, ÷

1 How far do the 3 boats stretch along the quayside?

2 How much longer is
(a) Sepia than Tern **(b)** Sepia than Dawn **(c)** Tern than Dawn?

3 John stacks boxes of fish on the quay.
(a) What is the total height of 5 of these boxes in centimetres?
(b) 6 boxes are laid end to end. How far do they stretch
- in centimetres
- in metres and centimetres?

85·5 cm

4 In 8 minutes, Alex gutted 77·6 kg of fish.
In 9 minutes, Peter gutted 92·7 kg of fish.
On average, what weight of fish did each man gut in 1 minute?

5 The 7 crew members of the Sepia were at sea for 10 days.
(a) On average, how much of each item was used each day?
(b) On average, how much did each crew member use each day?

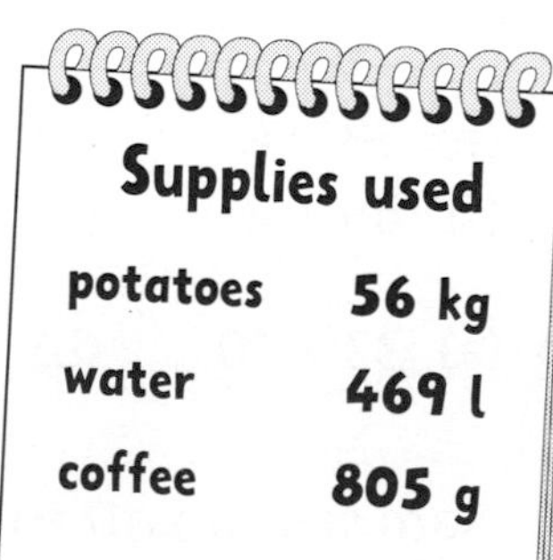

Problem solving

6 The length of the longest fish caught on the trip was ☐☐•8 cm
When its length is multiplied by 7, the **product** has
- the tens digit the same as the tenths digit
- a zero units digit
- a hundreds digit which is even.

What is the length of the fish?

47 out of the 100 light cells on this traffic sign are lit.
The fraction of the sign lit is 47 hundredths **or** $\frac{47}{100}$ **or** 0·47.

1 Each sign has 100 cells.
Write in **three** ways the fraction of each sign lit.

(a) 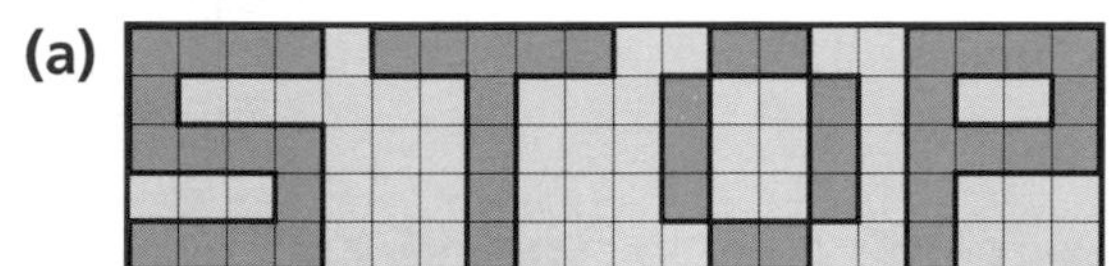

(b) 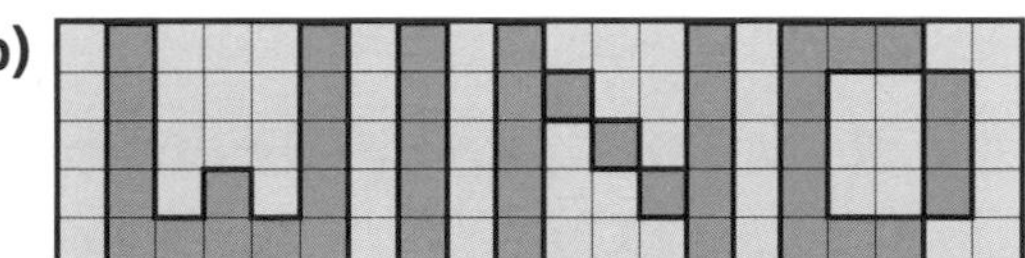

(c) 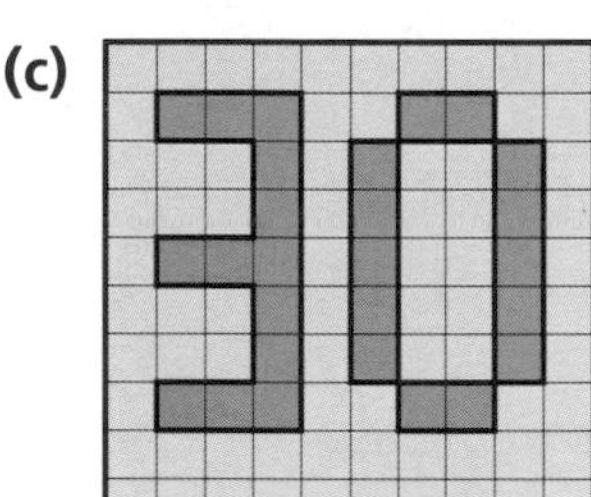

(d) 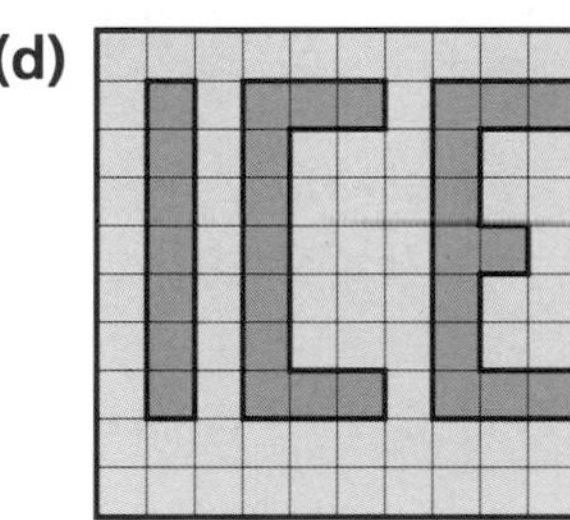

(e) 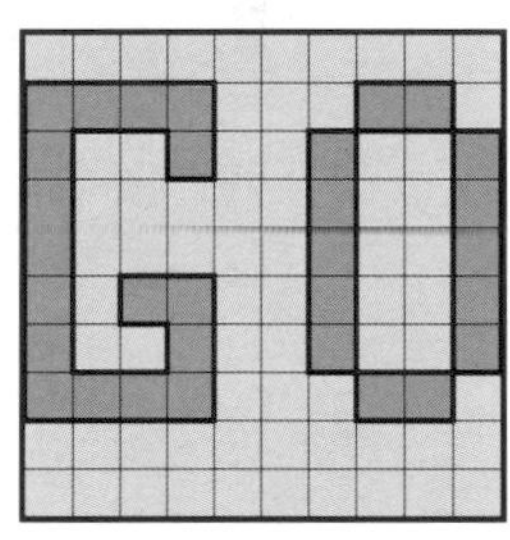

0·31 is the **decimal form** of 31 hundredths or $\frac{31}{100}$

0·03 is the decimal form of 3 hundredths or $\frac{3}{100}$

0·30 is the decimal form of 30 hundredths or $\frac{30}{100}$

2 Write in decimal form

(a) 23 hundredths **(b)** 50 hundredths **(c)** 4 hundredths

(d) $\frac{39}{100}$ **(e)** $\frac{70}{100}$ **(f)** $\frac{1}{100}$ **(g)** $\frac{62}{100}$ **(h)** $\frac{9}{100}$ **(i)** $\frac{20}{100}$

3 Write each of these decimals in **two** other ways:

(a) 0·51 **(b)** 0·92 **(c)** 0·40 **(d)** 0·55 **(e)** 0·08 **(f)** 0·83

4 Write the decimals in order, starting with the **smallest** each time.

(a) 0·38 0·31 0·37 0·39 0·35 0·32
(b) 0·16 0·56 0·86 0·26 0·96 0·46
(c) 0·21 0·01 0·12 0·02 0·22 0·11
(d) 0·05 0·08 0·11 0·06 0·01 0·10

Go to Workbook page 10.

43 Beach battle

Decimals: length, money

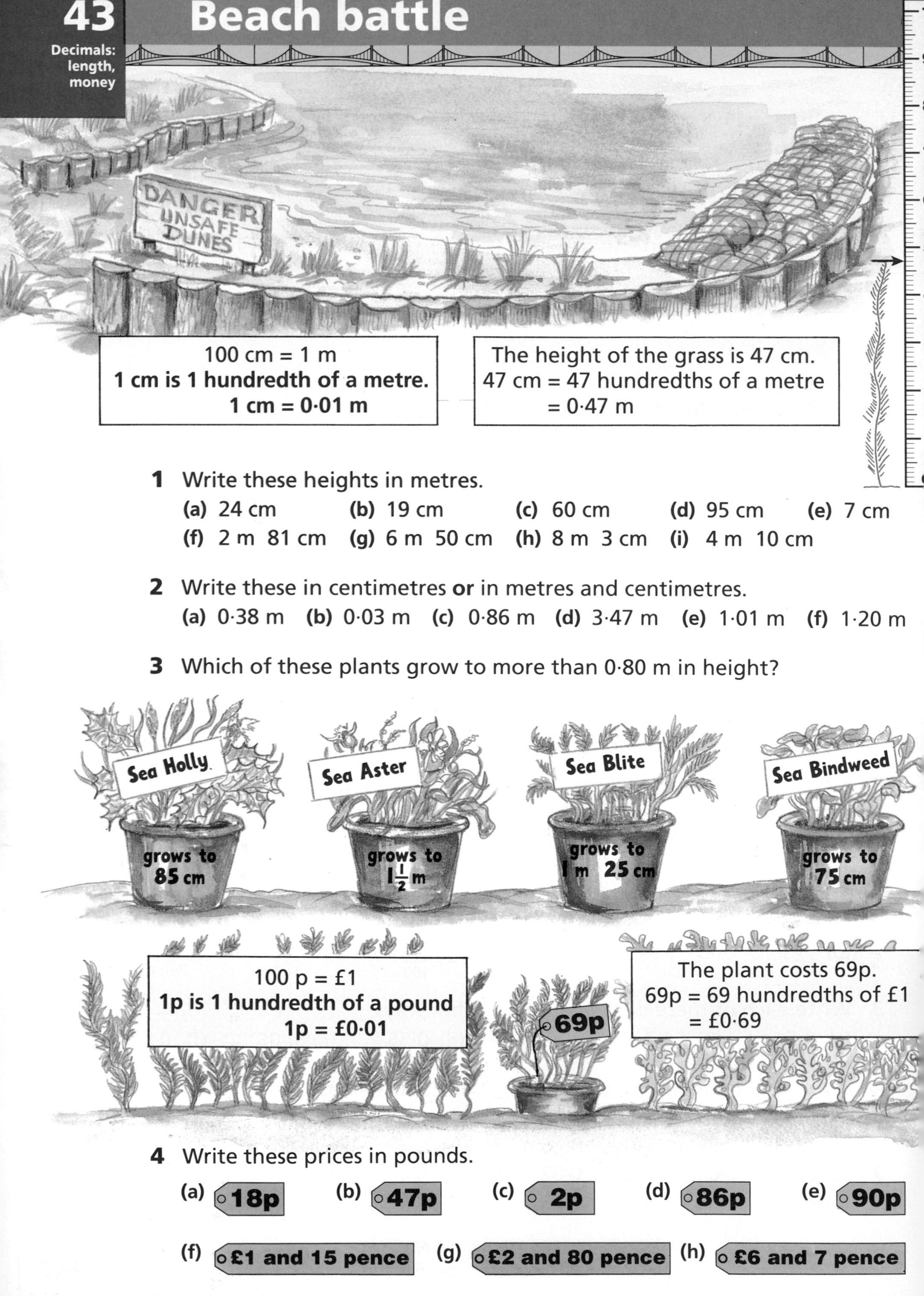

100 cm = 1 m
1 cm is 1 hundredth of a metre.
1 cm = 0·01 m

The height of the grass is 47 cm.
47 cm = 47 hundredths of a metre
= 0·47 m

1 Write these heights in metres.

(a) 24 cm **(b)** 19 cm **(c)** 60 cm **(d)** 95 cm **(e)** 7 cm
(f) 2 m 81 cm **(g)** 6 m 50 cm **(h)** 8 m 3 cm **(i)** 4 m 10 cm

2 Write these in centimetres **or** in metres and centimetres.

(a) 0·38 m **(b)** 0·03 m **(c)** 0·86 m **(d)** 3·47 m **(e)** 1·01 m **(f)** 1·20 m

3 Which of these plants grow to more than 0·80 m in height?

100 p = £1
1p is 1 hundredth of a pound
1p = £0·01

The plant costs 69p.
69p = 69 hundredths of £1
= £0·69

4 Write these prices in pounds.

(a) **18p** (b) **47p** (c) **2p** (d) **86p** (e) **90p**

(f) **£1 and 15 pence** (g) **£2 and 80 pence** (h) **£6 and 7 pence**

44 Decimals: tenths and hundredths

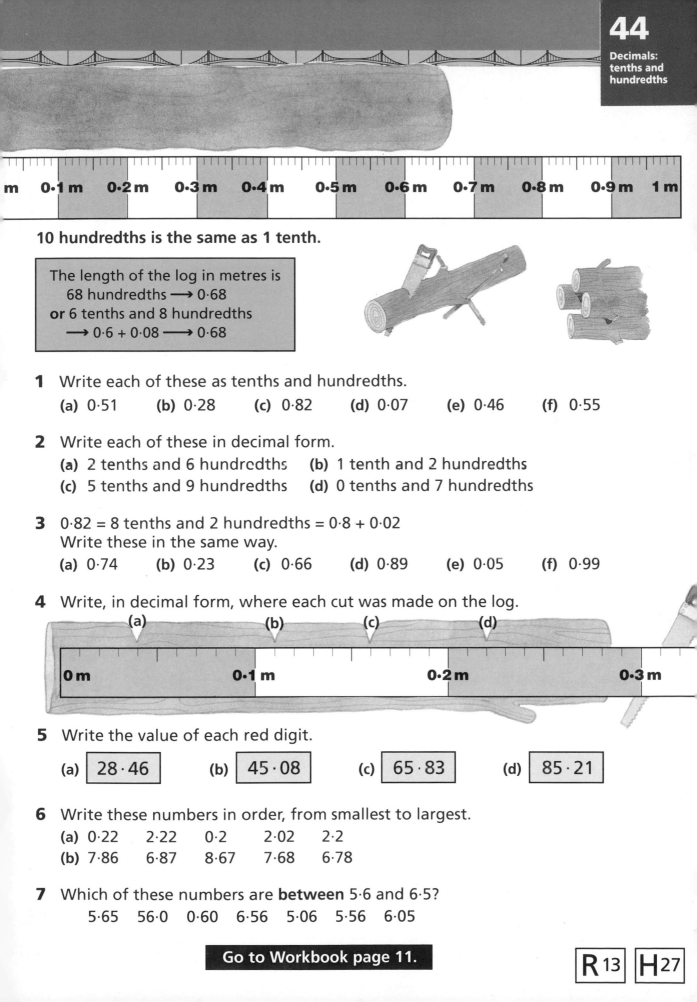

m 0·1 m 0·2 m 0·3 m 0·4 m 0·5 m 0·6 m 0·7 m 0·8 m 0·9 m 1 m

10 hundredths is the same as 1 tenth.

> The length of the log in metres is
> 68 hundredths ⟶ 0·68
> **or** 6 tenths and 8 hundredths
> ⟶ 0·6 + 0·08 ⟶ 0·68

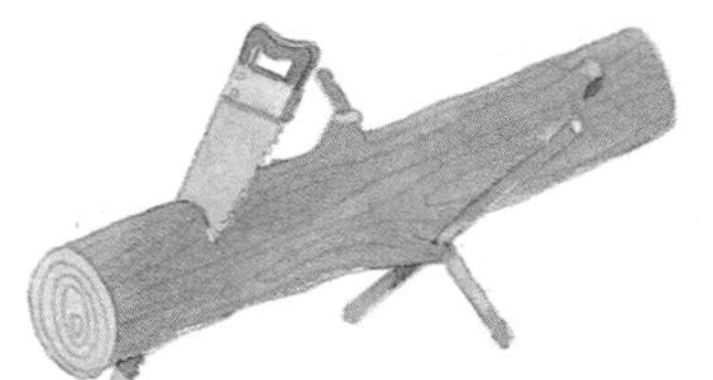

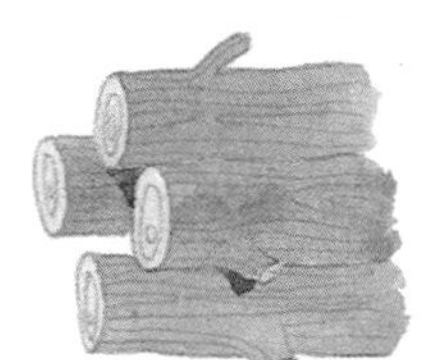

1 Write each of these as tenths and hundredths.

(a) 0·51 **(b)** 0·28 **(c)** 0·82 **(d)** 0·07 **(e)** 0·46 **(f)** 0·55

2 Write each of these in decimal form.

(a) 2 tenths and 6 hundredths **(b)** 1 tenth and 2 hundredths
(c) 5 tenths and 9 hundredths **(d)** 0 tenths and 7 hundredths

3 0·82 = 8 tenths and 2 hundredths = 0·8 + 0·02
Write these in the same way.

(a) 0·74 **(b)** 0·23 **(c)** 0·66 **(d)** 0·89 **(e)** 0·05 **(f)** 0·99

4 Write, in decimal form, where each cut was made on the log.

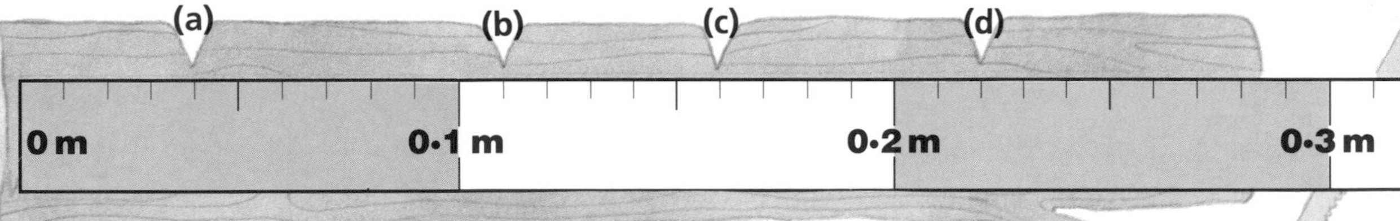

5 Write the value of each red digit.

(a) 28·46 **(b)** 45·08 **(c)** 65·83 **(d)** 85·21

6 Write these numbers in order, from smallest to largest.

(a) 0·22 2·22 0·2 2·02 2·2
(b) 7·86 6·87 8·67 7·68 6·78

7 Which of these numbers are **between** 5·6 and 6·5?

5·65 56·0 0·60 6·56 5·06 5·56 6·05

Go to Workbook page 11.

45 Waiting for the ferry

Decimals: second decimal place, addition

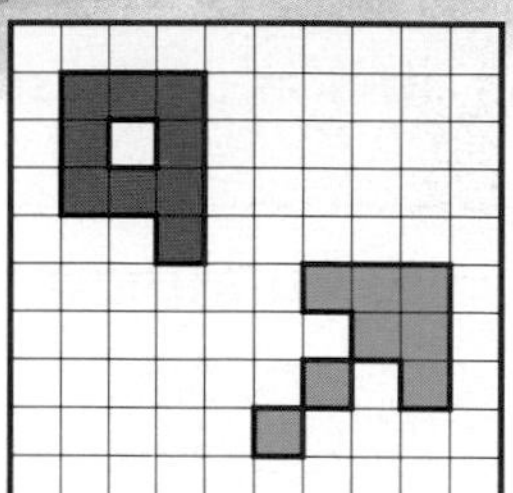

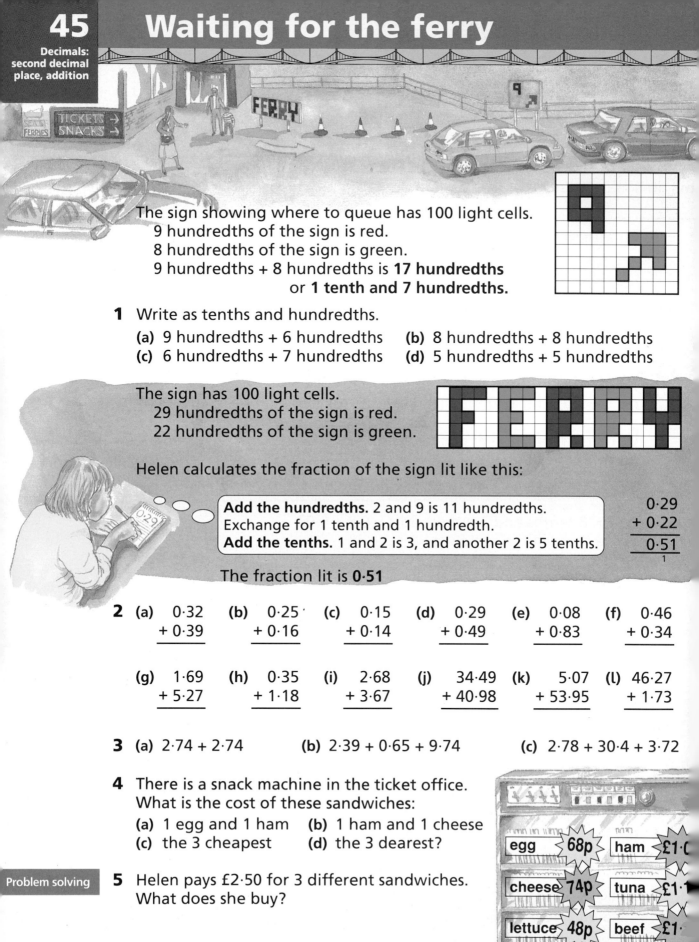

The sign showing where to queue has 100 light cells.
9 hundredths of the sign is red.
8 hundredths of the sign is green.
9 hundredths + 8 hundredths is **17 hundredths**
or **1 tenth and 7 hundredths.**

1 Write as tenths and hundredths.

(a) 9 hundredths + 6 hundredths (b) 8 hundredths + 8 hundredths
(c) 6 hundredths + 7 hundredths (d) 5 hundredths + 5 hundredths

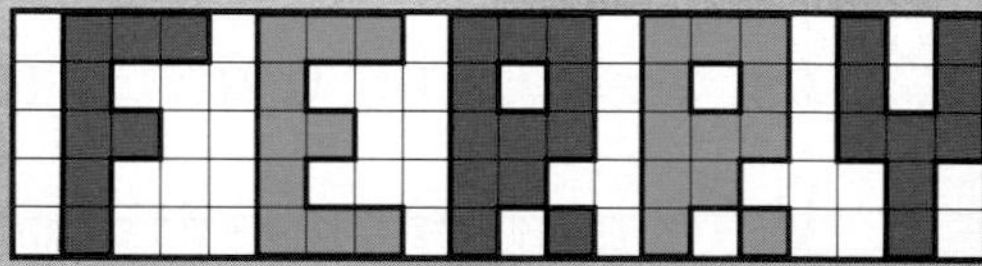

The sign has 100 light cells.
29 hundredths of the sign is red.
22 hundredths of the sign is green.

Helen calculates the fraction of the sign lit like this:

Add the hundredths. 2 and 9 is 11 hundredths.
Exchange for 1 tenth and 1 hundredth.
Add the tenths. 1 and 2 is 3, and another 2 is 5 tenths.

$$\begin{array}{r} 0{\cdot}29 \\ +\ 0{\cdot}22 \\ \hline 0{\cdot}51 \\ \hline {\scriptstyle 1} \end{array}$$

The fraction lit is **0·51**

2

(a) 0·32 + 0·39 (b) 0·25 + 0·16 (c) 0·15 + 0·14 (d) 0·29 + 0·49 (e) 0·08 + 0·83 (f) 0·46 + 0·34

(g) 1·69 + 5·27 (h) 0·35 + 1·18 (i) 2·68 + 3·67 (j) 34·49 + 40·98 (k) 5·07 + 53·95 (l) 46·27 + 1·73

3 (a) 2·74 + 2·74 (b) 2·39 + 0·65 + 9·74 (c) 2·78 + 30·4 + 3·72

4 There is a snack machine in the ticket office.
What is the cost of these sandwiches:

(a) 1 egg and 1 ham (b) 1 ham and 1 cheese
(c) the 3 cheapest (d) the 3 dearest?

Problem solving

5 Helen pays £2·50 for 3 different sandwiches.
What does she buy?

DRY CLEANERS
4·69 m

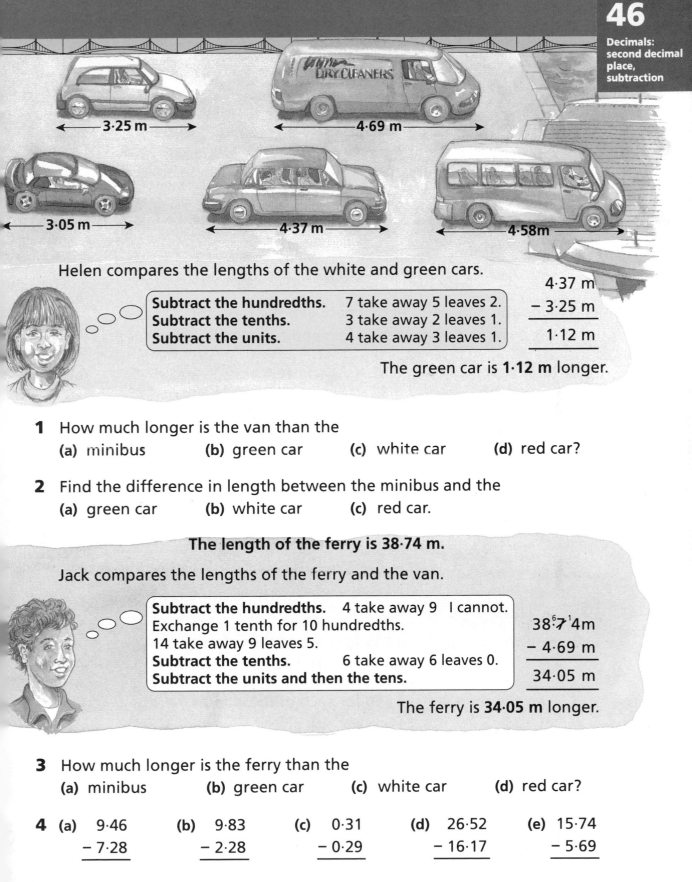

Helen compares the lengths of the white and green cars.

Subtract the hundredths.	7 take away 5 leaves 2.
Subtract the tenths.	3 take away 2 leaves 1.
Subtract the units.	4 take away 3 leaves 1.

$$\begin{array}{r} 4{\cdot}37\text{ m} \\ -\ 3{\cdot}25\text{ m} \\ \hline 1{\cdot}12\text{ m} \\ \hline \end{array}$$

The green car is **1·12 m** longer.

1 How much longer is the van than the
(a) minibus (b) green car (c) white car (d) red car?

2 Find the difference in length between the minibus and the
(a) green car (b) white car (c) red car.

The length of the ferry is 38·74 m.

Jack compares the lengths of the ferry and the van.

Subtract the hundredths. 4 take away 9 I cannot.
Exchange 1 tenth for 10 hundredths.
14 take away 9 leaves 5.
Subtract the tenths. 6 take away 6 leaves 0.
Subtract the units and then the tens.

$$\begin{array}{r} 38{\cdot}\overset{6}{\not7}{}^{1}4\text{m} \\ -\ 4{\cdot}69\text{ m} \\ \hline 34{\cdot}05\text{ m} \\ \hline \end{array}$$

The ferry is **34·05 m** longer.

3 How much longer is the ferry than the
(a) minibus (b) green car (c) white car (d) red car?

4 (a) $\begin{array}{r} 9{\cdot}46 \\ -\ 7{\cdot}28 \\ \hline \end{array}$ (b) $\begin{array}{r} 9{\cdot}83 \\ -\ 2{\cdot}28 \\ \hline \end{array}$ (c) $\begin{array}{r} 0{\cdot}31 \\ -\ 0{\cdot}29 \\ \hline \end{array}$ (d) $\begin{array}{r} 26{\cdot}52 \\ -\ 16{\cdot}17 \\ \hline \end{array}$ (e) $\begin{array}{r} 15{\cdot}74 \\ -\ 5{\cdot}69 \\ \hline \end{array}$

5 (a) 5·35 − 2·16 (b) 11·80 − 8·34 (c) 13·87 − 9·79 (d) 37·86 − 15·47
(e) 14·58 − 11·29 (f) 8·66 − 8·19 (g) 10·71 − 8·17 (h) 73·35 − 12·47

6 (a) 9·7 − 3·45 (b) 6·5 − 1·07 (c) 9·8 − 2·06 (d) 8·23 − 2·9

47 Boarding the ferry

Decimals: second decimal place, subtraction

Ferry fares

Adult	**£5·40**
Child	**£2·85**
Car	**£12·85**
Van	**£17·62**
Minibus	**£19·50**

An adult's fare is £5·40
A child's fare is £2·85

```
  £5·40
– £2·85
  £2·55
```

The difference in cost is **£2·55**

1 Find the difference in cost between the fares for
(a) a car and a van **(b)** a van and a minibus **(c)** a car and a minibus.

2 **(a)** 8·34 − 3·49 **(b)** 6·85 − 4·89 **(c)** 10·43 − 8·46 **(d)** 5·42 − 4·79 **(e)** 4·33 − 1·85

3 **(a)** 8·22 − 5·46 **(b)** 2·21 − 1·63 **(c)** 3·22 − 1·23 **(d)** 5·31 − 2·63
(e) 10·71 − 7·75 **(f)** 10·48 − 9·99 **(g)** 8·34 − 1·77 **(h)** 6·81 − 1·86

The fare for a van and driver is £23·02.
What is the driver's change from £25?

```
  £25·00
– £23·02
  £ 1·98
```

The change is **£1·98**

4 Find the change from **£35** for each of these fares:
(a) £31·57 **(b)** £33·45 **(c)** £33·82 **(d)** £34·12 **(e)** £31·27

5 Find the change from **£50** for each of these fares:
(a) £34·75 **(b)** £44·85 **(c)** £28·42 **(d)** £31·57 **(e)** £36·97

6 Find the difference between
(a) 18 and 16·03 **(b)** 9·3 and 6·81 **(c)** 1·58 and 4·75
(d) 4·08 and 6·24 **(e)** 3·39 and 7·3 **(f)** 3·45 and 2·57

7 An adult and three children go on board the ferry in a vehicle. The total cost is £33·45. What kind of vehicle are they in?

Problem solving

8 Three people go on board the ferry in a car. The total cost of the tickets is £23·95. What tickets do they buy?

H29 R14

Alltbay Marina

~ Sailing, Fishing, Camping ~

Sun Cruisers

Make	Length
Sunstar	5·05 m
Sunseeker	5·44 m
Sunray	6·05 m
Sunbeam	6·58 m

1 (a) The Sunbeam is towed on a trailer which is 7·5 m long. How much longer is the trailer than the boat?

(b) The towing car is 4·35 m long. What is the total length of the car and trailer?

(c) How much longer is the Sunray than the Sunseeker?

(d) What length of quay is taken up by these four cruisers moored end to end?

2 The charge for keeping a boat in the marina is £9 for each metre length of the boat.
What is the charge for a boat with a length of

(a) 4·7 m (b) 7·6 m (c) 8·3 m (d) 9·9 m?

3

16 kg anchor £23·55

7 m chain £15·80

10 m rope £11·45

(a) What is the total cost of the anchor, chain and rope?

(b) Each metre of chain weighs 5·7 kg. Each metre of rope weighs 0·2 kg. What is the total weight of the anchor, chain and rope?

4 A Sunstar uses 46·8 litres of fuel during a 6-hour trip. What is the average amount of fuel used each hour?

5

Sailing lessons

£5·60 for 1 hour
£10·00 for 2 hours
£14·10 for 3 hours
£17·64 for 4 hours

(a) What is the total cost of
- three 2-hour lessons
- two 3-hour lessons?

(b) What is the cheapest way to buy six hours of lessons?

Problem solving

49 Alltbay fishing club

Decimals: consolidation, 1 and 2 decimal places

Hire charges

boat	£12·60
rod	£ 8·55
lifejacket	£ 2·35

1 (a) How much does it cost to hire all three items from the fishing club?
(b) Jill brings her own rod. What does she pay to hire the other items?

2 Jill catches 3 salmon each weighing 5·8 kg, and 2 sea trout each weighing 2·7 kg.
What is the total weight of her catch?

Problem solving

3 Find the length, in metres, of one of Jill's sea trout.

- the units digit and the tenths digit add to 3
- all the digits add to 7
- the hundredths digit is 1 more than the tenths digit

4 These are the heaviest fish caught this year by club members.

(a) Find the difference in weight between the heaviest and the lightest f
(b) What is the total weight of the four fish?
(c) What is their average weight?

5 Jill's caravan is 4 m 85 cm long.
She spends 3 nights on the site.
(a) What is the total cost for parking her caravan?
(b) How much does it cost to hire all four items from the camp shop?

Problem solving

(c) Jill hires 3 of the items listed.
The total charge is £7·85.
Which items does she hire?

Caravan site fees

up to 4 m: £8·75 a night
more than 4 m: £9·50 a night

Items for hire

barbecue	£3·85
fridge	£4·05
heater	£1·35
TV set	£2·65

Hire all 4. Save £2!

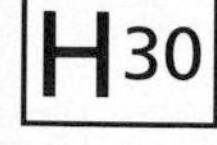

Point of Allt

Decimals: second decimal place, calculator

The table shows the depth of water at the Point of Allt causeway at different times during Saturday 14th May.

1 Copy and complete the table.

Time	8 am	9 am	10 am	11 am	noon	1 pm	2 pm	3 pm	4 pm
Depth of water	1·88 m	1·49 m	1·07 m	0·70 m	0·34 m	0·65 m	1·05 m		
Change in depth each hour		down 0·39 m				up 0·31 m		up 0·41 m	up 0·38 m

2 What is the difference between the water depths
(a) at 8 am and at noon **(b)** at noon and at 4 pm?

3 It is safe to cross the causeway when the water is less than 1 m 50 cm deep.
Between which times is it safe to cross?

4 How much does each of these groups pay to visit the lighthouse:
(a) 1 adult and 1 child
(b) 2 adults and 2 children?

5 Find the total cost, **including parking**, for each of these groups to visit the lighthouse.
(a) 2 adults and 4 children in a car
(b) 12 children in a minibus
(c) 36 children in a coach
(d) 8 children and 2 adults in a minibus
(e) 29 children and 4 adults in a coach

6 A group of 13 travelling by minibus pays a total of £13 for parking and visiting the lighthouse.
How many adults and how many children are in the group?

Problem solving

51 At the lighthouse

Decimals: second decimal place, calculator

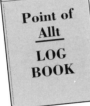

Point of Allt
LOG BOOK

1 **(a)** Use the information in this table to find the **average** number of visitors each day. Give your answer in decimal form **and** then rounded to the nearest whole number.

Lighthouse visitors

Thu	Fri	Sat	Sun
16	45	61	51

(b) On the other three days that week there were 63 visitors altogether. Find, to the nearest whole number, the average number of visitors each day of the week.

2 Many sea birds visit the island.

Lighthouse log book

	Tern	Fulmar	Kittiwake	Diver	Gannet
Number of sightings	170	215	389	222	188
Number of months	8	4	6	5	9

For each type of bird find, to the nearest whole number, the average number of sightings in a month.

3 The drawing shows one of the stones used to build the lighthouse wall. Find

0·13 m

0·56 m

(a) the height of the wall – it has 15 layers of stones.

(b) the length of the wall – it has 467 stones end-to-end.

Problem solving

4 **(a)** Follow these instructions to find out when the lighthouse was built.

- Write a 4-digit **starting number** with 2 decimal places.
- Enter it in your calculator then double it.
- Add 38·04 then divide your answer by 2.
- Subtract your starting number then multiply your answer by 100.

(b) Do all this again for different starting numbers. What do you notice?

Ask your teacher what to do next

Merlin Castle

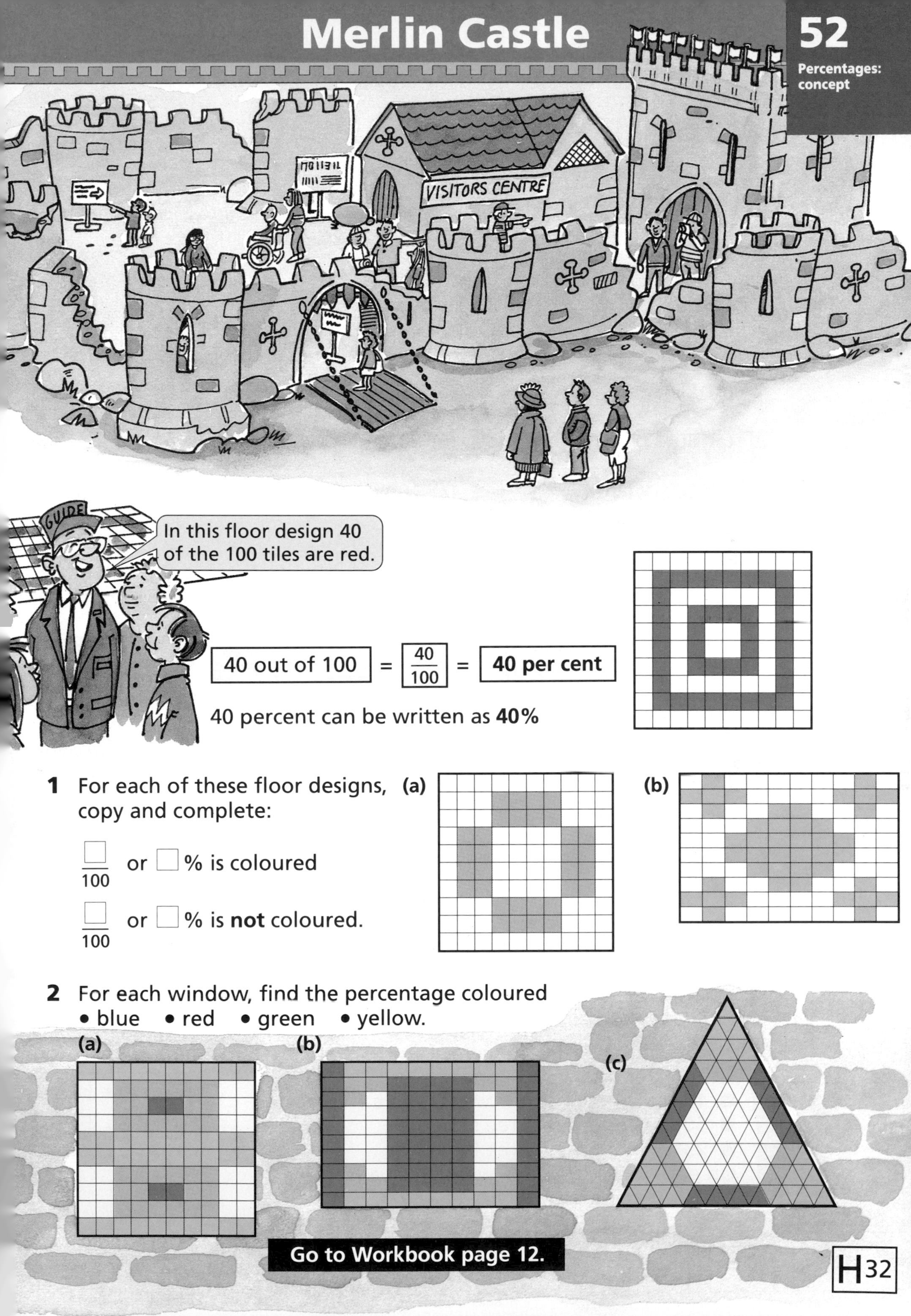

40 out of 100 = $\frac{40}{100}$ = **40 per cent**

40 percent can be written as **40%**

1 For each of these floor designs, copy and complete:

(a) (b)

$\frac{\square}{100}$ or $\square$ % is coloured

$\frac{\square}{100}$ or $\square$ % is **not** coloured.

2 For each window, find the percentage coloured
• blue • red • green • yellow.

(a) (b) (c)

Go to Workbook page 12.

53 Castle visitors

Percentages: of a quantity

$50\% = \frac{1}{2}$	$25\% = \frac{1}{4}$	$10\% = \frac{1}{10}$

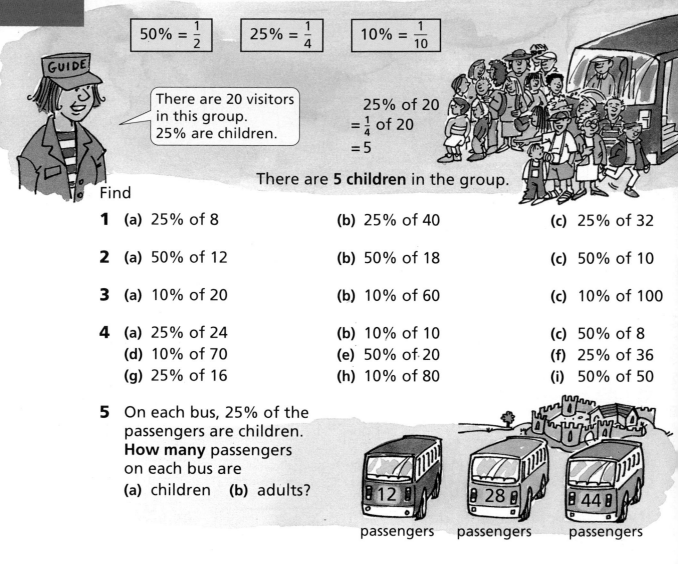

There are 20 visitors in this group. 25% are children.

25% of 20
$= \frac{1}{4}$ of 20
$= 5$

There are **5 children** in the group.

Find

1 **(a)** 25% of 8 **(b)** 25% of 40 **(c)** 25% of 32

2 **(a)** 50% of 12 **(b)** 50% of 18 **(c)** 50% of 10

3 **(a)** 10% of 20 **(b)** 10% of 60 **(c)** 10% of 100

4 **(a)** 25% of 24 **(b)** 10% of 10 **(c)** 50% of 8
(d) 10% of 70 **(e)** 50% of 20 **(f)** 25% of 36
(g) 25% of 16 **(h)** 10% of 80 **(i)** 50% of 50

5 On each bus, 25% of the passengers are children. **How many** passengers on each bus are
(a) children **(b)** adults?

12 passengers

28 passengers

44 passengers

6 Which bus has more passengers who are Senior Citizens? How many more?

50% Senior Citizens

16 passengers

50 passengers

10% Senior Citizens

7 The table shows the number of visitors during the weekend.
- 10% of these visitors were given a free poster
- 50% were given a free pencil
- 25% were given a free badge

On each day, how many were given a free
(a) poster **(b)** pencil **(c)** badge?

Celebration at Merlin Castle 500 years old this weekend

Number of visitors

Fri	Sat	Sun
180	300	260

H33 R16

Ask your teacher what to do next

Winning card

1 Which yellow card, in each set, can reach the **End** box?

(a)

10% | 30% | 100% | 75% | 40%

Start ▼ Greater than 20% ▼ yes ▼ Greater than $\frac{1}{2}$ ▼ yes ▼ Less than 1 ▼ yes ▼ **End**

(b)

0·83 | 0·25 | 0·11 | 0·36 | 0·65

Start ▼ Less than 0·8 ▼ yes ▼ Greater than two tenths ▼ yes ▼ Greater than $\frac{1}{2}$ ▼ yes ▼ **End**

(c)

25% | 0·75 | $\frac{1}{20}$ | $\frac{1}{2}$ | 0·2

Start ▼ Less than 0·5 ▼ yes ▼ Greater than $\frac{1}{10}$ ▼ yes ▼ Less than $\frac{1}{4}$ ▼ yes ▼ **End**

2 Look at these cards.

Problem solving

30% | 15% | 89% | 62% | 5%

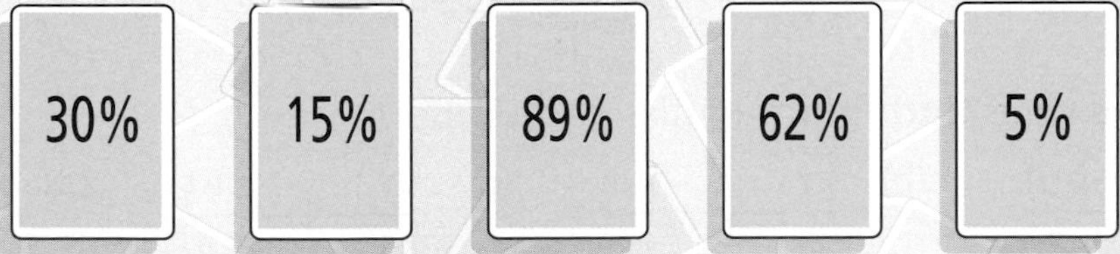

Write an instruction so that only **one** card reaches the end.
Which card is it? Why?

Start ▶ Greater than one tenth ▶ yes ▶ Less than $\frac{48}{100}$ ▶ yes ▶ ______ ▶ yes ▶ **End**

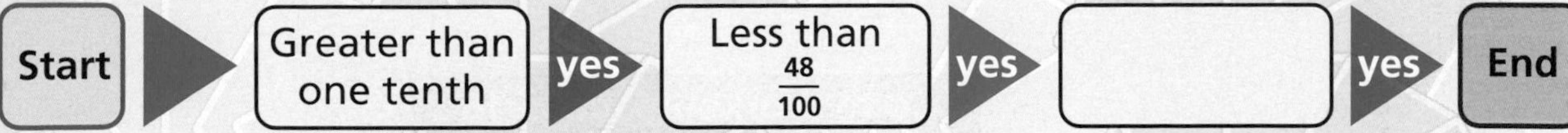

55 Function machines

Pattern: function machines

Do Workbook page 15.

The **rule** for each function machine is missing.

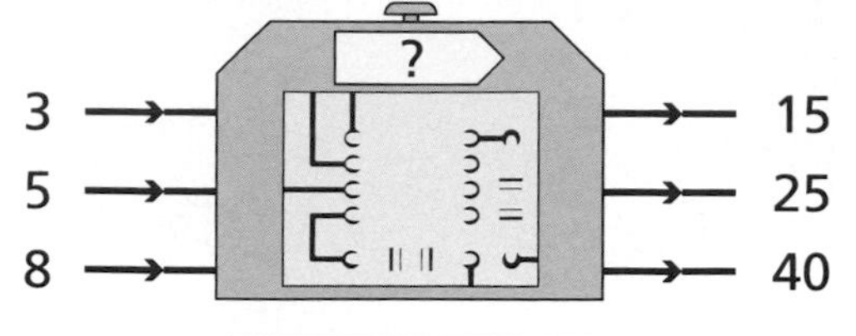

Rule: Multiply by 5

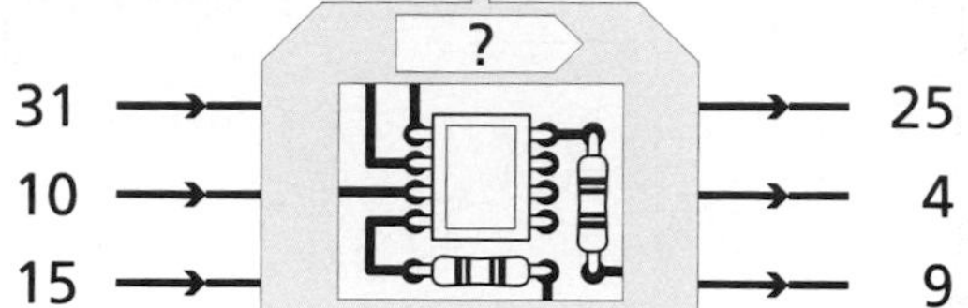

Rule: Subtract 6

1 Write the rule for each of these machines.

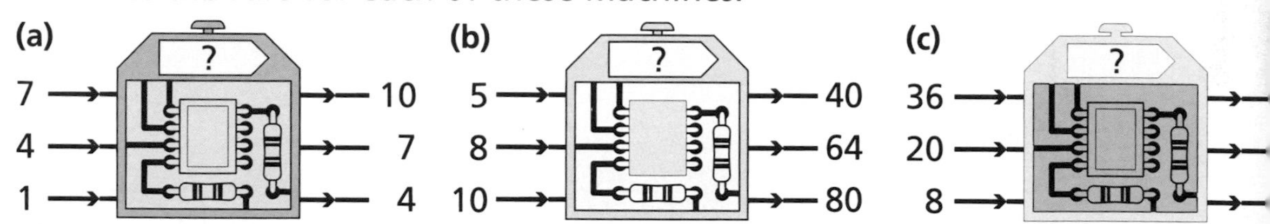

2 Write the rules.

(a)

16 ⟶ 18
12 ⟶ 14
8 ⟶ 10

(b)

20 ⟶ 15
30 ⟶ 25
40 ⟶ 35

(c)

3 ⟶ 30
7 ⟶ 70
9 ⟶ 90

(d)

12 ⟶ 2
18 ⟶ 3
30 ⟶ 5

3 Write the rules.

(a)

in	out
3	21
8	56
10	70

(b)

in	out
35	15
42	22
51	31

(c)

in	out
9	16
12	19
17	24

(d)

in	ou
50	10
40	8
35	[illegible]

(e)

in	out
1	5
3	7
6	10

(f)

in	out
18	9
14	7
6	3

(g)

in	out
1	3
4	12
7	21

(h)

in	ou
20	12
16	8
10	2

4 Write the rules and find the missing numbers.

(a)

in	out
49	7
21	3
7	1
14	■

(b)

in	out
2	12
5	15
7	17
10	■

(c)

in	out
30	24
25	19
16	10
11	■

(d)

in	ou
3	27
5	45
10	90
■	72

Go to Workbook page 16.

The banquet tables

56

Pattern: word formulae

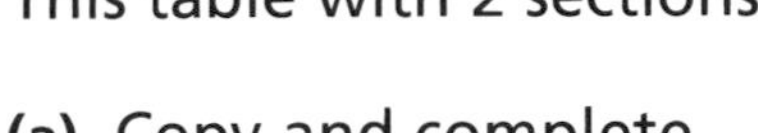

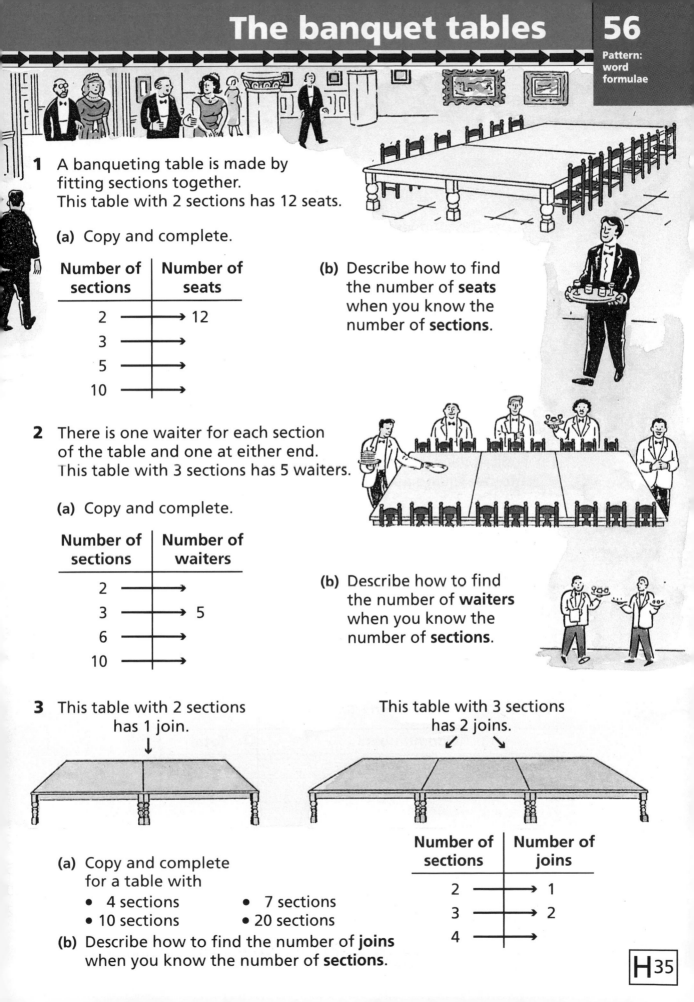

1 A banqueting table is made by fitting sections together.
This table with 2 sections has 12 seats.

(a) Copy and complete.

Number of sections	Number of seats
2 →	12
3 →	
5 →	
10 →	

(b) Describe how to find the number of **seats** when you know the number of **sections**.

2 There is one waiter for each section of the table and one at either end.
This table with 3 sections has 5 waiters.

(a) Copy and complete.

Number of sections	Number of waiters
2 →	
3 →	5
6 →	
10 →	

(b) Describe how to find the number of **waiters** when you know the number of **sections**.

3 This table with 2 sections has 1 join.

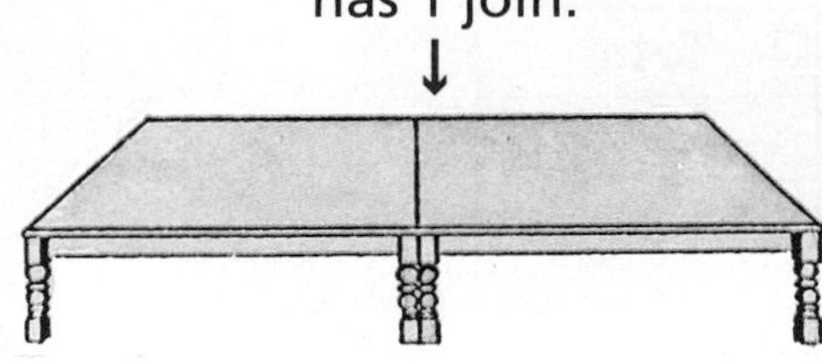

This table with 3 sections has 2 joins.

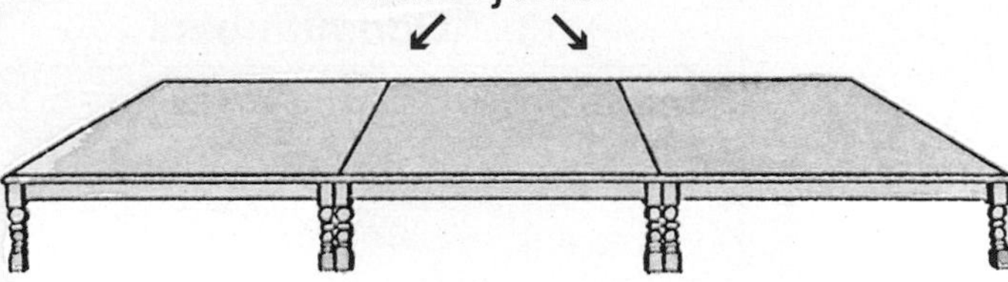

(a) Copy and complete for a table with

- 4 sections
- 7 sections
- 10 sections
- 20 sections

Number of sections	Number of joins
2 →	1
3 →	2
4 →	

(b) Describe how to find the number of **joins** when you know the number of **sections**.

57 Pippa's pin patterns

Pattern: square numbers

1 Pippa makes patterns of squares using coloured pins.

(a) Write the number of pins in each pattern.
(b) Use counters or draw dots to make the next two patterns. Write the number of counters or dots in each.

Each square pattern shows a **square number**. To find a square number multiply a number by itself.

1 × 1 =	**1**
2 × 2 =	**4**
3 × 3 =	**9**
4 × 4 =	**16**

2 (a) List **all** the square numbers up to 100.
(b) Look at your list. Find pairs of square numbers which add to give another square number.

3 Colin makes square patterns this way.

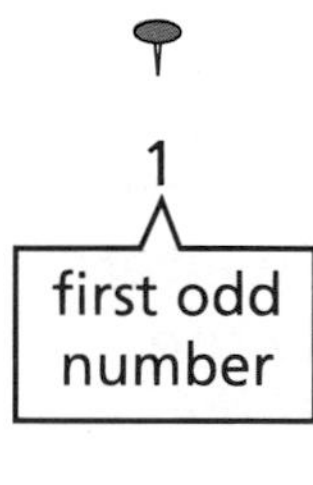

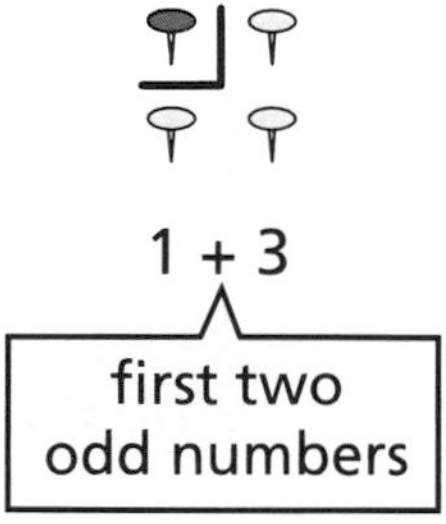

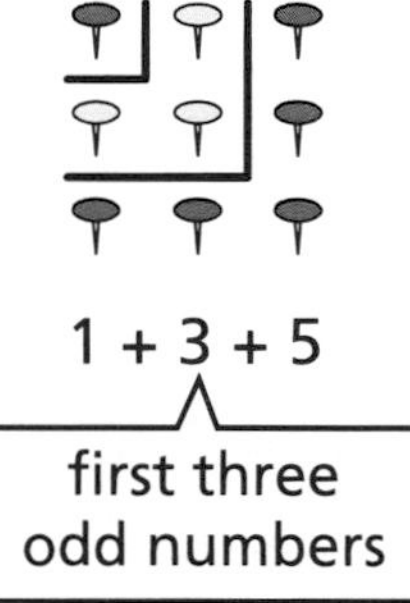

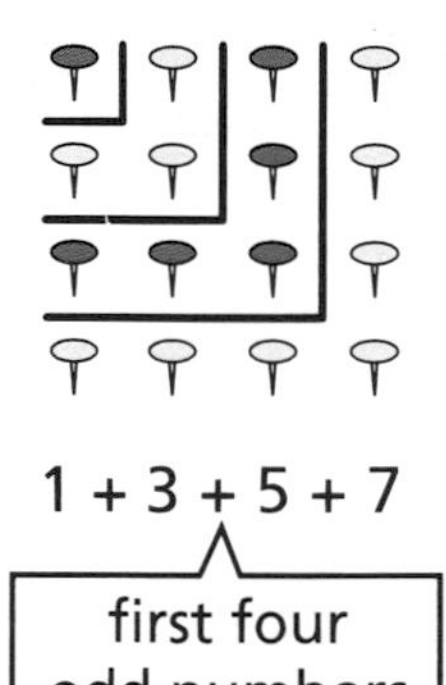

Copy and complete Colin's table.

Odd numbers	Total
1	
1 + 3	
1 + 3 + 5	
1 + 3 + 5 + 7	

Problem solving

4 **Without adding** find the sum of the first twenty odd numbers.

Colin's counters

1 Colin uses counters to make **triangular** patterns.

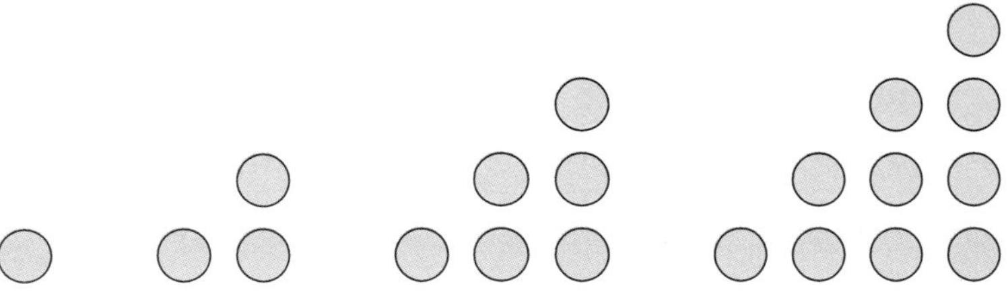

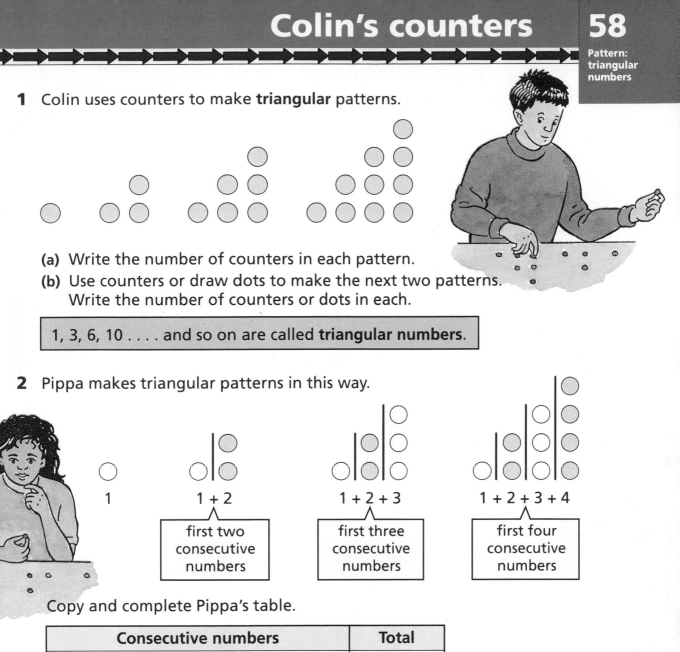

(a) Write the number of counters in each pattern.

(b) Use counters or draw dots to make the next two patterns. Write the number of counters or dots in each.

1, 3, 6, 10 . . . . and so on are called **triangular numbers.**

2 Pippa makes triangular patterns in this way.

1

1 + 2

first two consecutive numbers

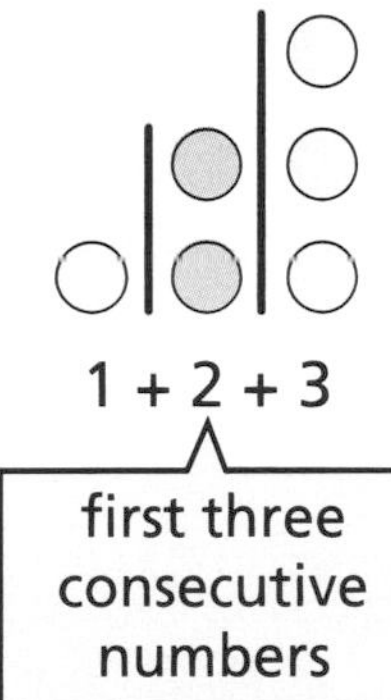

1 + 2 + 3

first three consecutive numbers

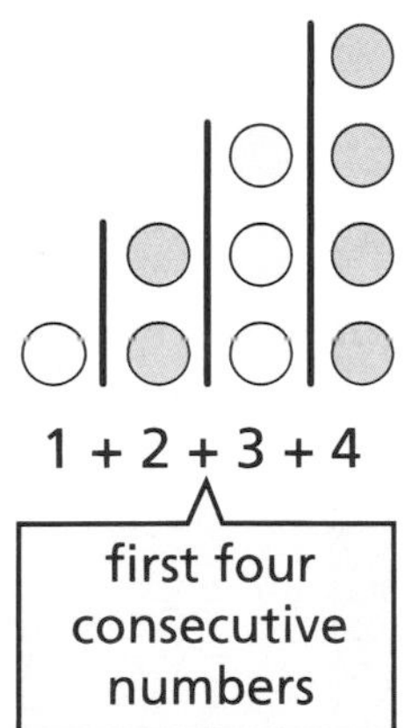

1 + 2 + 3 + 4

first four consecutive numbers

Copy and complete Pippa's table.

Consecutive numbers	Total
1	
1 + 2	
1 + 2 + 3	
1 + 2 + 3 + 4	

3 **(a)** Copy and complete: 1, 3, 6, 10, 15, 21, 28, _____, _____, _____.

(b) Which **triangular** number is also a **square** number?

(c) Investigate what happens when you add two consecutive triangular numbers.

Ask your teacher what to do next

59

Other activity: sequences and relationships

Hidden patterns

There are sequences of **four** numbers hidden in the grid.

Each sequence is arranged like this □□□□ or like this □□□□ (vertical).

1 Find and record a sequence of

(a) multiples of 5 **(b)** multiples of 4 **(c)** consecutive odd numbers

(d) multiples of 3 **(e)** square numbers **(f)** triangular numbers.

	9	11	13	15	19	
11	14		1	3	6	10
16	21		4			8
20	30	12	6	5	4	10
24			9		9	12
28	20	14	12		16	14
	8	10	15	20	25	

2 Write a rule which connects these sets of numbers on the grid.

(a)

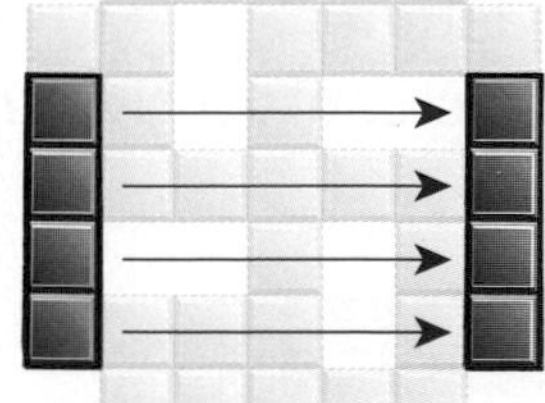

(b)

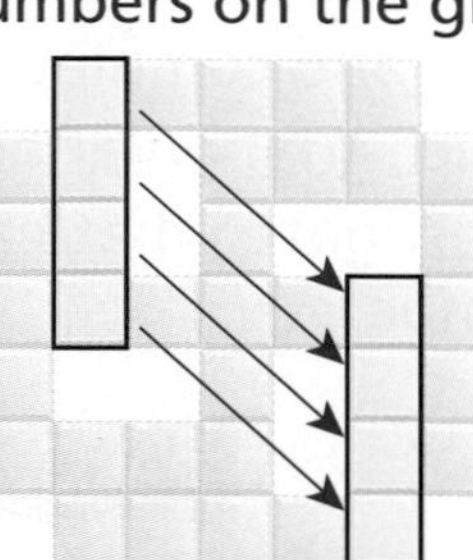

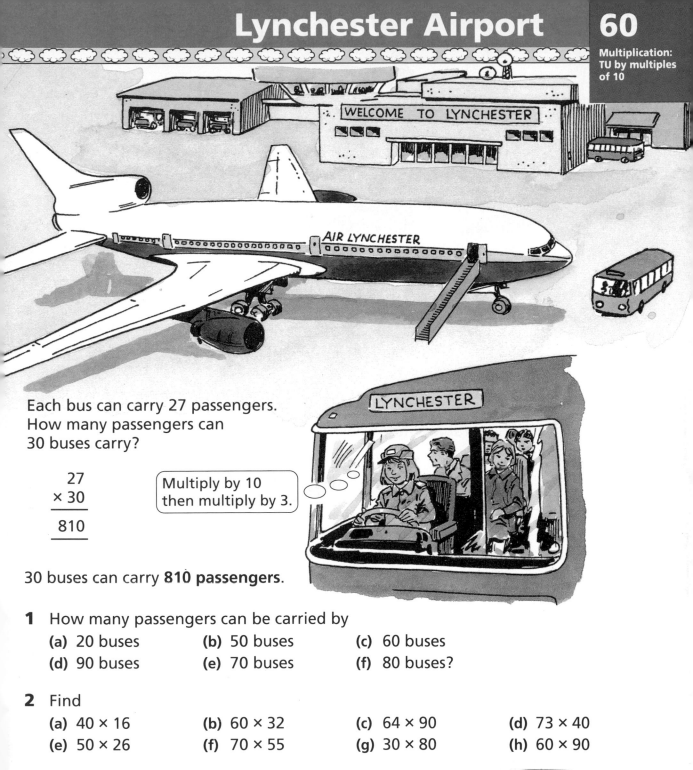

Each bus can carry 27 passengers. How many passengers can 30 buses carry?

$$\begin{array}{r} 27 \\ \times\ 30 \\ \hline 810 \\ \hline \end{array}$$

Multiply by 10 then multiply by 3.

30 buses can carry **810 passengers**.

1 How many passengers can be carried by

(a) 20 buses **(b)** 50 buses **(c)** 60 buses
(d) 90 buses **(e)** 70 buses **(f)** 80 buses?

2 Find

(a) 40 × 16 **(b)** 60 × 32 **(c)** 64 × 90 **(d)** 73 × 40
(e) 50 × 26 **(f)** 70 × 55 **(g)** 30 × 80 **(h)** 60 × 90

3 Each van can carry 36 sacks of mail. How many sacks can be carried in

(a) 20 vans **(b)** 30 vans **(c)** 80 vans?

4 The table shows car park charges at the airport. Find the cost of parking each type of vehicle for

(a) 15 hours
(b) 24 hours
(c) 29 hours.

	Cost per hour
car	20p
bus	30p

Air freight

There are 24 TV sets on the trolley.
Each weighs 23 kg.
Find their total weight.

4 sets	+	20 sets	→	24 sets
23 kg × 4 = 92 kg		23 kg × 20 = 460 kg		92 kg + 460 kg = 552 kg

Their total weight is **552 kg**.

1 Find the total weight on each trolley.

(a)

25 computers each weighing 21 kg

(b)

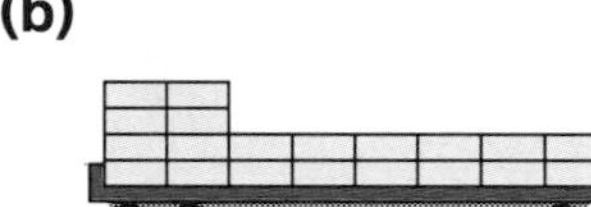

36 video recorders each weighing 17 kg

(c)

48 boxes of circuit each weighing 48

(d)

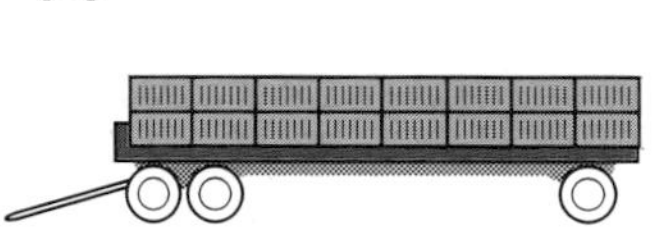

32 crates of pears each weighing 29 kg

(e)

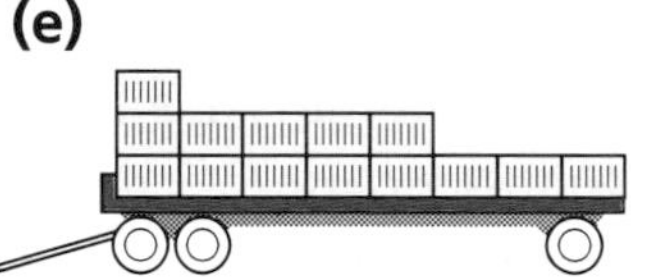

27 crates of plums each weighing 34 kg

(f)

44 crates of apple each weighing 26

2 Find

(a) 53 × 46 **(b)** 65 × 62 **(c)** 72 × 84 **(d)** 86 × 67
(e) 97 × 56 **(f)** 61 × 73 **(g)** 78 × 54 **(h)** 83 × 49

3 Find the weight in each container.

Container	Number of crates	Weight of each crate
A	75	28 kg
B	93	64 kg
C	69	39 kg

An Amber A10 can carry 26 passengers on each flight. How many passengers can it carry on 13 flights?

Amber A10 – 26 passengers

	26
	× 13
3 × 26 ⟶	78
10 × 26 ⟶	+ 260
13 × 26 ⟶	338

An Amber A10 can carry **338 passengers** on 13 flights.

1 Find the number of passengers an Amber A10 can carry on
(a) 12 flights **(b)** 17 flights **(c)** 15 flights **(d)** 18 flights.

2 **(a)** 25 × 17 **(b)** 32 × 16 **(c)** 58 × 14 **(d)** 39 × 13 **(e)** 28 × 19

Flightbus – 27 passengers

Tri-blade 35 passengers

3 How many passengers can be carried by
(a) a Flightbus on 14 flights
(b) a Tri-blade on 13 flights
(c) a Bi-Star on 11 flights
(d) a Flightbus on 16 flights
(e) a Tri-blade on 15 flights
(f) a Bi-Star on 19 flights?

Bi-Star 46 passengers

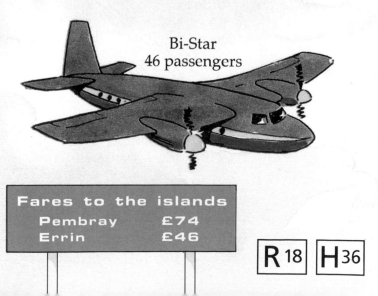

4 12 passengers flew to Pembray and 17 flew to Errin. How much did they pay altogether in fares?

Fares to the islands	
Pembray	£74
Errin	£46

63 Customs

Multiplication: TU by 21 to 99

We brought back 24 of them.
CD PLAYERS

You have to pay £36 tax on each one.

Amount to pay = 24 × £36

= **£864**

```
            36
          × 24
4 × 36 →   144
20 × 36 → + 720
           864
```

1 Find these amounts.

(a) 21 × £35 **(b)** 31 × £43 **(c)** 43 × £32 **(d)** 27 × £64

2 Multiply

(a) 52 × 26 **(b)** 35 × 49 **(c)** 28 × 41 **(d)** 58 × 44

(e) 87 × 56 **(f)** 47 × 47 **(g)** 79 × 34 **(h)** 54 × 82

3 Alex is listing the items held by Customs.
Find the total number of each item.

(a) 22 envelopes with 75 diamonds in each

(b) 38 bags, each with 33 watches

(c) 26 sheets of 48 stamps

(d) 72 boxes with 45 bottles of perfu in each

(e) Videos: 53 crates of 36

(f) 62 boxes of jeans, with 21 in each box

(g) 37 bags of gold coins, 85 in each

(h) 29 boxes with 24 cigars in each

4 **(a)** Alex is paid £65 per day. How much is he paid for 28 days?

(b) How many **more** days must he work to make his total pay just over £2000?

R19 H37

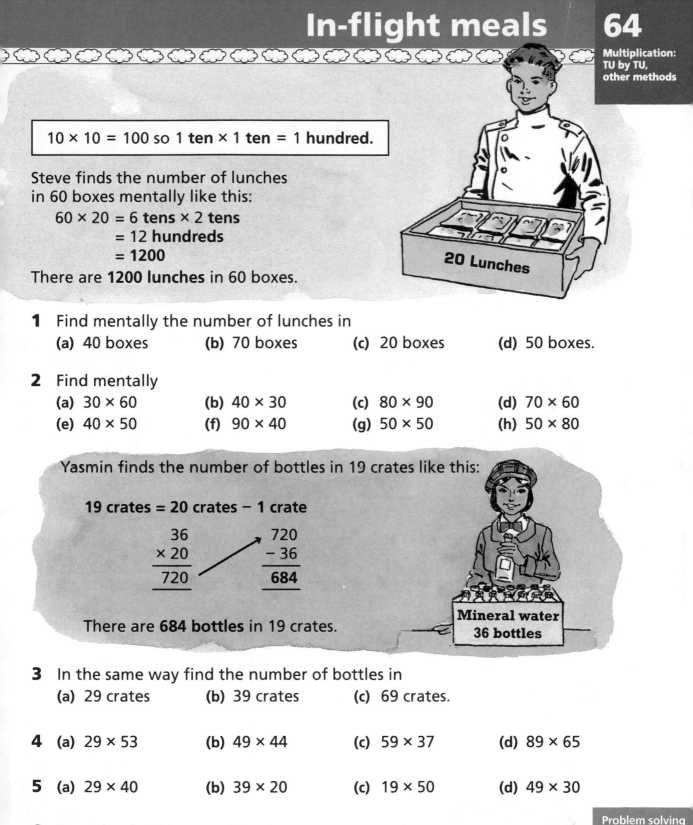

10 × 10 = 100 so 1 **ten** × 1 **ten** = 1 **hundred.**

Steve finds the number of lunches in 60 boxes mentally like this:

60 × 20 = 6 **tens** × 2 **tens**
= 12 **hundreds**
= **1200**

There are **1200 lunches** in 60 boxes.

1 Find mentally the number of lunches in
(a) 40 boxes **(b)** 70 boxes **(c)** 20 boxes **(d)** 50 boxes.

2 Find mentally
(a) 30 × 60 **(b)** 40 × 30 **(c)** 80 × 90 **(d)** 70 × 60
(e) 40 × 50 **(f)** 90 × 40 **(g)** 50 × 50 **(h)** 50 × 80

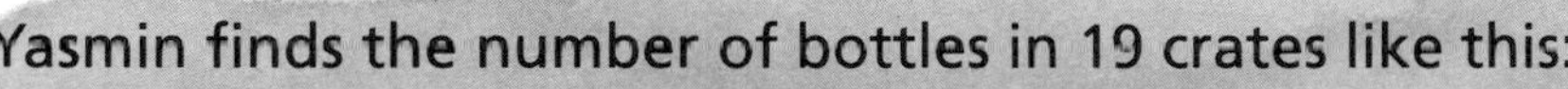

Yasmin finds the number of bottles in 19 crates like this:

19 crates = 20 crates − 1 crate

$$\begin{array}{r} 36 \\ \times\ 20 \\ \hline 720 \\ \hline \end{array} \quad \nearrow \quad \begin{array}{r} 720 \\ -\ 36 \\ \hline \mathbf{684} \\ \hline \end{array}$$

There are **684 bottles** in 19 crates.

3 In the same way find the number of bottles in
(a) 29 crates **(b)** 39 crates **(c)** 69 crates.

4 **(a)** 29 × 53 **(b)** 49 × 44 **(c)** 59 × 37 **(d)** 89 × 65

5 **(a)** 29 × 40 **(b)** 39 × 20 **(c)** 19 × 50 **(d)** 49 × 30

Problem solving

6 Steve loads 88 boxes of lunches.
Yasmin loads 49 crates of mineral water.
Has Yasmin loaded enough, to give one bottle of mineral water with each lunch?
Explain.

65 Flight delayed

Division: by TU

Share 56 sandwiches equally among 17 passengers.
How many sandwiches does each receive? How many are left over?

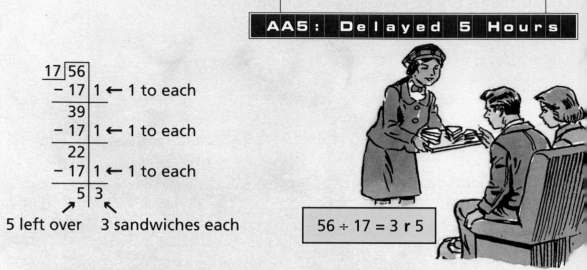

```
17|56
 - 17 | 1 ← 1 to each
   39 |
 - 17 | 1 ← 1 to each
   22 |
 - 17 | 1 ← 1 to each
    5 | 3
   ↗     ↖
5 left over    3 sandwiches each
```

Each passenger receives **3 sandwiches** and there are **5 left over**.

1 Share these sandwiches equally among the passengers.
How many does each passenger receive? How many are left over?

Type of sandwich	beef	egg	tuna	ham	cheese	salad
Number of sandwiches	54	60	100	120	86	290
Number of passengers	27	28	31	45	39	88

2 **(a)** $19\overline{)42}$ **(b)** $61\overline{)183}$ **(c)** $25\overline{)98}$ **(d)** $50\overline{)166}$

(e) $35\overline{)117}$ **(f)** $74\overline{)208}$ **(g)** $69\overline{)207}$ **(h)** $37\overline{)85}$

3 Aeroblot Airlines has £171 to divide equally among the 57 passengers on its delayed flight AA5.
How much should each passenger receive?

4 Flight AA7 is also delayed.
There are 64 passengers, including 15 children.
Share equally:

(a) 192 bags of crisps among **all** the passengers
(b) 98 drinks among the **adults** only
(c) 45 comics among the **children** only.

5 **(a)** 169 ÷ 62 **(b)** 140 ÷ 43 **(c)** 147 ÷ 49

Free gifts

Share 159 mugs equally among 13 stewards.

Free gift
when you fly
from Lynchester

$13\overline{)159}$		
− 130	10	← 10 to each
29		
− 13	1	← 1 to each
16		
− 13	1	← 1 to each
3	12	

159 ÷ 13 = 12 **r** 3

Each steward receives **12 mugs** and there are **3** left over.

1 Share equally:
- **(a)** 192 pens among 16 stewards
- **(b)** 315 stickers among 27 stewards
- **(c)** 420 badges among 32 stewards.

2 Find:
- **(a)** $18\overline{)234}$ **(b)** $29\overline{)350}$ **(c)** $22\overline{)248}$
- **(d)** 560 ÷ 42 **(e)** 638 ÷ 58 **(f)** 317 ÷ 25

Share 359 travel packs equally among 17 stewards.

TRAVEL
PACK

$17\overline{)359}$		
− 170	10	← 10 to each
189		
− 170	10	← 10 to each
19		
− 17	1	← 1 to each
2	21	

359 ÷ 17 = 21 **r** 2

Each steward receives **21 packs** and there are **2** left over.

3 Share equally:
- **(a)** 360 posters among 12 stewards
- **(b)** 451 comics among 20 stewards
- **(c)** 748 flags among 24 stewards.

4 Find:
- **(a)** $28\overline{)874}$ **(b)** $16\overline{)336}$ **(c)** $23\overline{)513}$
- **(d)** 775 ÷ 25 **(e)** 339 ÷ 11 **(f)** 756 ÷ 34

67

Division: by TU

Around the airport

315 children are taken on a tour of the airport in groups of 15. How many groups are there?

$$
\begin{array}{r|l}
15 \overline{)\,315} & \\
-\,150 & 10 \leftarrow 10 \text{ groups} \\
\hline
165 & \\
-\,150 & 10 \leftarrow 10 \text{ groups} \\
\hline
15 & \\
-\,15 & 1 \leftarrow 1 \text{ group} \\
\hline
0 & 21
\end{array}
$$

There are **21 groups**.

$315 \div 15 = 21$

1 How many groups of 15 can be formed from
(a) 165 children (b) 195 children (c) 465 children?

2 Cars are parked in rows of 18.
(a) How many rows can be **filled** from 560 cars?
(b) How many are in the next row?

3 Magazines are put in bundles of 36.
How many bundles can be made from 780 magazines?
How many are left over?

4 Helicopter trips can carry 23 passengers on each flight. How many flights are needed to carry 506 passengers?

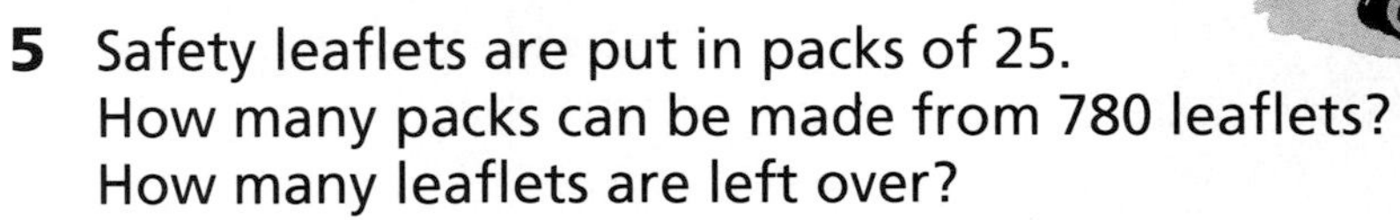

5 Safety leaflets are put in packs of 25.
How many packs can be made from 780 leaflets?
How many leaflets are left over?

6 A ticket for the viewing area costs 45p.
How many tickets can be bought with £5?
How much money is left over?

Ask your teacher what to do next

What's the difference?

1 **(a)** Choose a 2-digit number, say 23.

(b) Subtract 1 and add 1 to give a sequence.

22 23 24

(c) Multiply

- the smallest number by the largest ⟶ 22 × 24 =
- the middle number by itself ⟶ 23 × 23 =

(d) Find the difference between the two answers.

2 Repeat question 1 for other 2-digit numbers. What do you notice about the differences?

3 **(a)** Choose a 2-digit number.

(b) Subtract **2** and add **2** to make a sequence.

(c) Repeat questions 1(c), (d) for your sequence.

(d) Do this again for other 2-digit numbers. What do you notice about the differences?

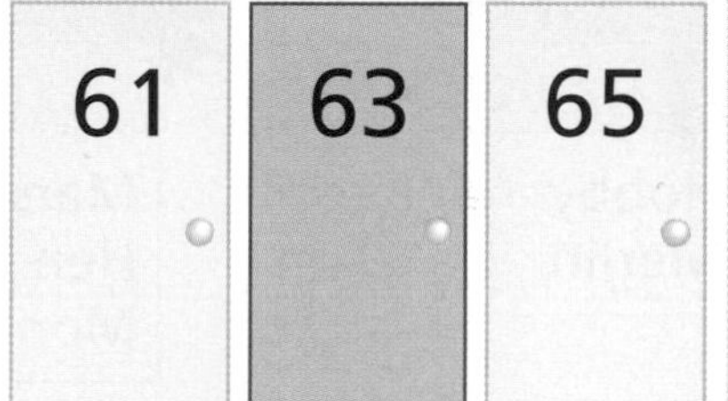

4 Investigate what happens when you

- start with a 2-digit number
- subtract **3** and add **3** to make a sequence
- multiply and find the difference.

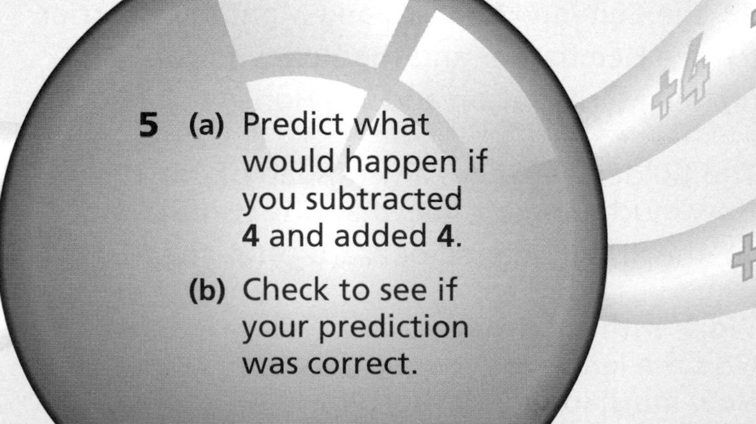

5 **(a)** Predict what would happen if you subtracted **4** and added **4**.

(b) Check to see if your prediction was correct.

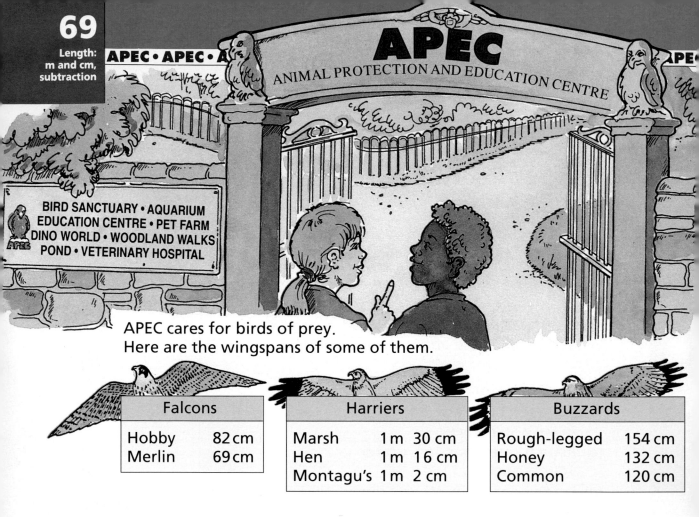

APEC cares for birds of prey.
Here are the wingspans of some of them.

Falcons	
Hobby	82 cm
Merlin	69 cm

Harriers	
Marsh	1 m 30 cm
Hen	1 m 16 cm
Montagu's	1 m 2 cm

Buzzards	
Rough-legged	154 cm
Honey	132 cm
Common	120 cm

1 Write in **centimetres** the wingspan of each harrier.

2 Write in **metres** and **centimetres** the wingspan of each buzzard.

3 Which of the birds has
(a) the longest wingspan (b) the shortest wingspan?

4 Find the difference between the wingspans of
(a) the Rough-legged buzzard and the Marsh harrier
(b) the Common buzzard and Montagu's harrier
(c) the Hen harrier and the Hobby falcon
(d) the Merlin falcon and the Honey buzzard.

5 The Golden eagle has a wingspan of 2 m 18 cm.
How much longer is this than the wingspan of
(a) the Rough-legged buzzard (b) the Marsh harrier?

6 **Work with a partner.**
Find the length of **your** arm span.
How much longer or shorter is
your span than the wingspan of the
(a) Hobby falcon (b) Honey buzzard
(c) Marsh harrier (d) Rough-legged buzzard?

1 Find the length of wood needed to make each of these perches.

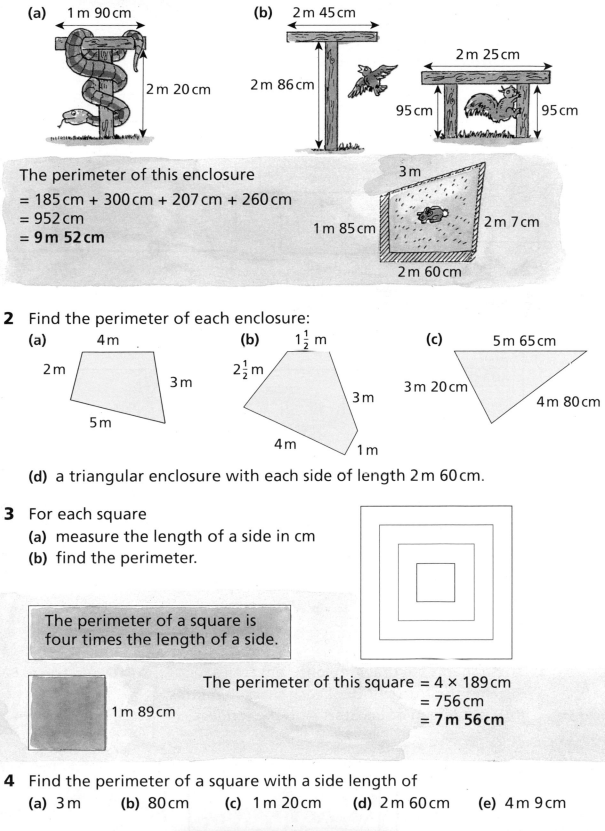

(a)

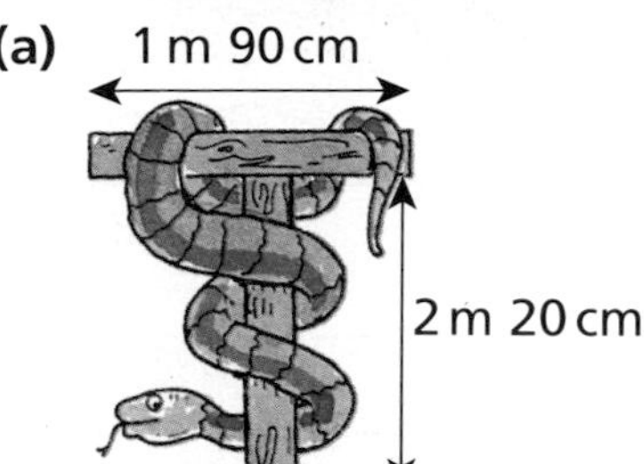

(b)

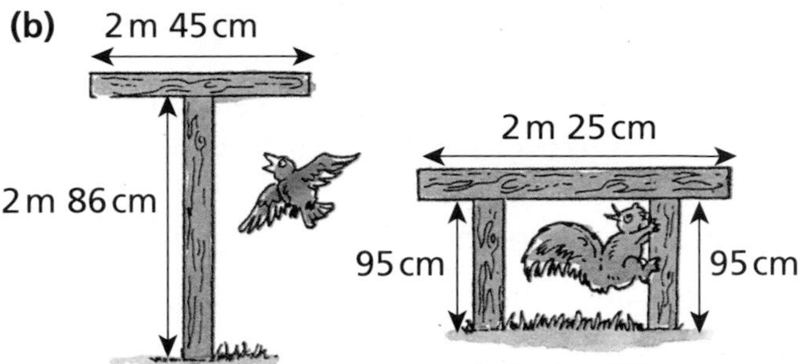

The perimeter of this enclosure
= 185 cm + 300 cm + 207 cm + 260 cm
= 952 cm
= **9 m 52 cm**

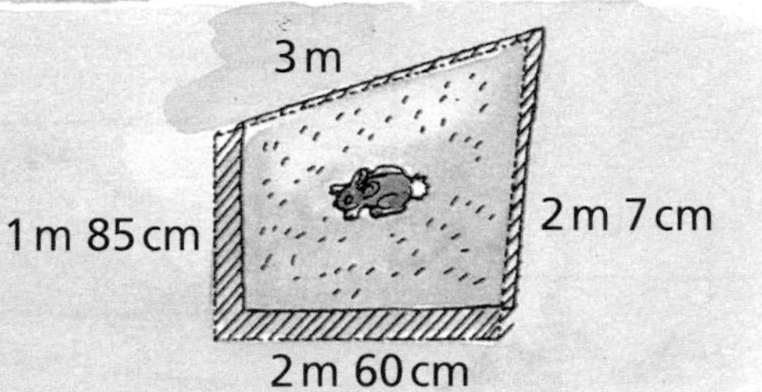

2 Find the perimeter of each enclosure:

(a)

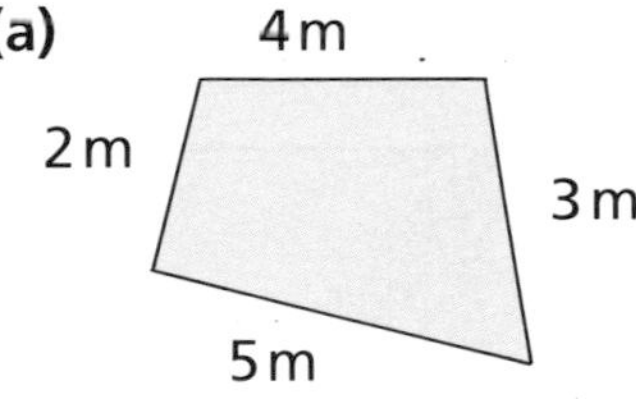

(b)

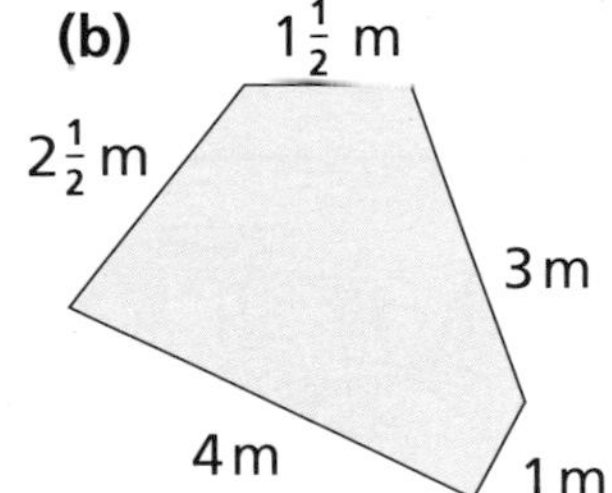

(c)

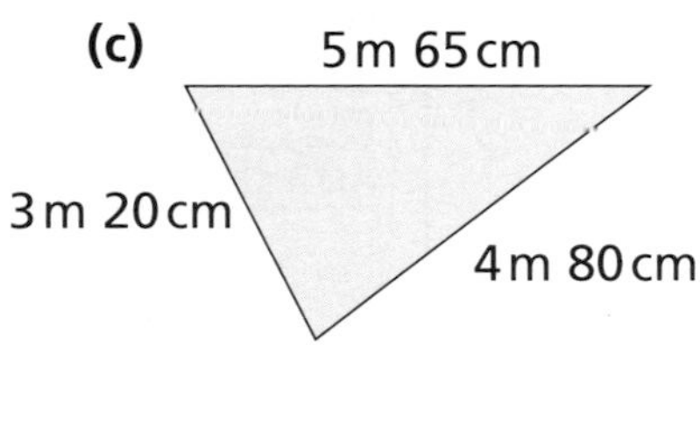

(d) a triangular enclosure with each side of length 2 m 60 cm.

3 For each square

(a) measure the length of a side in cm

(b) find the perimeter.

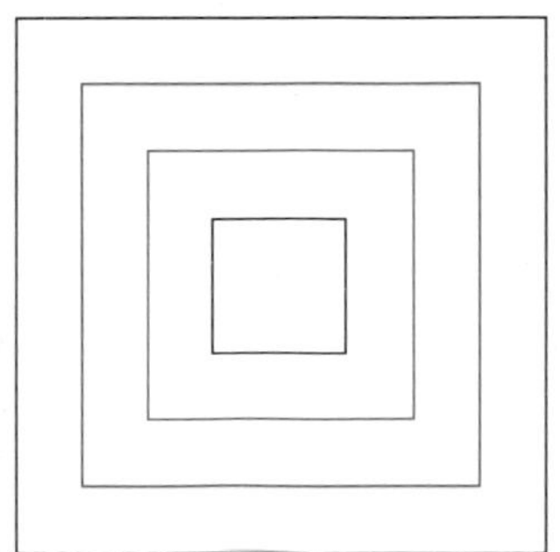

The perimeter of a square is four times the length of a side.

1 m 89 cm

The perimeter of this square = 4 × 189 cm
= 756 cm
= **7 m 56 cm**

4 Find the perimeter of a square with a side length of

(a) 3 m **(b)** 80 cm **(c)** 1 m 20 cm **(d)** 2 m 60 cm **(e)** 4 m 9 cm

Go to Workbook page 17.

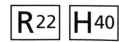

Fish scales

Measure to check that this fish is 6 cm long.
The fish is drawn to scale.
The scale is **1 cm to 5 cm**.
Each centimetre represents 5 centimetres.
The **true length** is 6 × 5 cm = **30 cm**

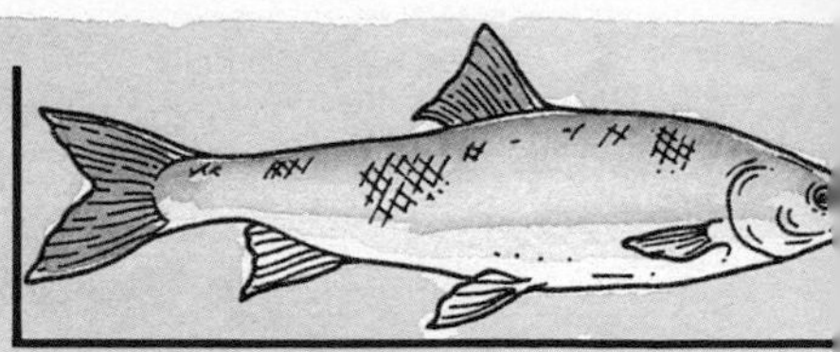
Dace

1 Measure each fish and calculate its true length.

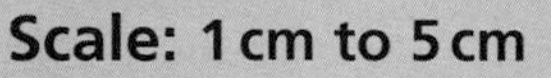

Silver Bream

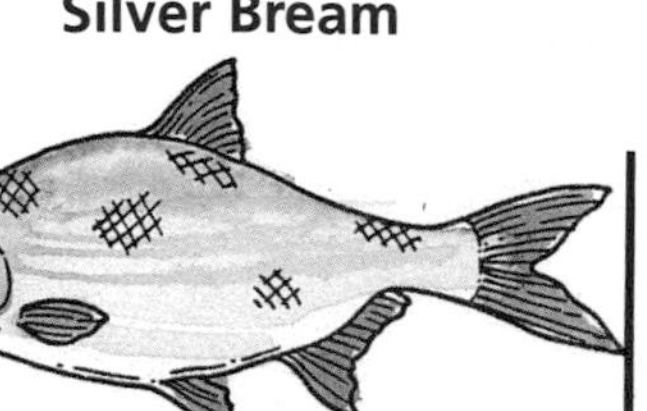

Anchovy

Minnow

Red Mullet

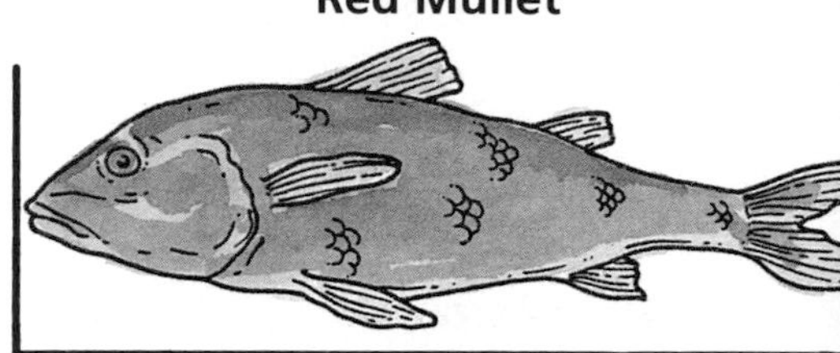

2 **(a)** Measure and then calculate to find the true length of the
- tank
- fish
- rock
- submarine.

(b) Find the true height of the
- tank
- castle
- diver
- plant.

(c) Is the water more or less than 40 cm deep? Explain.

3 These sharks are drawn to different scales.

(a) Find the true length of each shark **in metres**.

(b) List them in order. Start with the longest.

Great Blue: 1 cm to 80 cm

Nurse: 1 cm to 60 cm

Crocodile: 1 cm to 20 cm

Mako: 1 cm to 90 cm

This Tyrannosaurus is drawn to a scale of **1 cm to 2 m.**

Each centimetre represents 2 metres.

Its true length = 7 × 2 m
= **14 m**

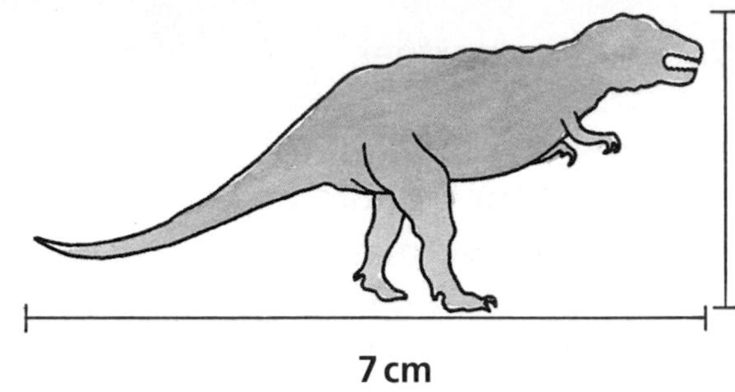

1 Find the true length of each of these dinosaurs.

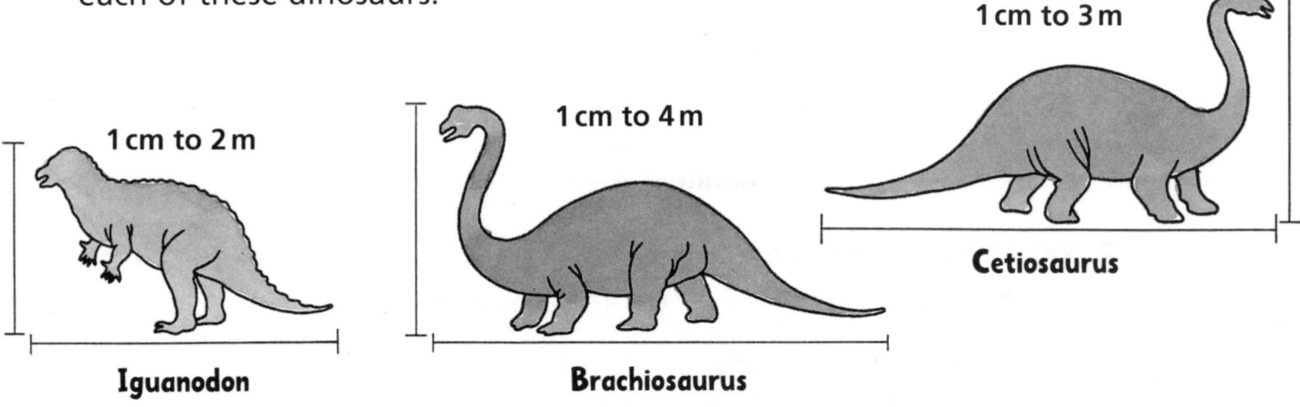

2 **(a)** Which of these dinosaurs was the longest? How many times longer than the shortest one was it?

(b) How much longer or shorter than your classroom was the Iguanodon?

(c) Which mammal living today can be longer than any of these dinosaurs?

3 **(a)** Find the true height of each of the **four** dinosaurs.

(b) Which was the tallest of these dinosaurs? About how many times the height of your classroom was it?

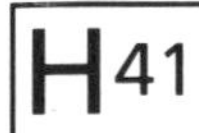

This plan of Dino World and its grounds is drawn to scale.

4 **(a)** Find the true length and breadth of
- Dino World
- its grounds.

(b) How many Cetiosaurus lengths would fit into the length of the grounds?

(c) Would 3 Brachiosaurus lengths fit into the length of Dino World? Explain.

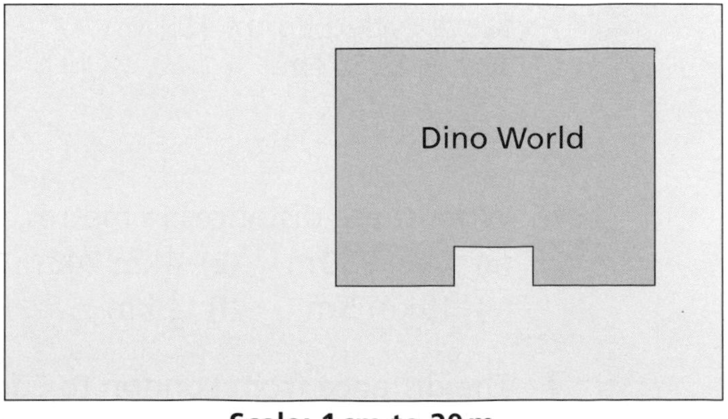

Scale: 1 cm to 20 m

Race for APEC

Length: introducing the kilometre

APEC • APEC • APEC • APEC • APEC • APEC • APEC • APEC • APEC • APEC • APE

Work with a partner.

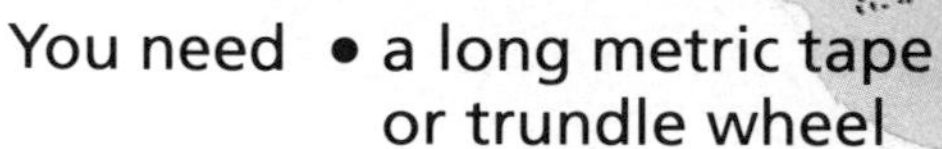

You need
- a long metric tape or trundle wheel
- two marker cones
- a watch.

1 Measure and mark out a length of 50 m.

2 **(a)** Find how long it takes you to walk 100 m.
(b) **Estimate** how long it would take you to walk 1000 m.

A distance of 1000 metres is called 1 kilometre. **1000 m = 1 km**

3 How long are these races in kilometres?
(a) 3000 m **(b)** 5000 m **(c)** 10 000 m **(d)** 25 000 m

MARATHON FOR APE

The marathon distance is 42 195 m.
This is **42 km 195 m.**

42 195 m = 42 000 m + 195 m
= **42 km 195 m**

4 In half an hour Yvonne ran 8437 m.
How far is this in kilometres and metres?

5 Write these distances in kilometres and metres.
(a) 3960 m **(b)** 4936 m **(c)** 6174 m **(d)** 18 258 m
(e) 3055 m **(f)** 12 090 m **(g)** 5005 m **(h)** 70 000 m

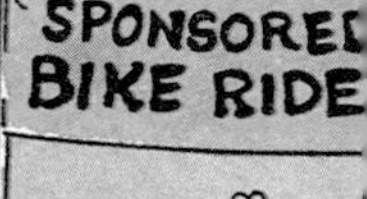

Steve cycled 26 km 102 m.
This is **26 102 m.**

26 km 102 m = 26 000 m + 102 m
= **26 102 m**

6 Write these distances in metres.
(a) 2 km 350 m **(b)** 4 km 746 m **(c)** 11 km 400 m **(d)** 3 km 25 m
(e) 15 km 5 m **(f)** $\frac{1}{2}$ km **(g)** $1\frac{1}{2}$ km **(h)** $3\frac{1}{2}$ km

7 The distance from London to Edinburgh is 610 km.
Find the distance, in km, from **your** town to 3 other towns.

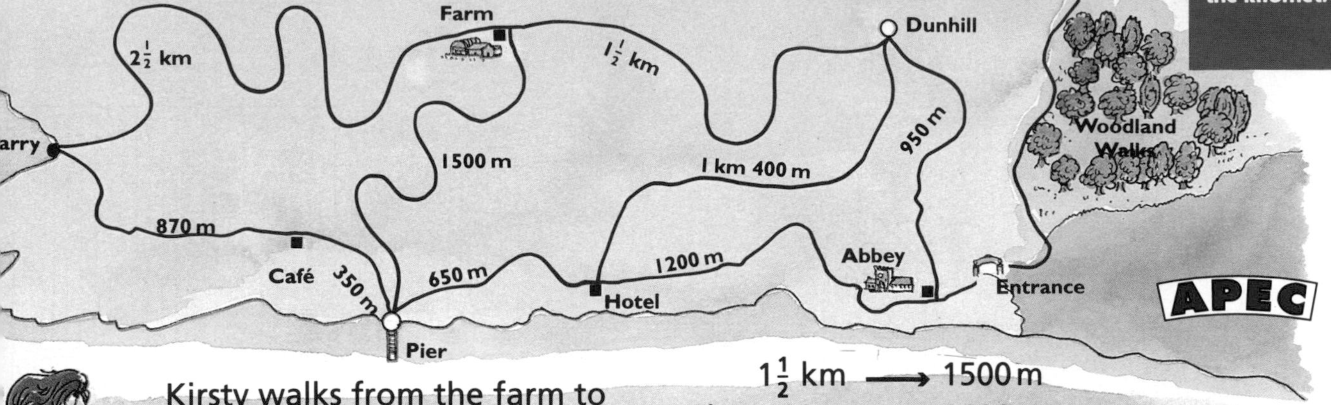

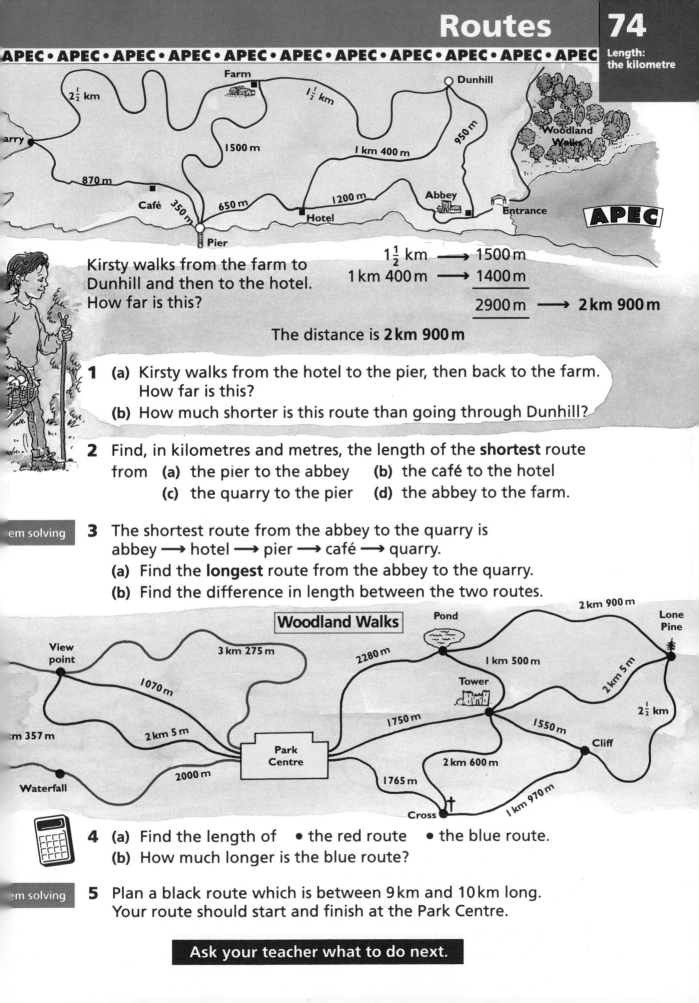

Kirsty walks from the farm to Dunhill and then to the hotel. How far is this?

$1\frac{1}{2}$ km ⟶ 1500 m
1 km 400 m ⟶ 1400 m
2900 m ⟶ **2 km 900 m**

The distance is **2 km 900 m**

1 (a) Kirsty walks from the hotel to the pier, then back to the farm. How far is this?
(b) How much shorter is this route than going through Dunhill?

2 Find, in kilometres and metres, the length of the **shortest** route from (a) the pier to the abbey (b) the café to the hotel (c) the quarry to the pier (d) the abbey to the farm.

em solving

3 The shortest route from the abbey to the quarry is abbey ⟶ hotel ⟶ pier ⟶ café ⟶ quarry.
(a) Find the **longest** route from the abbey to the quarry.
(b) Find the difference in length between the two routes.

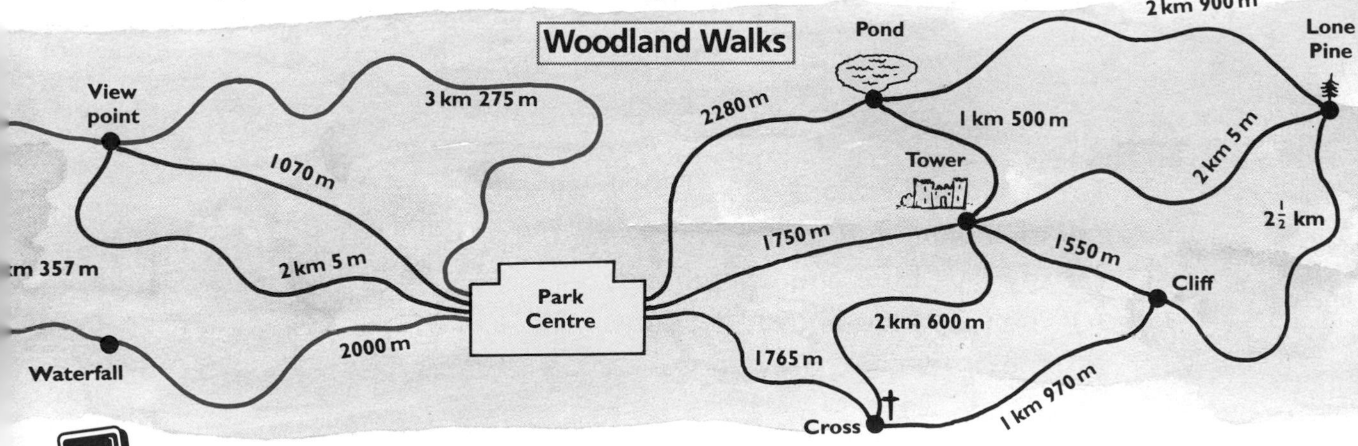

4 (a) Find the length of • the red route • the blue route.
(b) How much longer is the blue route?

em solving

5 Plan a black route which is between 9 km and 10 km long. Your route should start and finish at the Park Centre.

Ask your teacher what to do next.

75 Weighing at APEC

Weight: kg and g, +, −

APEC • APEC • APEC • APEC • APEC • APEC • APEC • APEC • APEC • APEC • APEC

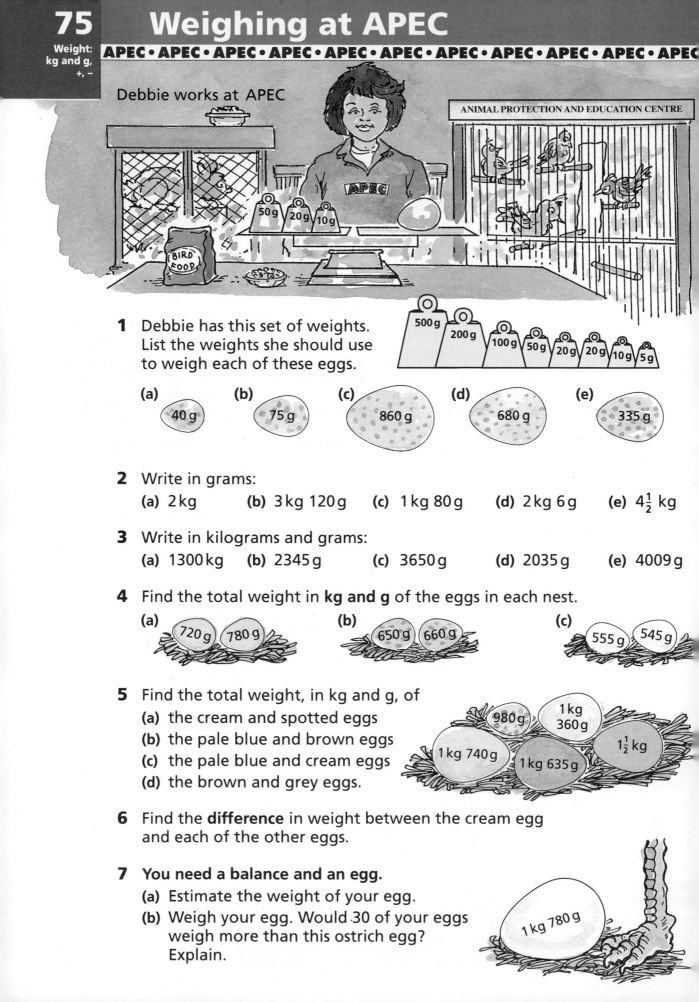

Debbie works at APEC

1 Debbie has this set of weights. List the weights she should use to weigh each of these eggs.

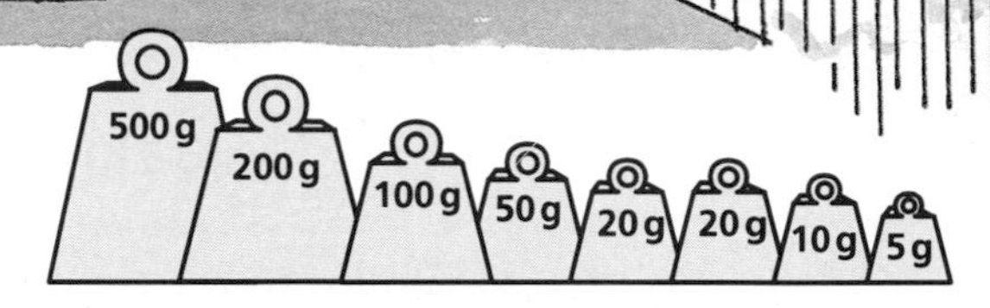

(a) 40 g (b) 75 g (c) 860 g (d) 680 g (e) 335 g

2 Write in grams:

(a) 2 kg (b) 3 kg 120 g (c) 1 kg 80 g (d) 2 kg 6 g (e) $4\frac{1}{2}$ kg

3 Write in kilograms and grams:

(a) 1300 kg (b) 2345 g (c) 3650 g (d) 2035 g (e) 4009 g

4 Find the total weight in **kg and g** of the eggs in each nest.

(a)

(b)

(c)

5 Find the total weight, in kg and g, of
- **(a)** the cream and spotted eggs
- **(b)** the pale blue and brown eggs
- **(c)** the pale blue and cream eggs
- **(d)** the brown and grey eggs.

980 g 1 kg 360 g 1 kg 740 g 1 kg 635 g $1\frac{1}{2}$ kg

6 Find the **difference** in weight between the cream egg and each of the other eggs.

7 **You need a balance and an egg.**
- **(a)** Estimate the weight of your egg.
- **(b)** Weigh your egg. Would 30 of your eggs weigh more than this ostrich egg? Explain.

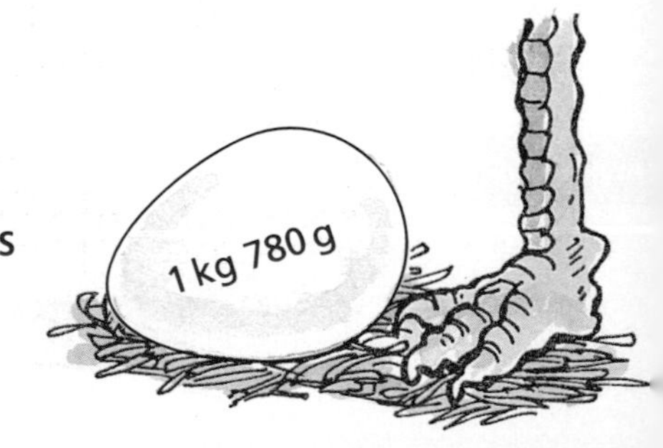

Feeding time at APEC

PEC • APEC • APEC • APEC • APEC • APEC • APEC • APEC • APEC • APEC • APEC

APEC

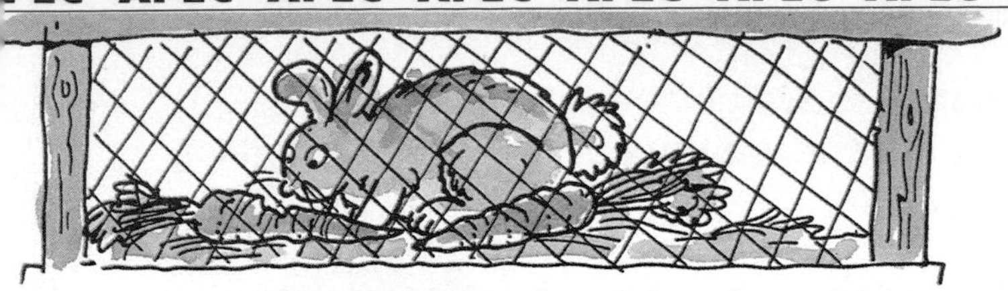

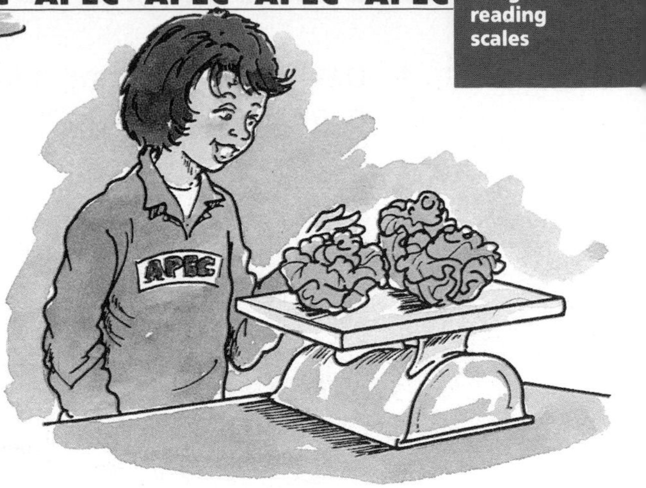

1 Debbie is weighing food for the rabbits. What weight is shown on each scale?

(a)

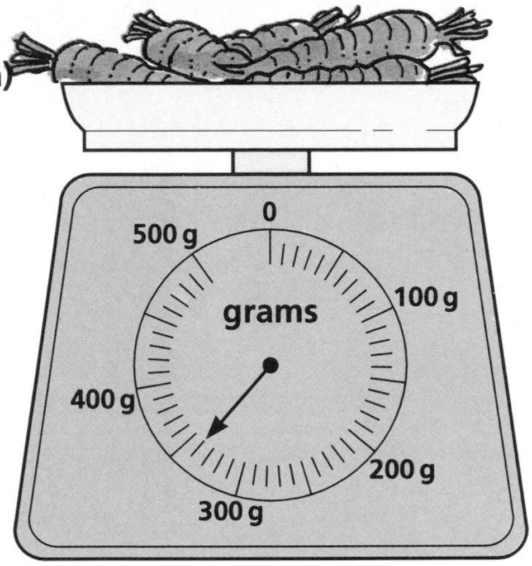

0
100 g
200 g
300 g
400 g
500 g
grams

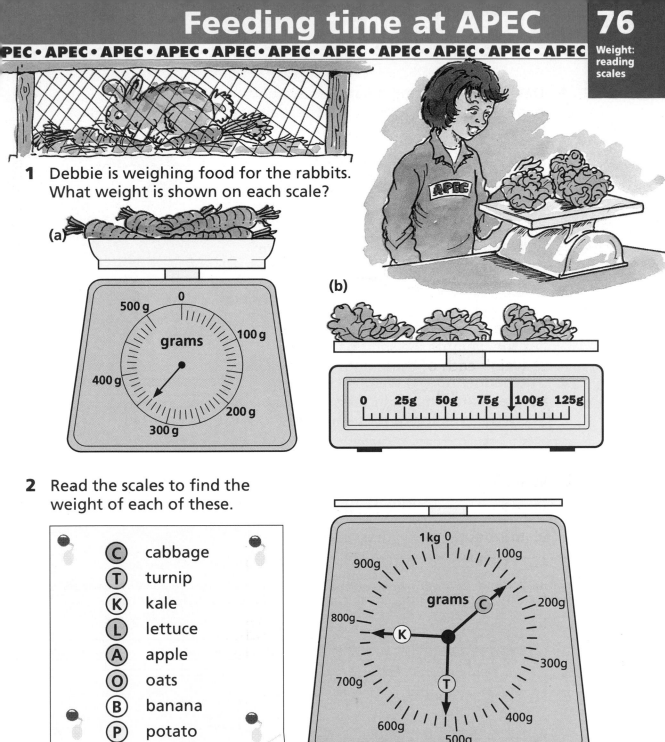

(b)

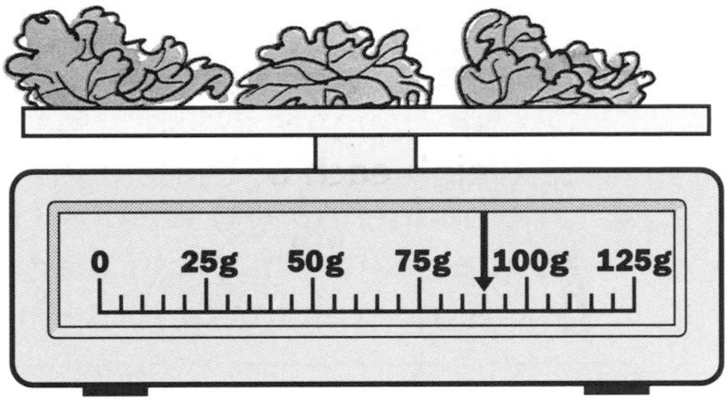

0
25g
50g
75g
100g
125g

2 Read the scales to find the weight of each of these.

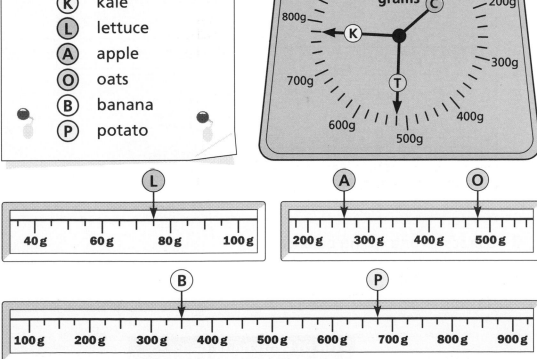

- (C) cabbage
- (T) turnip
- (K) kale
- (L) lettuce
- (A) apple
- (O) oats
- (B) banana
- (P) potato

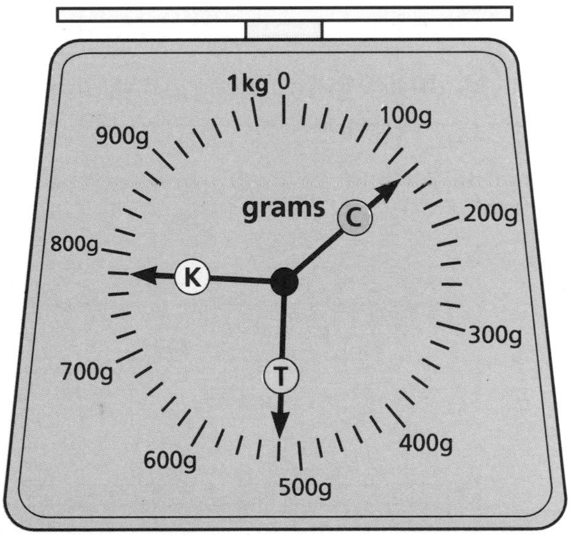

1 kg 0
100g
200g
300g
400g
500g
600g
700g
800g
900g
grams
C
K
T

L
40 g
60 g
80 g
100 g

A
O
200 g
300 g
400 g
500 g

B
P
100 g
200 g
300 g
400 g
500 g
600 g
700 g
800 g
900 g

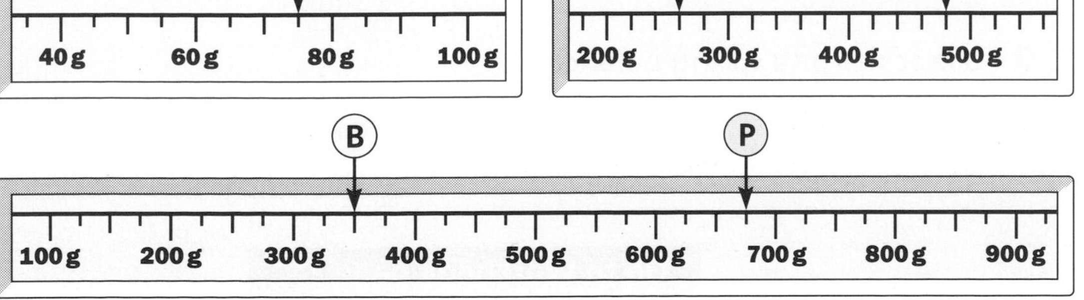

The weigh-in

1 Debbie uses a **spring balance** to weigh the rabbit.
It weighs 1kg 200g. What are the weights of the other animals?

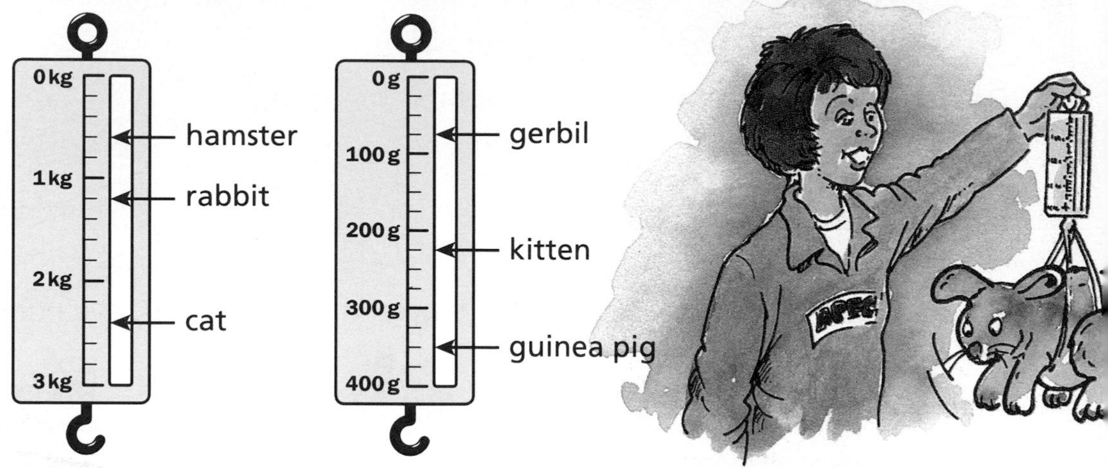

2 The hedgehog (H) weighs 1 kg 300 g **to the nearest mark**. In the same way, write the weights of these animals.

(R) rat	(S) seagull
(P) pigeon	(M) mole
(C) cat	(F) field mouse
(D) dormouse	(G) grass snake

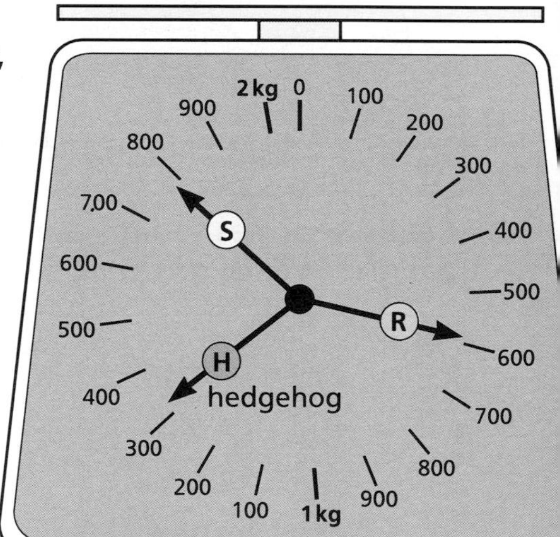

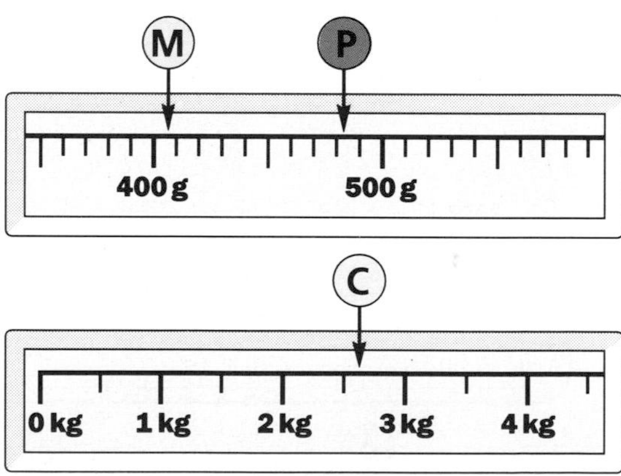

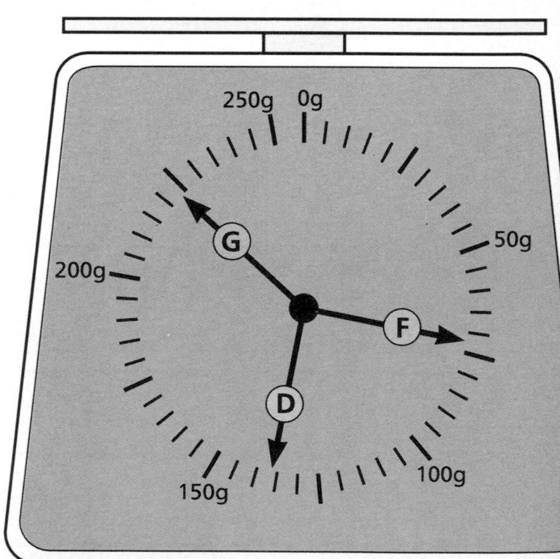

3 Use scales or a spring balance.
Estimate then find the weight of

(a) your jacket or coat

(b) this book.

Go to Workbook page 24.

APEC foodstore

APEC • APEC • APEC • APEC • APEC • APEC • APEC • APEC • APEC • APEC • APEC

1 Find the total weight, in kilograms and grams, of

(a) 10 bags of

(b) 6 bags of

(c) 8 bags of

(d) 7 bags of

mixed vegetables $4\frac{1}{2}$ kg

(e) 9 bags of

(f) 20 bags of

2 Five bags of dog biscuits have the same weight as two bags of another food. Which food?

3 Use scales, sand and plastic bags.
Weigh out a bag of sand with the same weight as **one** bag of the
(a) dried milk (b) dog biscuits.

4 Find and list things in your classroom which have **about** the same weight as one bag of the
(a) nuts (b) dried fruit (c) mixed vegetables.

Some things are difficult to weigh using scales or balances.

m solving

5 Find the weight of
(a) your chair
(b) 1 litre of sand
(c) 1 litre of water.

Write about how you found each of these weights.

Ask your teacher what to do next

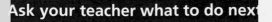

79 The Guard Room

Area: rectangles

Do Workbook pages 25 and 26.

1 What is the area in squares of each rectangular shield?

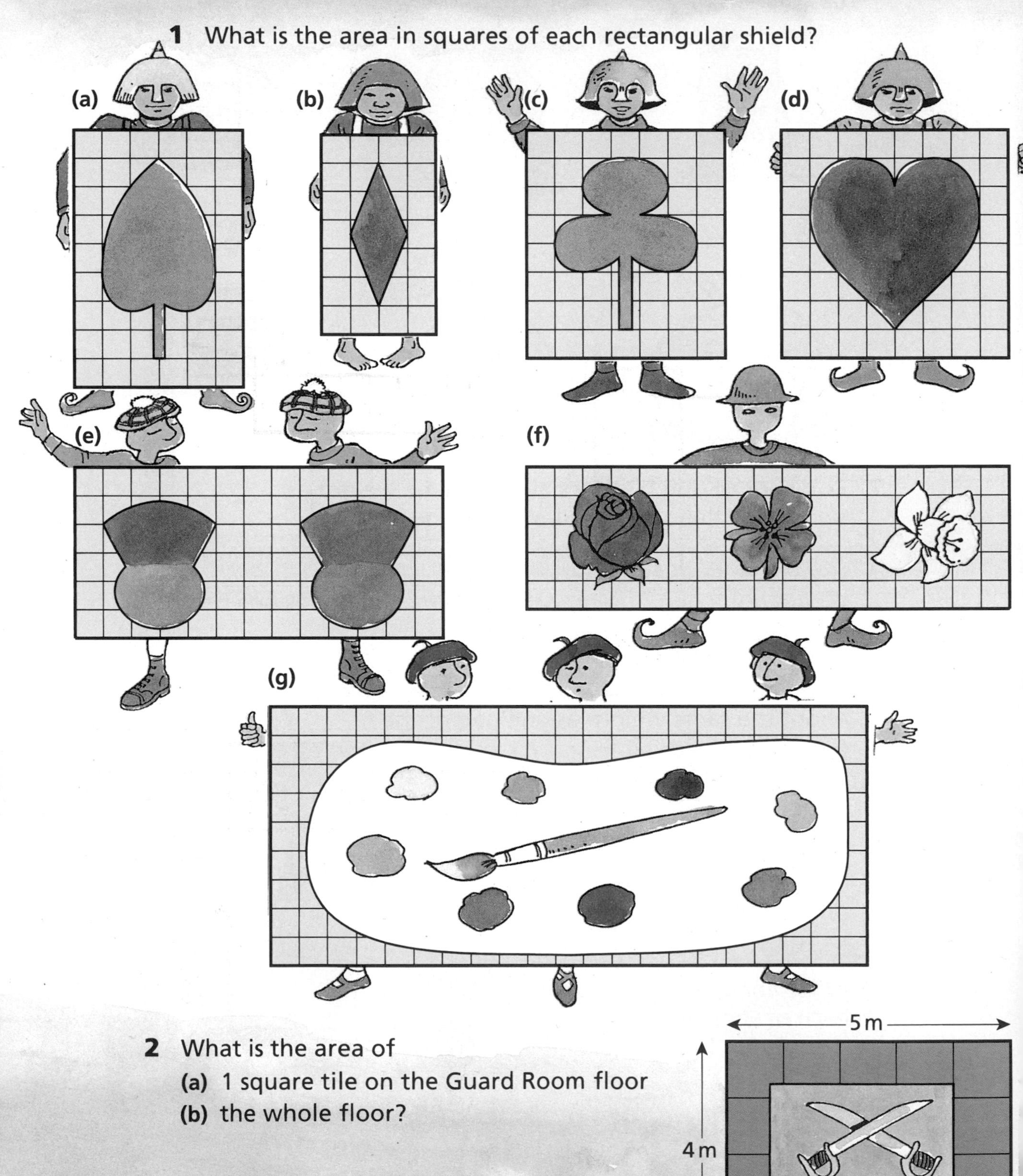

2 What is the area of

(a) 1 square tile on the Guard Room floor

(b) the whole floor?

5 m

4 m

Groovy gallery

Area: composite shapes

1 This design has been made using 2 rectangles and 1 square.
Find the area, in squares, of

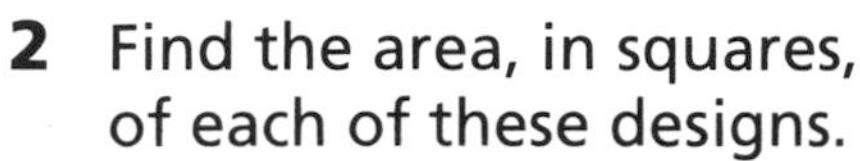

(a) the red rectangle
(b) the blue rectangle
(c) the green square
(d) the **whole** design.

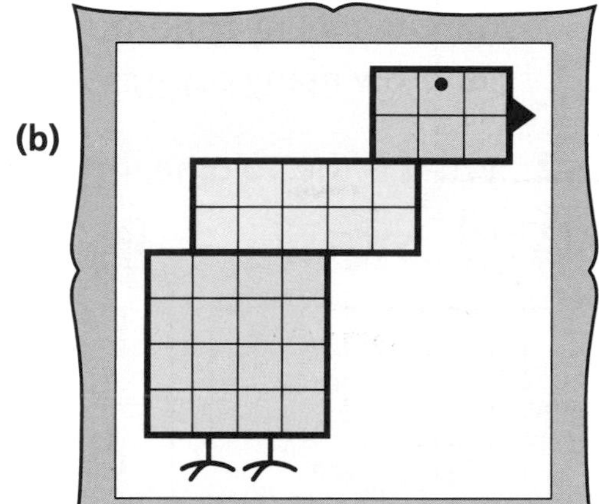

2 Find the area, in squares, of each of these designs.

(a)

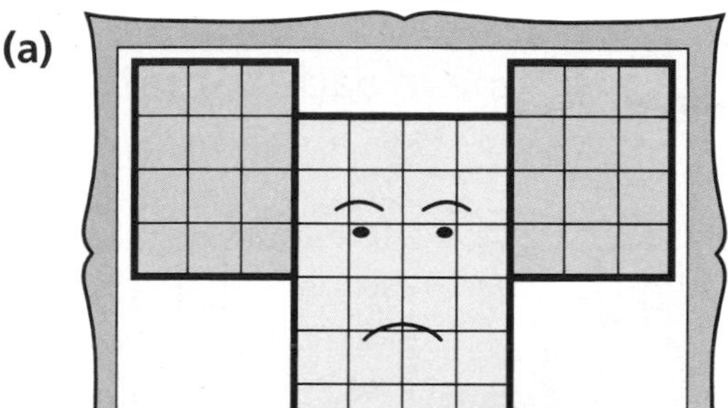

(b)

3 What is the area, in squares, of each design?

(a)

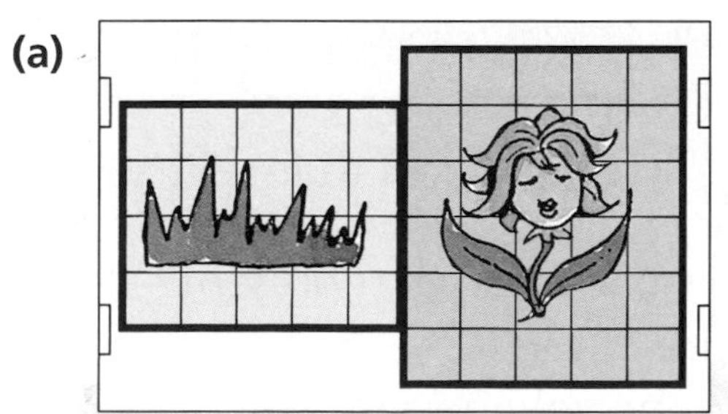

(b)

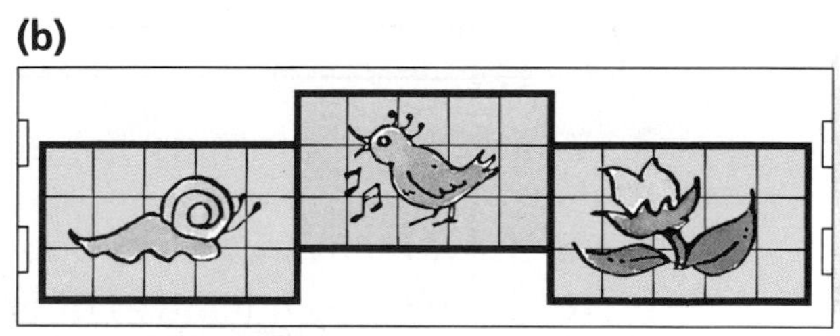

(c)

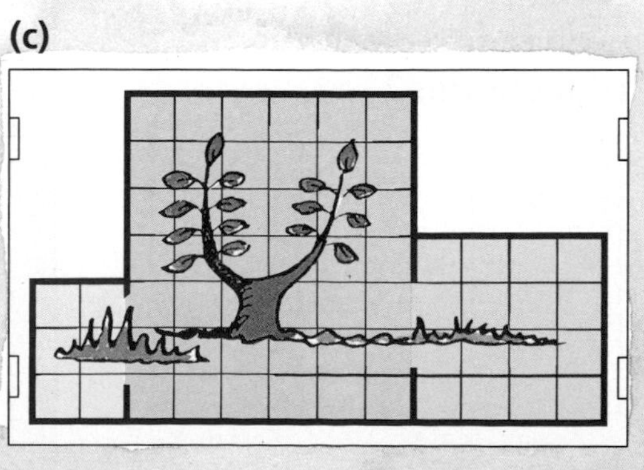

(d)

Go to Workbook page 27.

81 Medicine

Volume: millilitres

APEC • APEC • APEC • APEC • APEC • APEC • APEC • APEC • APEC • APEC • APE

The jug holds **1 litre** or **1000** millilitres of medicine.

1 litre = 1000 ml

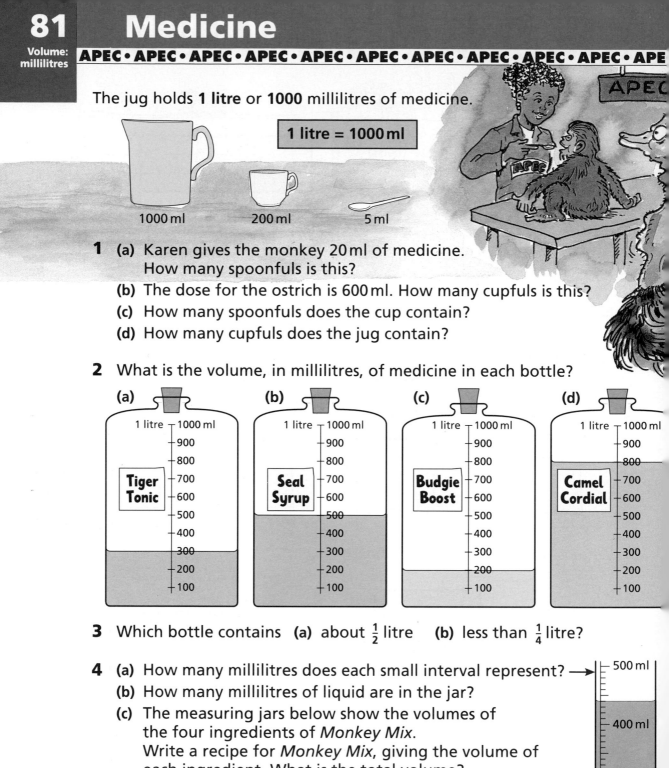

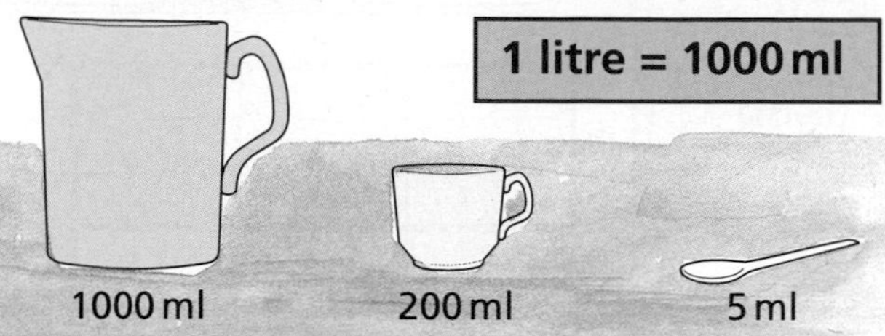

1 **(a)** Karen gives the monkey 20 ml of medicine. How many spoonfuls is this?
(b) The dose for the ostrich is 600 ml. How many cupfuls is this?
(c) How many spoonfuls does the cup contain?
(d) How many cupfuls does the jug contain?

2 What is the volume, in millilitres, of medicine in each bottle?

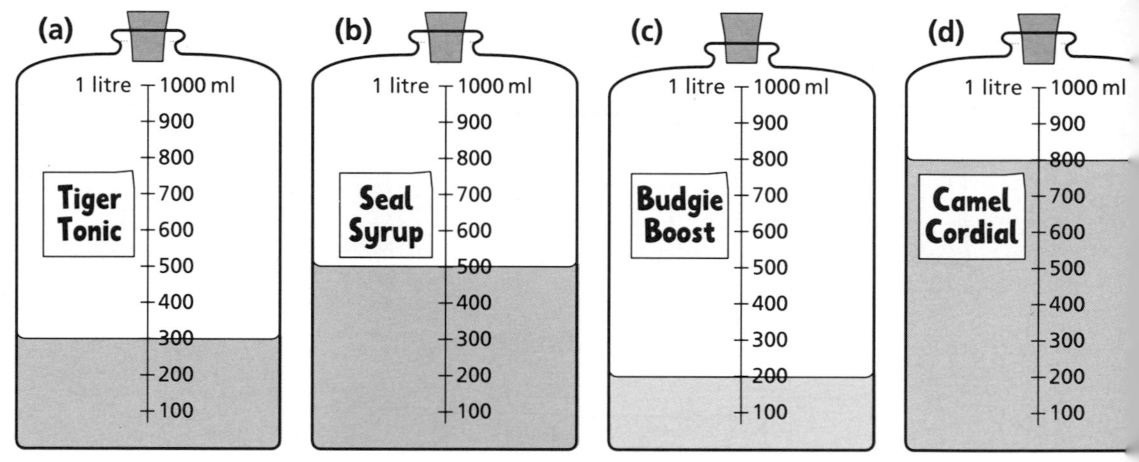

3 Which bottle contains **(a)** about $\frac{1}{2}$ litre **(b)** less than $\frac{1}{4}$ litre?

4 **(a)** How many millilitres does each small interval represent?
(b) How many millilitres of liquid are in the jar?
(c) The measuring jars below show the volumes of the four ingredients of *Monkey Mix*. Write a recipe for *Monkey Mix*, giving the volume of each ingredient. What is the total volume?

500 ml
400 ml
300 ml
200 ml
100 ml

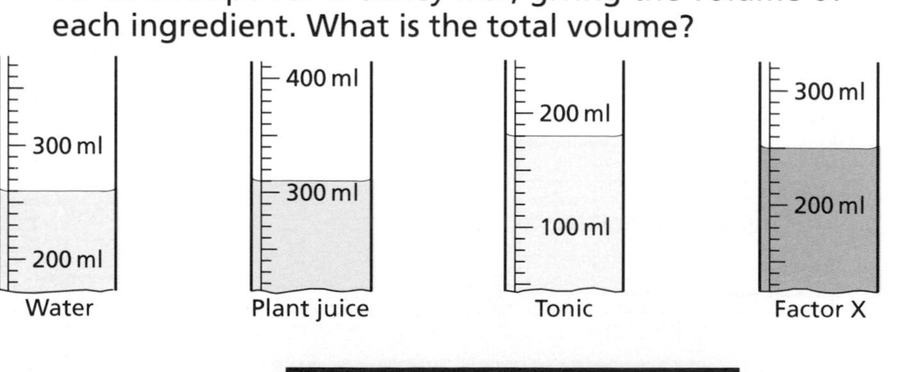

Go to Workbook page 28.

To the nearest mark

1 Which measuring jar below contains the

- Antiseptic
- Lotion
- Balm
- Spirit?

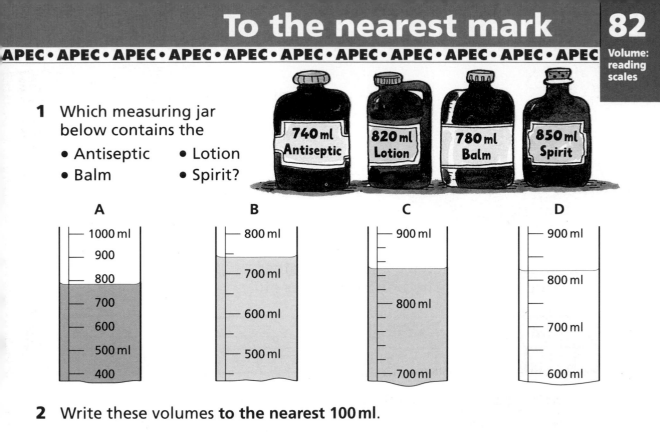

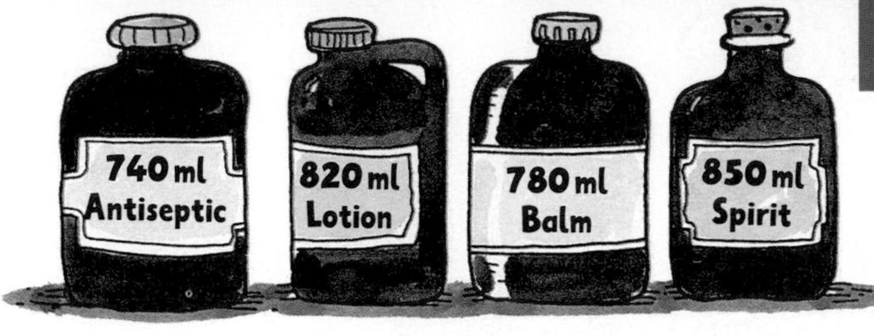

A

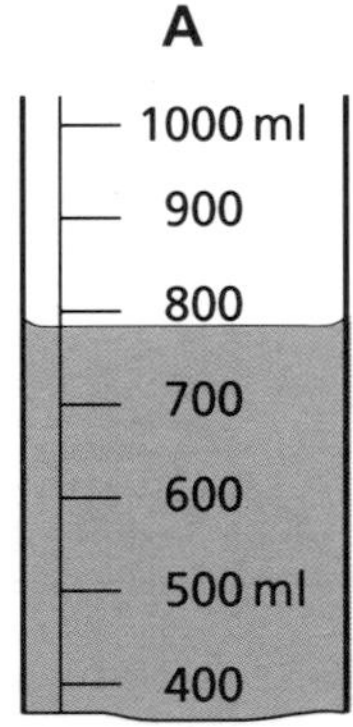

B

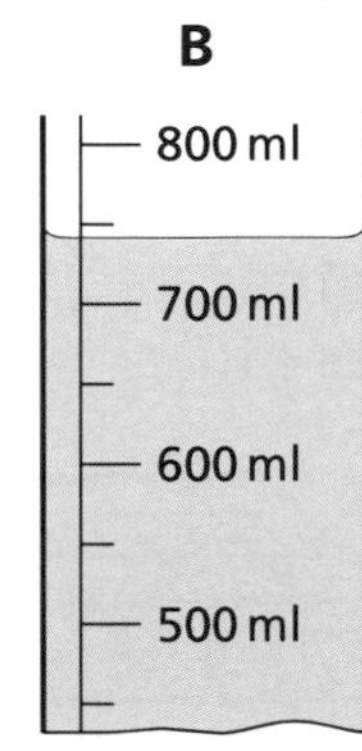

C

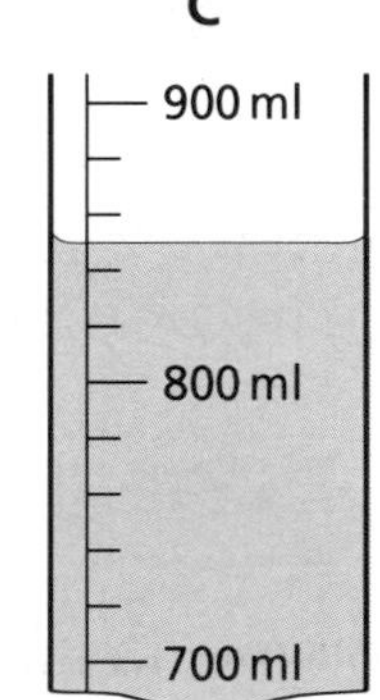

D

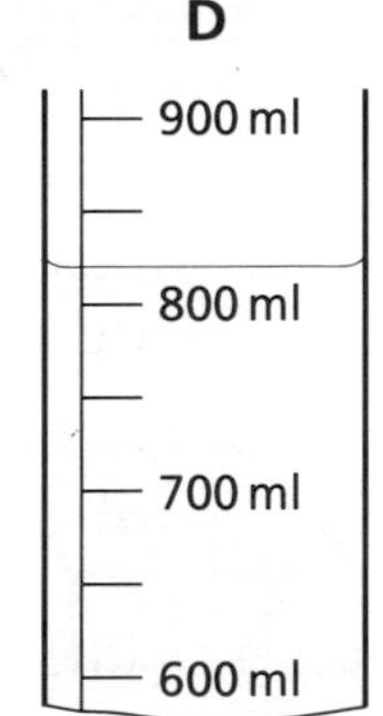

2 Write these volumes **to the nearest 100 ml**.

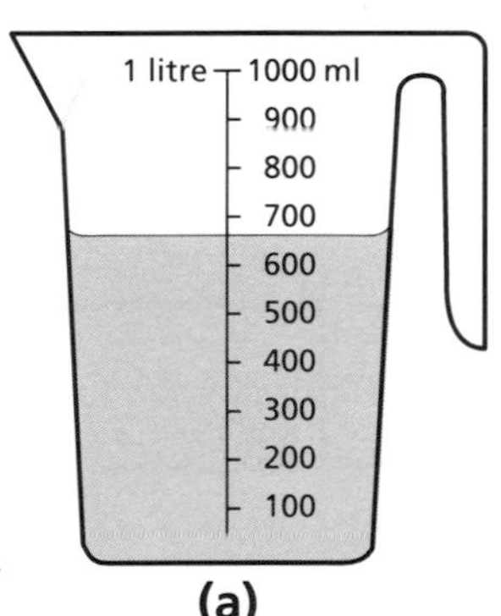

(a)

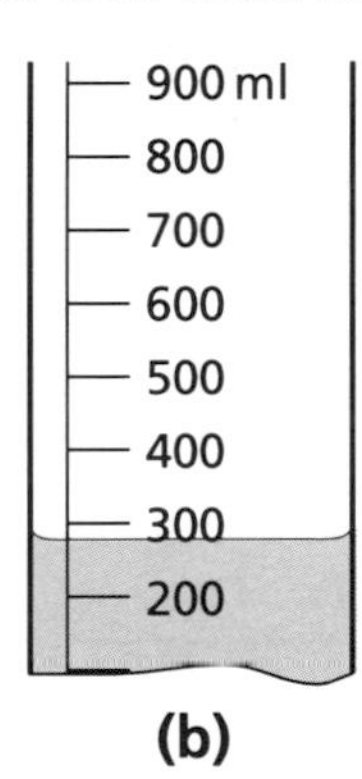

(b)

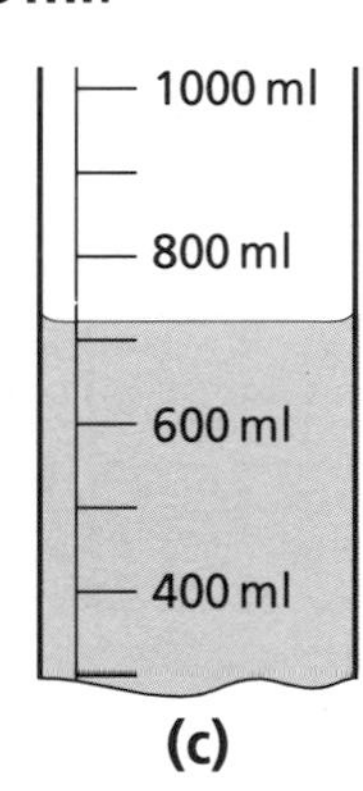

(c)

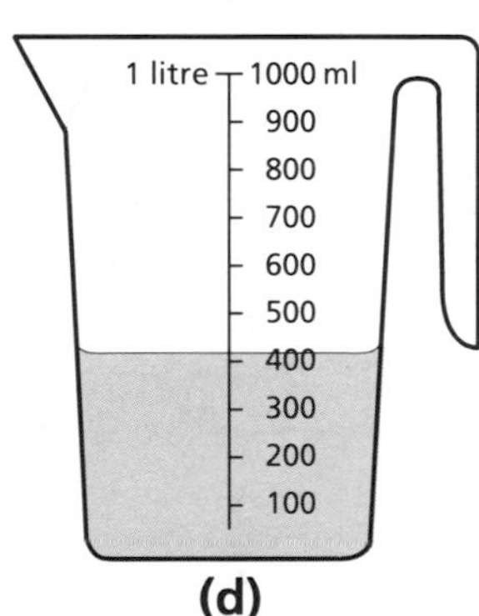

(d)

3 Read these volumes **to the nearest mark**.

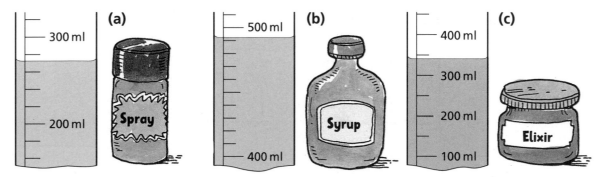

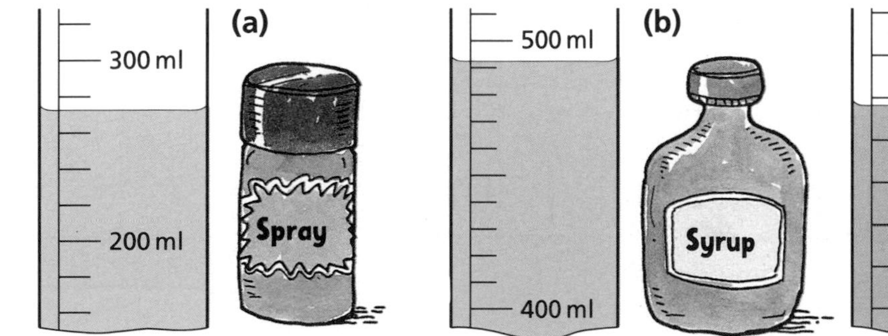

4 Ask your teacher for some containers and measuring jars.
Find the volume which each container holds.

R25

H44

83 Vitamin cubes

Volume: cubic centimetre, cm^3

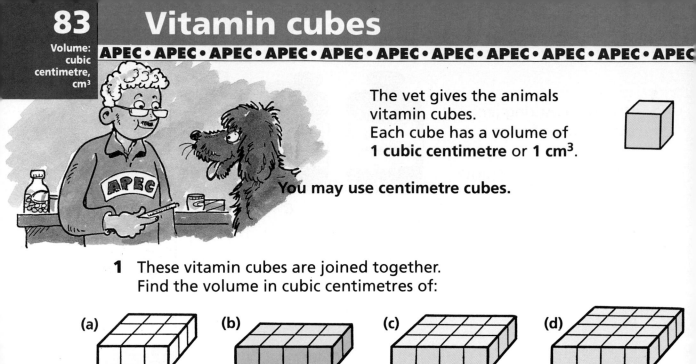

The vet gives the animals vitamin cubes.
Each cube has a volume of **1 cubic centimetre** or **1 cm^3**.

You may use centimetre cubes.

1 These vitamin cubes are joined together.
Find the volume in cubic centimetres of:

(a) 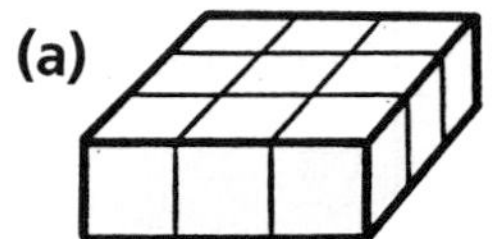

(b) 

(c) 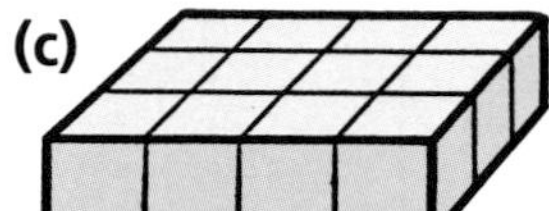

(d) 

2 The cubes are packed in boxes.

- How many **layers** can each box hold?
- Find the volume of each box.

(a) 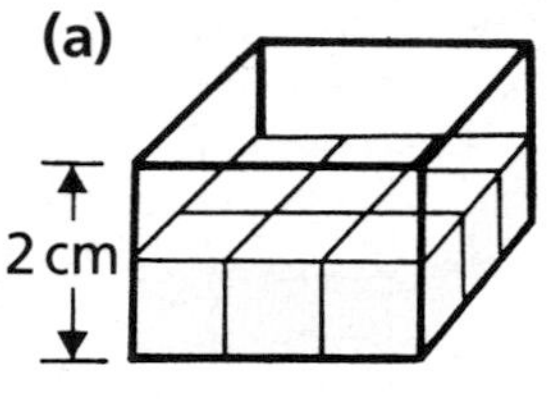

(b) 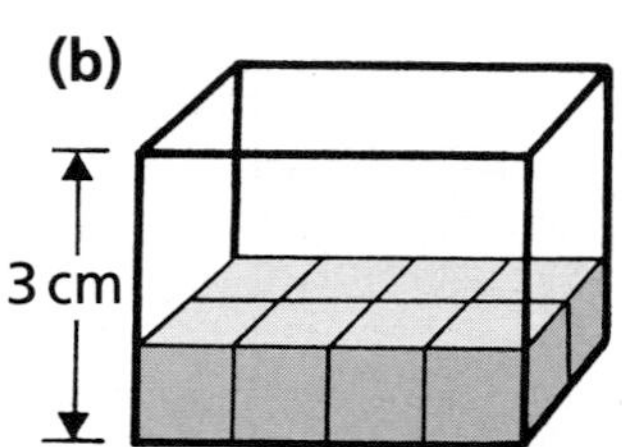

(c) 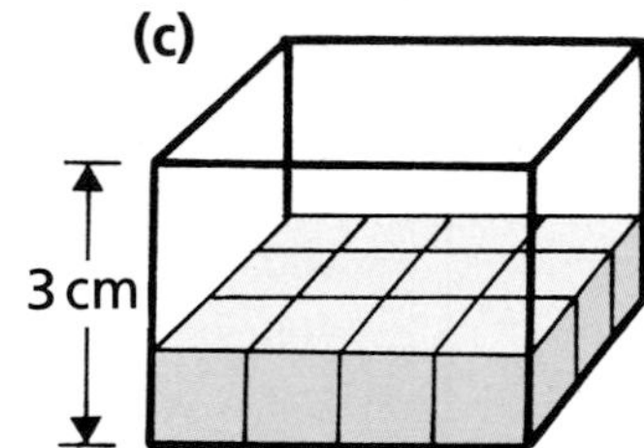

(d) 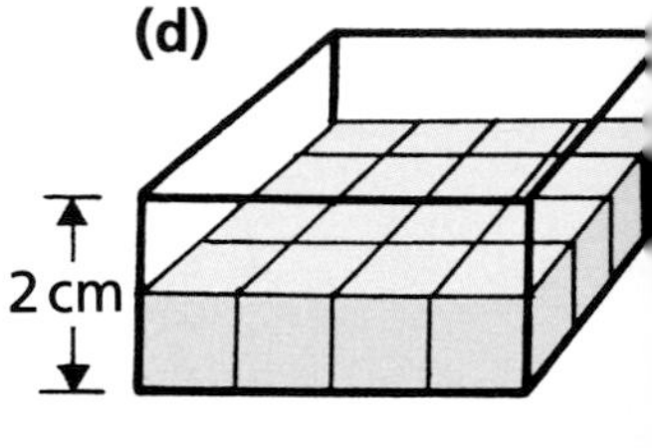

3 Find the volume of each box of vitamins.

(a) 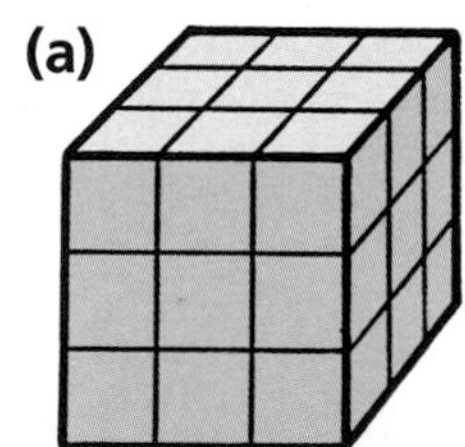

(b) 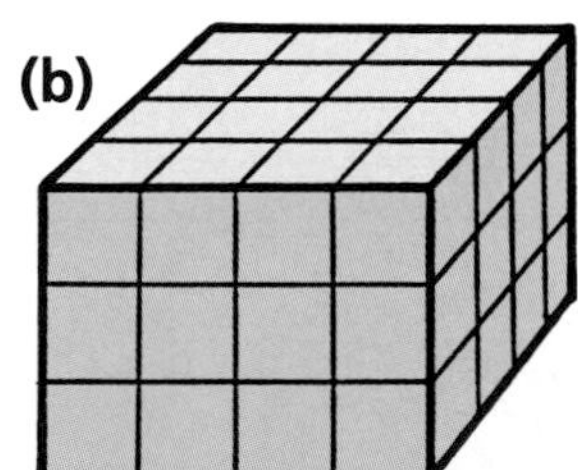

(c) 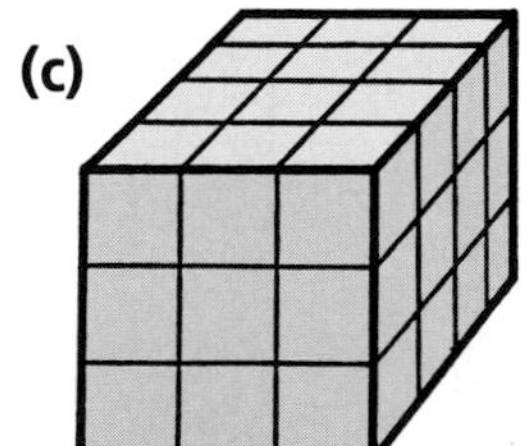

(d) 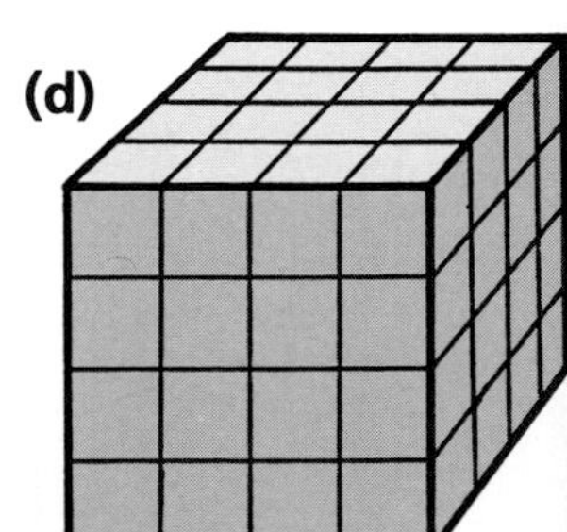

4 Use centimetre cubes to find the volumes of small boxes.

Litre of cubes

Volume: 1 litre = 1000 cm^3

1 **(a)** Build a layer of centimetre cubes like this.

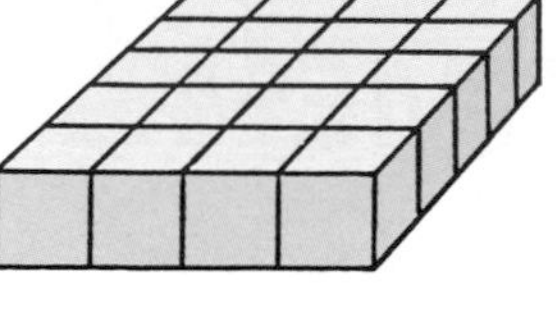

What is the volume of this layer?

(b) How many of these layers are needed to build a cuboid with a volume of
- 60 cm^3
- 100 cm^3
- 1000 cm^3 ?

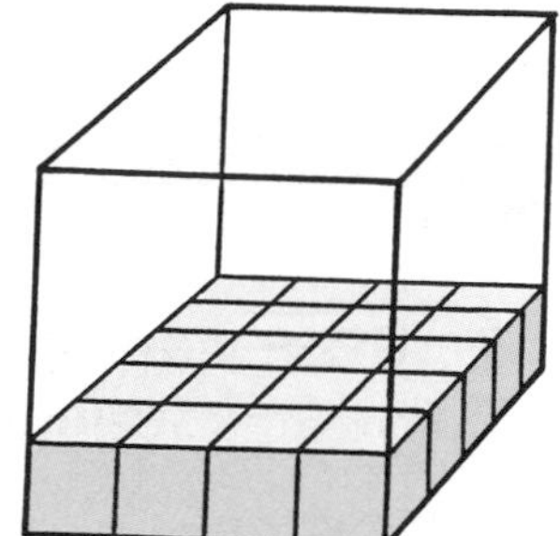

Work as a group.
You need 'flats' like these.

2 What is the volume in cm^3 of 1 flat?

3 Make a cube using flats.
(a) How many flats did you use?
(b) What is the volume of the cube?

4 Ask your teacher for the special cube.
Find its volume in cm^3 using flats.

5 Pour one litre of water into the empty special cube.
What do you notice?

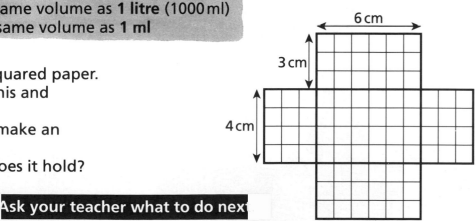

> **1000 cm^3** is the same volume as **1 litre** (1000 ml)
> **1 cm^3** is the same volume as **1 ml**

6 Use **centimetre** squared paper.
Draw a net like this and cut it out.
Fold your net to make an open box.
How many cm^3 does it hold?

6 cm
3 cm
4 cm

Ask your teacher what to do next

Class 6 is watching **TIME WARP**

The presenter asks them to keep a **Time Diary** for one school day.

School starts

1 Write the starting time for each school event in two ways.

(a) Play rehearsal

(b) Maths project

(c) In the gym

(d) Feeding pets

(e) Computer club

(f) Music time

(g) Road safety talk

2 Now write the events and times **in order**, to make a **Time Diary** for Class 6.

Time Diary: Tuesday

School starts 8.50 am

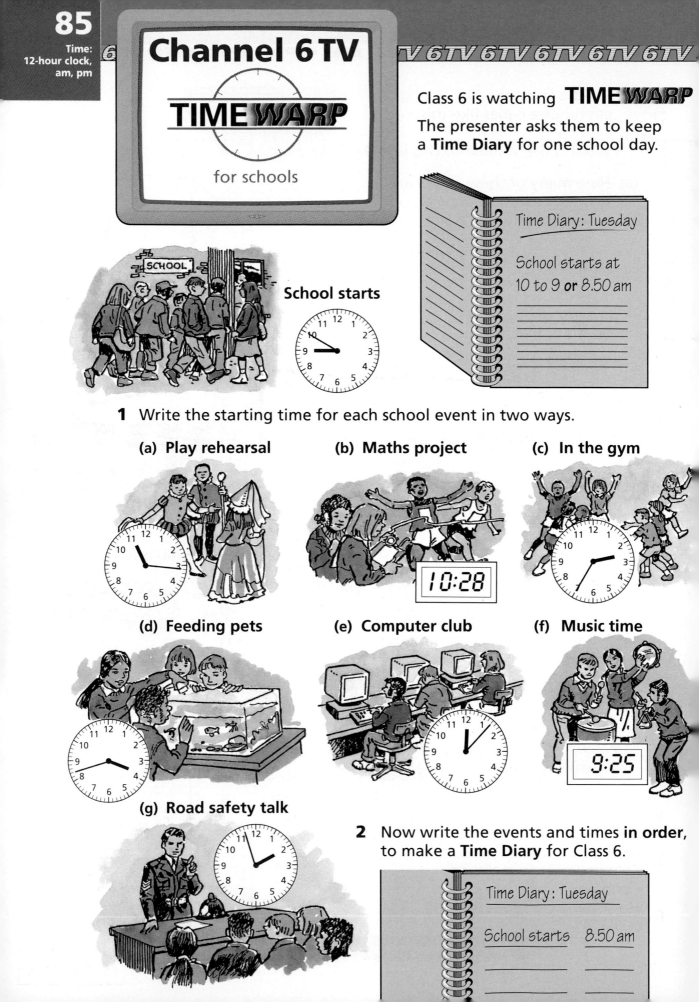

Going to 6TV

6TV 6TV 6TV 6TV 6TV 6TV 6TV 6TV 6TV 6TV 6TV

Class 6 is going to visit the 6TV studios.
The children use these timetables to plan the journey.

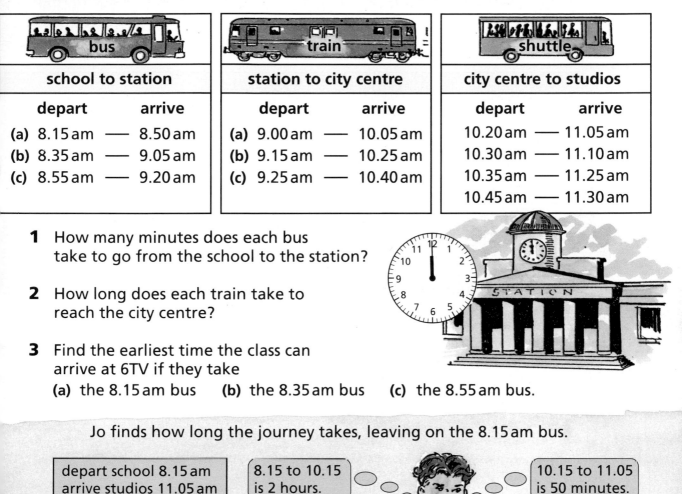

bus		train		shuttle	
school to station		**station to city centre**		**city centre to studios**	
depart	**arrive**	**depart**	**arrive**	**depart**	**arrive**
(a) 8.15 am	8.50 am	(a) 9.00 am	10.05 am	10.20 am	11.05 am
(b) 8.35 am	9.05 am	(b) 9.15 am	10.25 am	10.30 am	11.10 am
(c) 8.55 am	9.20 am	(c) 9.25 am	10.40 am	10.35 am	11.25 am
				10.45 am	11.30 am

1 How many minutes does each bus take to go from the school to the station?

2 How long does each train take to reach the city centre?

3 Find the earliest time the class can arrive at 6TV if they take
(a) the 8.15 am bus **(b)** the 8.35 am bus **(c)** the 8.55 am bus.

Jo finds how long the journey takes, leaving on the 8.15 am bus.

depart school 8.15 am
arrive studios 11.05 am

8.15 to 10.15 is 2 hours.
10.15 to 11.05 is 50 minutes.

The journey takes 2 hours 50 minutes.

4 How long does each of these journeys take?

(a)	depart	8.35 am	arrive	11.10 am
(b)	depart	8.55 am	arrive	11.30 am
(c)	depart	8.15 am	arrive	12 noon
(d)	depart	8.40 am	arrive	12.30 pm

5 The teacher leaves home at 8.20 am and returns at 5.15 pm. How long is she away from home?

6 Class 6 takes the 8.15 am bus from school. They miss the first train.
(a) When should they arrive at 6TV?
(b) How long does their journey take?

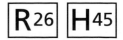

R26 H45

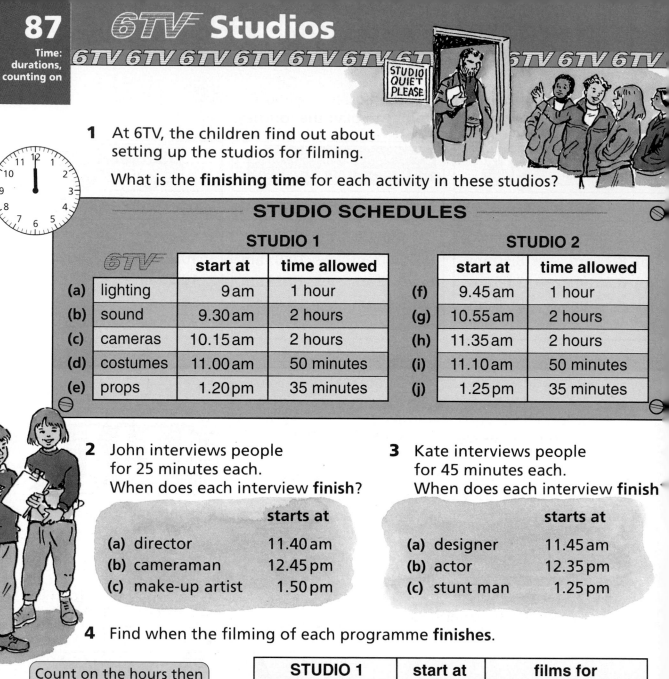

6TV Studios

1 At 6TV, the children find out about setting up the studios for filming.

What is the **finishing time** for each activity in these studios?

STUDIO SCHEDULES

STUDIO 1

	6TV	start at	time allowed
(a)	lighting	9am	1 hour
(b)	sound	9.30am	2 hours
(c)	cameras	10.15am	2 hours
(d)	costumes	11.00am	50 minutes
(e)	props	1.20pm	35 minutes

STUDIO 2

	start at	time allowed
(f)	9.45am	1 hour
(g)	10.55am	2 hours
(h)	11.35am	2 hours
(i)	11.10am	50 minutes
(j)	1.25pm	35 minutes

2 John interviews people for 25 minutes each.
When does each interview **finish**?

		starts at
(a)	director	11.40am
(b)	cameraman	12.45pm
(c)	make-up artist	1.50pm

3 Kate interviews people for 45 minutes each.
When does each interview **finish**?

		starts at
(a)	designer	11.45am
(b)	actor	12.35pm
(c)	stunt man	1.25pm

4 Find when the filming of each programme **finishes**.

	STUDIO 1	start at	films for
(a)	*Newsround*	6.30am	1 hour 15 minutes
(b)	*Scary Tales*	8.05am	2 hours 45 minutes
(c)	*Sailing*	11.35am	1 hour 5 minutes
(d)	*Quiz Time*	2.10pm	2 hours 50 minutes

	STUDIO 2	start at	films for
(e)	*Breakfast News*	6.45am	1 hour 20 minutes
(f)	*Cartoon*	8.30am	2 hours 40 minutes
(g)	*Cooking for Two*	11.20am	2 hours 50 minutes
(h)	*Golf*	3.50pm	3 hours 25 minutes
(i)	*Good Gardening*	8.15pm	1 hour 55 minutes
(j)	*Ghost Story*	10.30pm	2 hours 35 minutes

1 The children look at the sports filming schedule. Find the **starting time** for each film crew.

crew	sport	starts at	films for	finishes at
A	football		2 hours	4.45 pm
B	golf		3 hours	5.50 pm
C	cricket		3 hours	2.10 pm
D	sailing		35 minutes	10.45 am
E	motor racing		25 minutes	12.45 pm
F	snooker		45 minutes	11.50 pm

2 At what time before filming starts should each presenter report to the make-up artist?

Time needed for make-up	35 minutes	15 minutes	20 minutes	40 minutes	25 minutes
	Anne	Desmond	Shareen	Bill	Tracey
Filming starts at	10.30 am	6.00 pm	7.10 am	8.25 am	10.10 pm

3 The children meet Josh, the star of *Kidsklub*. Find when Josh should **start** each of these activities.

Count back the hours then count back the minutes.

		time needed	to finish at
(a)	make-up	1 hour 10 minutes	8.45 am
(b)	costume	1 hour 25 minutes	10.35 am
(c)	rehearsal	2 hours 15 minutes	1.20 pm
(d)	filming	1 hour 50 minutes	4.00 pm

4 Costumes are made for the actors. Find the time when each costume was **started**.

		time taken	finished at
(a)	mask	1 hour 20 minutes	3.10 pm
(b)	hat	1 hour 35 minutes	10.20 am
(c)	coat	2 hours 50 minutes	4.05 pm
(d)	long skirt	1 hour 25 minutes	12.15 pm
(e)	jacket	3 hours 30 minutes	1.20 pm
(f)	cloak	2 hours 45 minutes	2.25 pm

6TV

6TV Round the clock

6TV is a **24-hour** television station. It broadcasts programmes all day. The digital clock in the studio shows **24-hour times**.

Good Morning starts at 9 am.

9 am is written as **09.00**

Playaway starts at 5 pm.

5 pm is written as **17.00**

This chart in the director's room shows both 12-hour and 24-hour times.

12-hour time	10 am	11 am	12 noon	1 pm	2 pm
24-hour time	10.00	11.00	12.00	13.00	14.00

1 Write each programme time as a 24-hour time.

(a) *Daytime* 6 am **(b)** *Zoonooz* 3 pm **(c)** *Scary Tales* 11 pm
(d) *Sailing* 8 pm **(e)** *Video Box* 2 am **(f)** *Crackers* 7 am
(g) *Sounds Fine* 9 pm **(h)** *Crime Desk* 4 am **(i)** *Talkback* 4 pm

2 Write each time as a 12-hour time. Use am or pm.

(a) 03.00 **(b)** 20.00 **(c)** 05.00 **(d)** 19.00 **(e)** 22.00
(f) 18.00 **(g)** 12.00 **(h)** 01.00 **(i)** 11.00 **(j)** 13.00

8.45 am is written as **08.45**

24-hour times are always written with four figures.

3 Change each time to a 24-hour time.

(a) 6.15 am **(b)** 7.30 pm **(c)** 9.25 am **(d)** 10.20 pm **(e)** 5.40 am

4 Change each time to a 12-hour time. Use am or pm.

(a) 10.35 **(b)** 15.10 **(c)** 08.20 **(d)** 16.16 **(e)** 23.50 **(f)** 07.07

Find each time missing from the ON AIR chart.

	Studio 1	Studio 2	Studio 3	Studio 4	Studio 5	Studio 6
24-hour time	**(a)**	13.15	**(c)**	01.05	**(e)**	00.18
12-hour time	7.30 am	**(b)**	2.25 pm	**(d)**	12.50 am	**(f)**

These are 6TV **evening** programme times.

Wednesday	6TV
5.00	*News*
5.30	*Townscape*
6.15	*Pop Quiz*
7.00	*Police Call*
7.20	*Film on 6*
9.30	*Late News*
10.00	*Sportlook*
10.25	*Science Now*
11.00	*Stargazer*
11.30	*Into the Night*

1 Name the programme which starts at
(a) 17.30 **(b)** 19.00 **(c)** 23.30 **(d)** 22.25

2 Which programme is showing at
(a) 17.20 **(b)** 20.08 **(c)** 18.59 **(d)** 23.05?

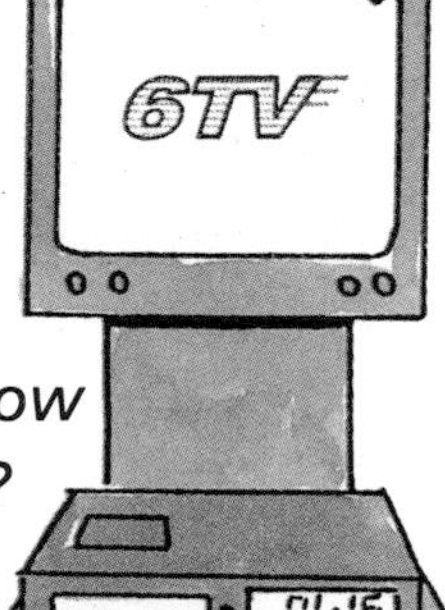

3 This video recorder has a 24-hour clock.
What starting time should be set to record
(a) *Police Call* **(b)** *Late News* **(c)** *Science Now*
(d) *Sportlook* **(e)** *Film on 6* **(f)** *Pop Quiz?*

Four of the children join the 6TV News team at the airport to film the arrival of performers for the Lynchester Pop Festival.

The flight arrival times are shown with **no dot**. 15.20 becomes 1520

European Arrivals	
Rome	0905
Madrid	1052
Lisbon	1144
Moscow	1319
London	1550
Paris	1744

International Arrivals	
Sydney	1010
Tokyo	1235
Nairobi	1420
Chicago	1605
Delhi	1705
New York	1928

4 Which flight arrives at
(a) 1.19 pm **(b)** 12.35 pm

(c) 3.50 pm **(d)** 5.05 pm?

5 Which flights arrive **(a)** before noon **(b)** after 2.25 pm?

6 Which flight arrives **just before** **(a)** 11.45 am **(b)** 1.20 pm **(c)** 7.30 pm?

7 Which flight arrives **just after** **(a)** 12.30 pm **(b)** 5 pm **(c)** 3.45 pm?

8 Dan Ely arrives on the flight from Chicago.
Two hours later he arrives at the 6TV studios to appear on *Pop Quiz*.
Is he on time for the start of the programme? Explain.

Go to Workbook page 29.

R28 H48,49

6TV TIME WARP

6TV 6TV 6TV 6TV 6TV 6TV 6TV 6TV 6TV 6TV 6T

We measure short periods of time in **seconds**.
There are **60 seconds** in **1 minute**.

The **red hand** shows that **35 seconds** have passed since the stopwatch was started.

1 Read each stopwatch. How long is each picture on the TV screen?

(a)

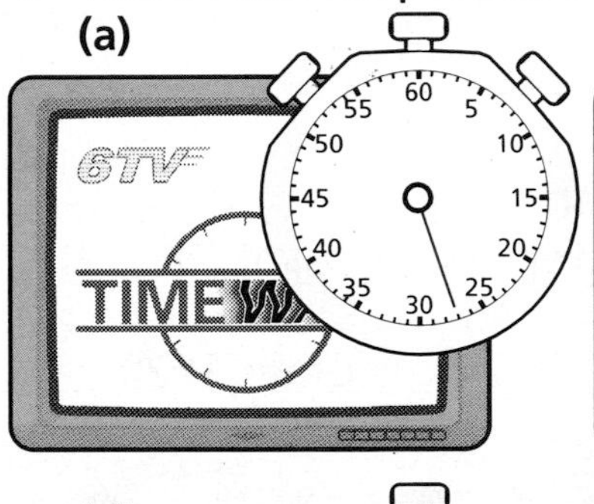

(b)

(c)

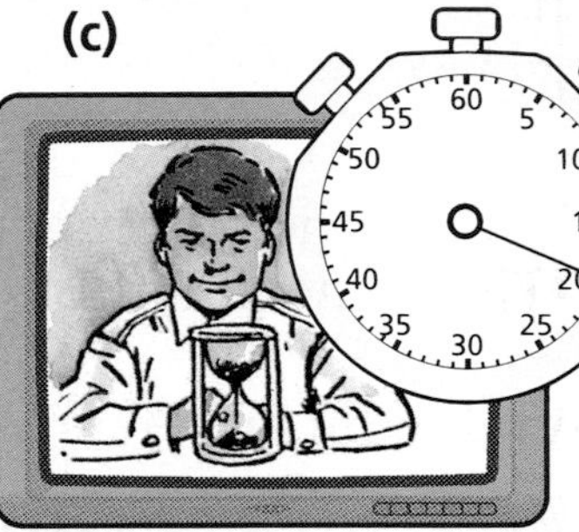

(d)

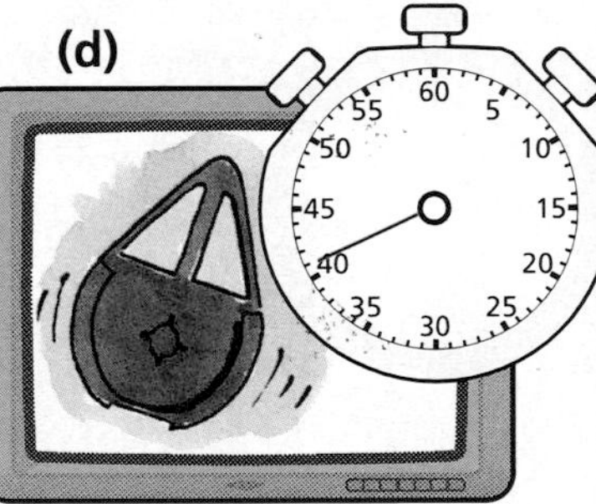

(e)

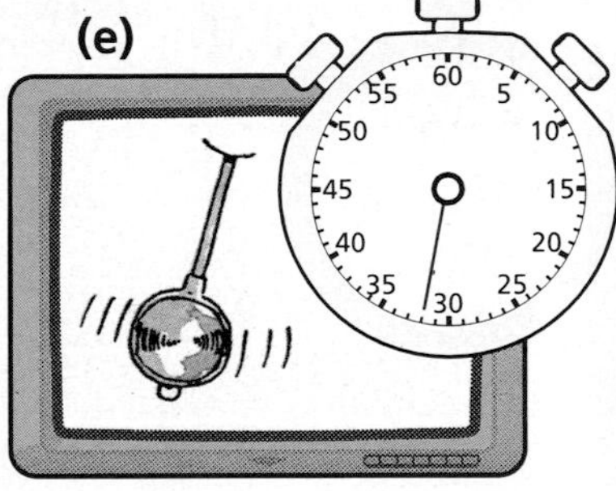

(f)

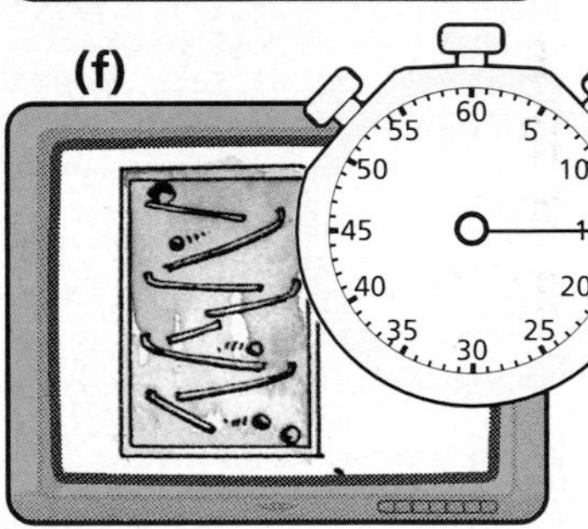

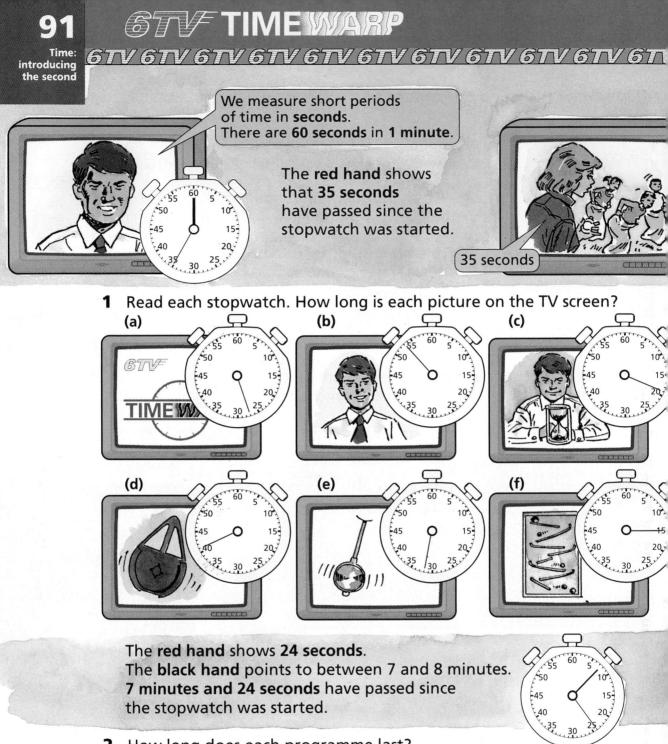

The **red hand** shows **24 seconds**.
The **black hand** points to between 7 and 8 minutes.
7 minutes and 24 seconds have passed since the stopwatch was started.

2 How long does each programme last?

Go to Workbook page 30.

1 In which month is each birthday?

(a) …d's is in the …th month.

(b) Gran's is two months later.

(c) Donna's is in the last month of the year.

(d) Kay's is in the month with fewest days.

(e) Anne's is three months before Kay's.

…se this calendar for questions 2 and 3.

…EPTEMBER

T	W	T	F	S	S
			1	2	3
5	6	7	8	9	10
2	13	14	15	16	17
9	20	21	22	23	24
6	27	28	29	30	

OCTOBER

M	T	W	T	F	S	S
						1
2	3	4	5	6	7	8
9	10	11	12	13	14	15
16	17	18	19	20	21	22
23	24	25	26	27	28	29
30	31					

2 On which date in **September** is each of these birthdays?

(a) Mum's is on the first Thursday.

(b) Roddy's is on the last Friday.

(c) Aunt Jean's is five days before Roddy's.

3 The family are planning a party in October. Find a date for the party.

…party must be …Saturday or …nday. Gran

I want to help but I work every Sunday. Anne

I work the last weekend every month. Dad

We go out every second Saturday. The 7th is the first outing in October. Mum

Problem solving

4 Roddy is 60 years younger than Gran. Gran is six times Roddy's age. How old are they?

93 Journeys

Other activity: timetables

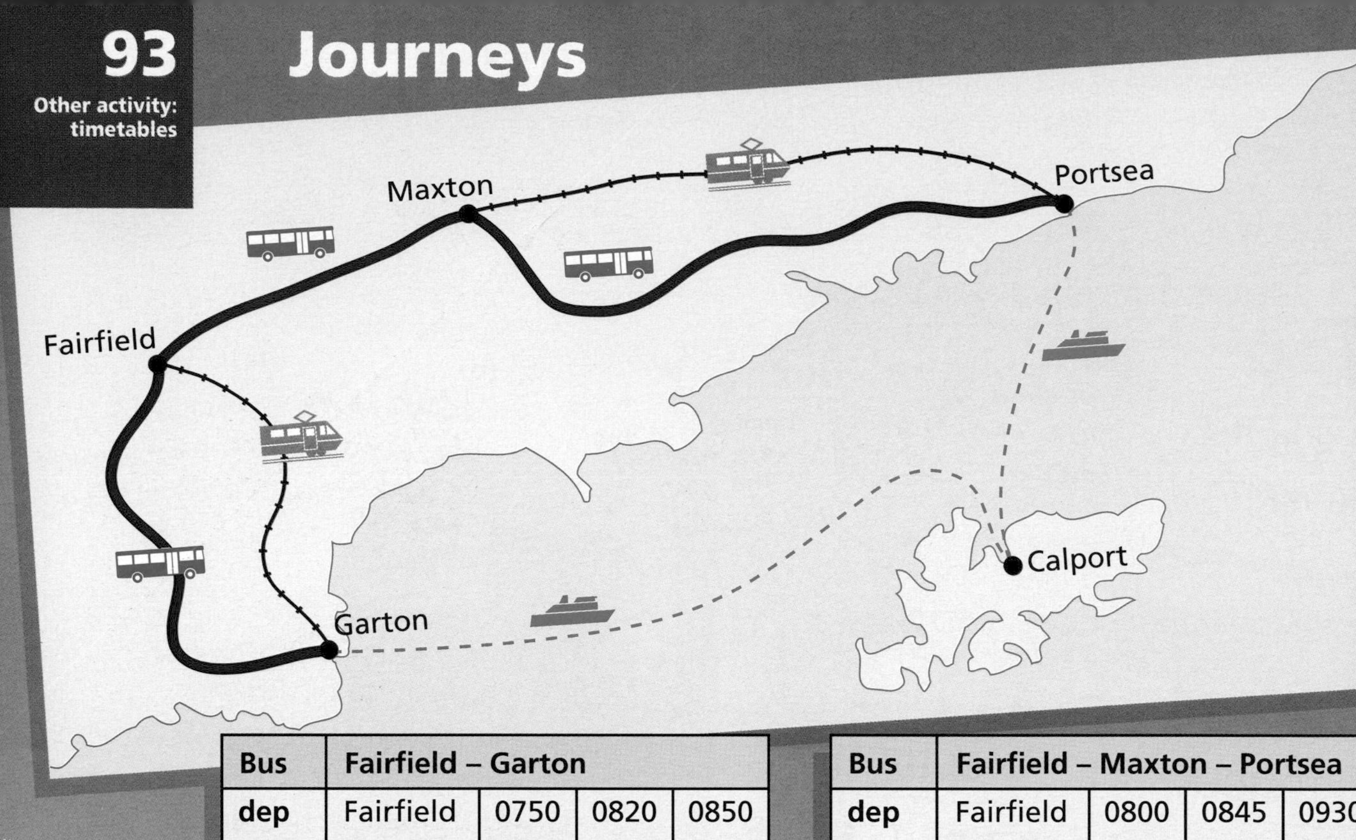

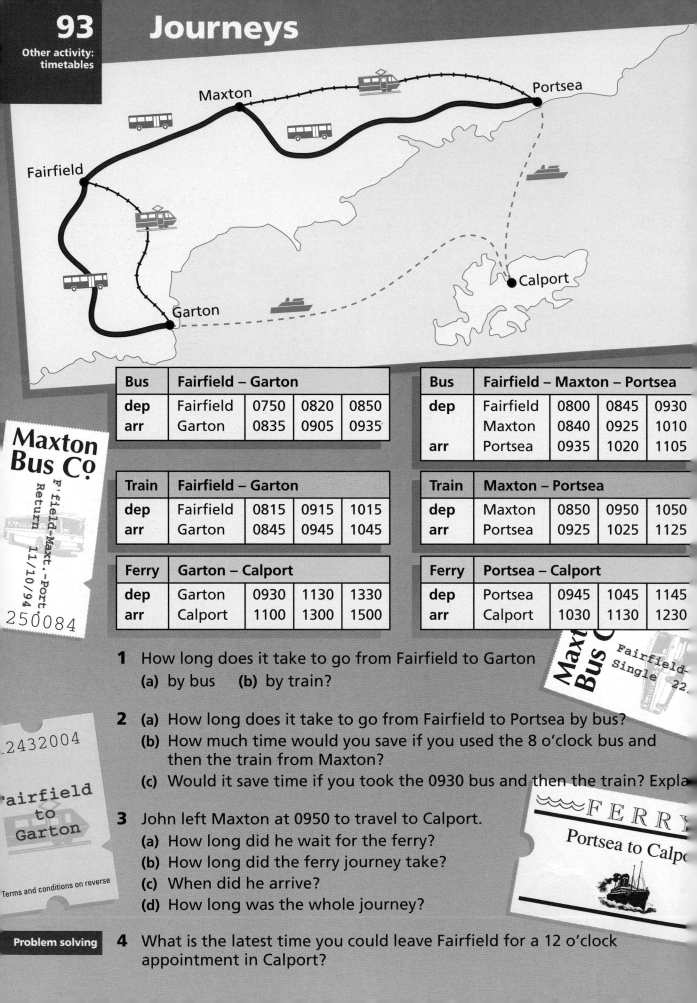

Bus	Fairfield – Garton			
dep	Fairfield	0750	0820	0850
arr	Garton	0835	0905	0935

Train	Fairfield – Garton			
dep	Fairfield	0815	0915	1015
arr	Garton	0845	0945	1045

Ferry	Garton – Calport			
dep	Garton	0930	1130	1330
arr	Calport	1100	1300	1500

Bus	Fairfield – Maxton – Portsea			
dep	Fairfield	0800	0845	0930
	Maxton	0840	0925	1010
arr	Portsea	0935	1020	1105

Train	Maxton – Portsea			
dep	Maxton	0850	0950	1050
arr	Portsea	0925	1025	1125

Ferry	Portsea – Calport			
dep	Portsea	0945	1045	1145
arr	Calport	1030	1130	1230

1 How long does it take to go from Fairfield to Garton
(a) by bus **(b)** by train?

2 **(a)** How long does it take to go from Fairfield to Portsea by bus?
(b) How much time would you save if you used the 8 o'clock bus and then the train from Maxton?
(c) Would it save time if you took the 0930 bus and then the train? Expla

3 John left Maxton at 0950 to travel to Calport.
(a) How long did he wait for the ferry?
(b) How long did the ferry journey take?
(c) When did he arrive?
(d) How long was the whole journey?

Problem solving

4 What is the latest time you could leave Fairfield for a 12 o'clock appointment in Calport?

Spaceflight control

The screen shows the positions of planets in the Alpha system.
Planet **A** is at the point **4 along** the **horizontal axis** and **3 up** the **vertical axis**.
Planet **A** has **co-ordinates (4, 3)**.
Planet **B** has **co-ordinates (0, 1)**.
The point with co-ordinates (0, 0) is called **the origin**.

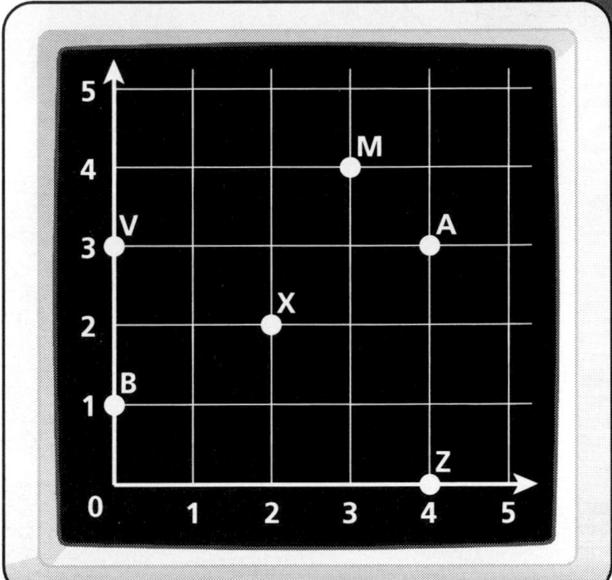

1 Write the co-ordinates of the Planets **M**, **V**, **X**, and **Z**.

This screen shows the positions of spaceships.

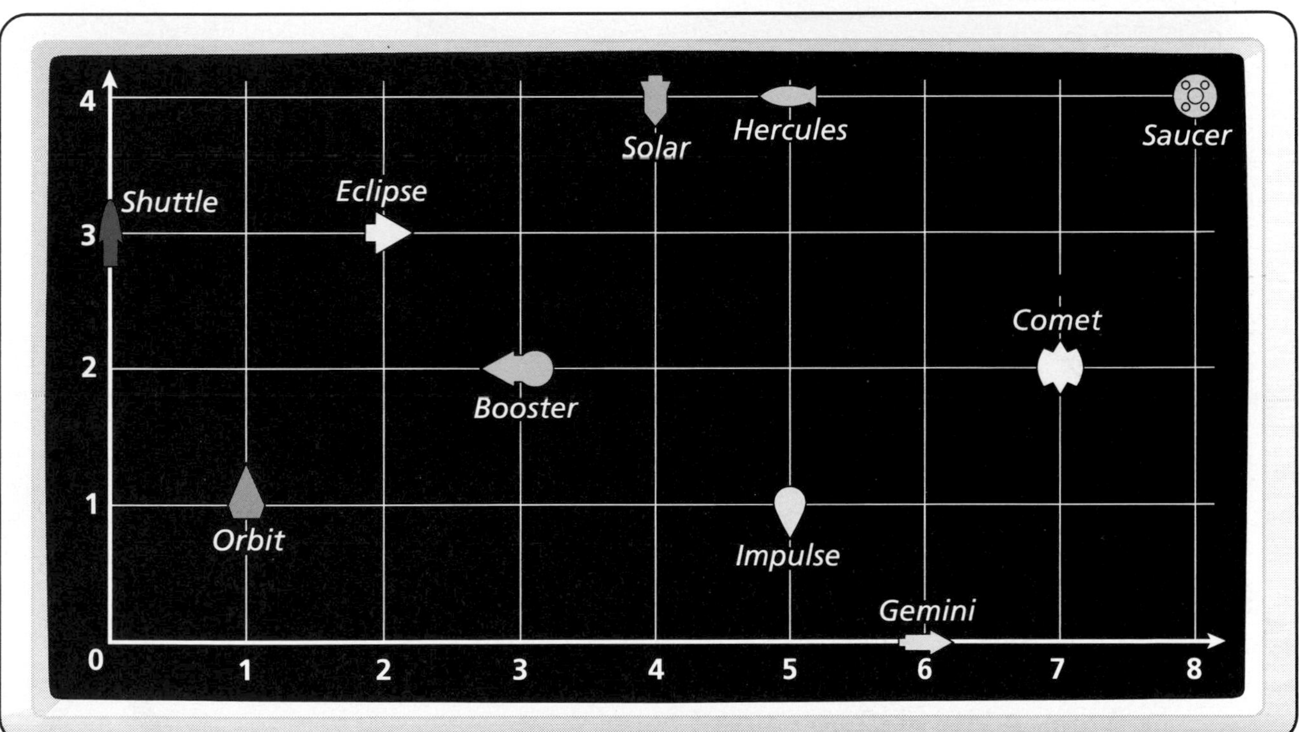

2 Which spaceship has co-ordinates
(a) (2, 3) **(b)** (5, 1) **(c)** (3, 2) **(d)** (0, 3) **(e)** (7, 2) **(f)** (4, 4)?

3 What are the co-ordinates of
(a) *Orbit* **(b)** *Saucer* **(c)** *Gemini* **(d)** *Hercules*?

4 Which spaceship is on **(a)** the horizontal axis **(b)** the vertical axis?

Go to Workbook page 31.

95 Shapes with four sides

2D shape: rhombus, parallelogram, kite

1 A **rhombus** has four equal sides.

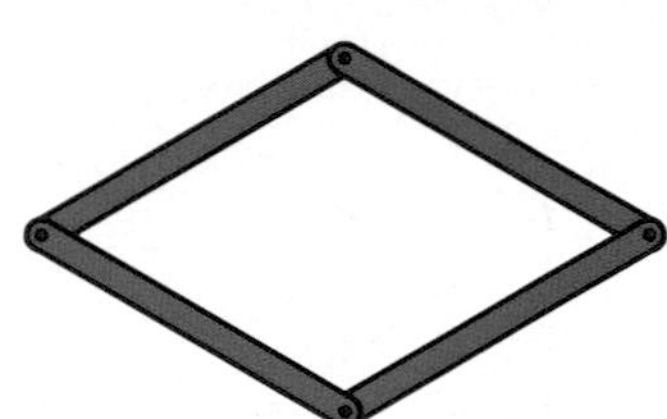

(a) Use strips to make a rhombus.
(b) Change your rhombus into a square.
(c) Compare the sides and angles of the square and the rhombus. What do you notice?

2 A **parallelogram** has two pairs of equal sides.

(a) Use strips to make a parallelogram.
(b) Change your parallelogram into a rectangle.
(c) Compare the sides and angles of the parallelogram and the rectangle. What do you notice?

3 **(a)** A **kite** has two pairs of equal sides. Use strips to make a kite like this.
(b) Compare the sides of the kite and the parallelogram. What do you notice?

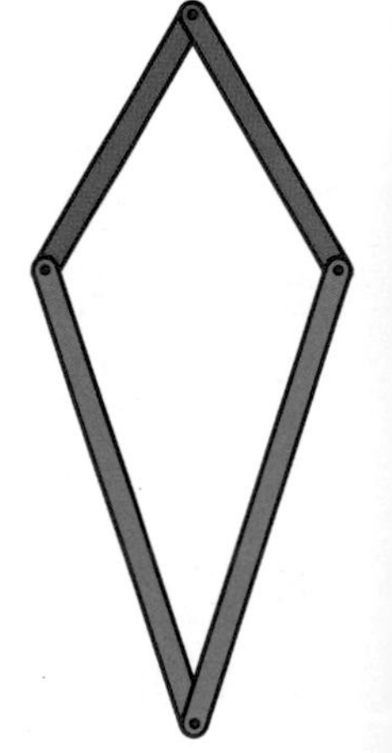

4 On each yellow shape on **Workbook page 18**,

- write its name
- draw along equal sides with the same colour
- mark any right angles.

1 (a) Cut out the yellow shapes from **Workbook page 18**.
(b) Fold each shape to find any lines of symmetry.
Draw each line of symmetry.

2 Which cut-out shapes have
(a) only one line of symmetry
(b) only two lines of symmetry
(c) four lines of symmetry
(d) no lines of symmetry?

Stick the yellow shapes in your jotter.

Each of these green lines is a **diagonal**.

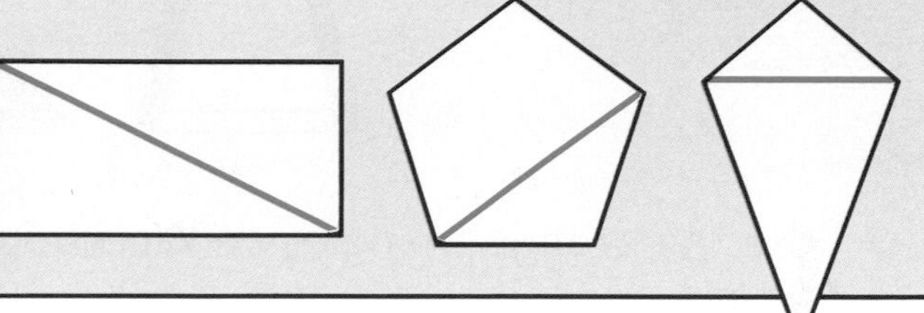

3 Which of these diagonals are also lines of symmetry?

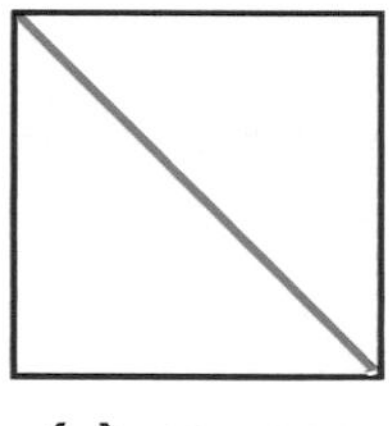

(a) square

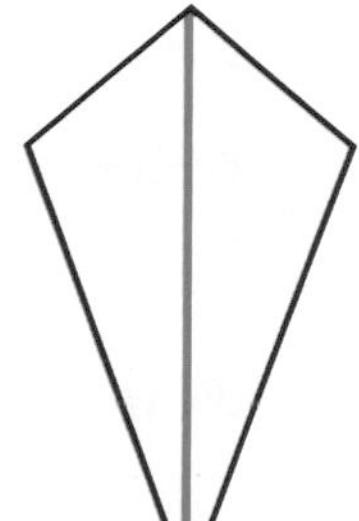

(b) kite

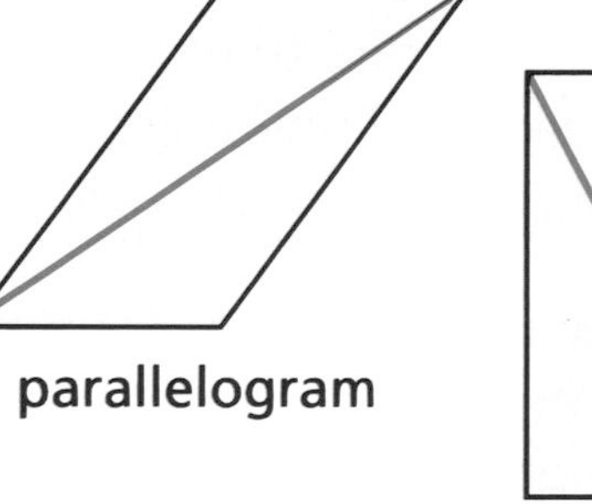

(c) parallelogram

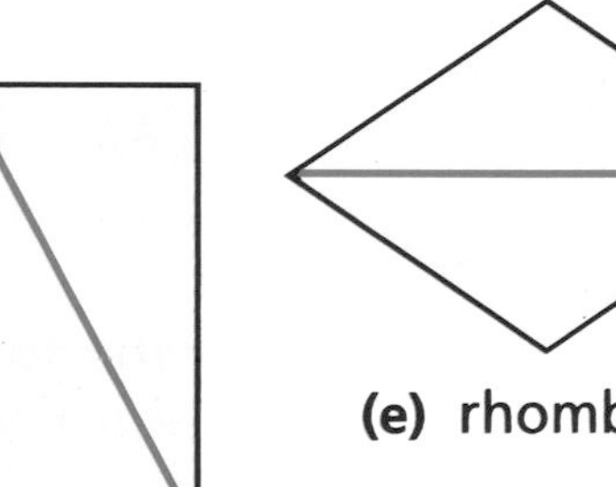

(d) rectangle

(e) rhombus

4 (a) Cut out the green rectangle from **Workbook page 20**.
Cut along the dotted diagonal.
Use the pieces green-side-up to make a different four-sided shape. What shape is it?
(b) Turn one piece over to make another four-sided shape.
Stick the shape in your jotter and name it.

5 Repeat question **4(a)** for the green kite on **Workbook page 20**.
Stick the new shape in your jotter.

6 **Use shapes.**
(a) Fit two parallelograms side by side like this.
What shape have you made?

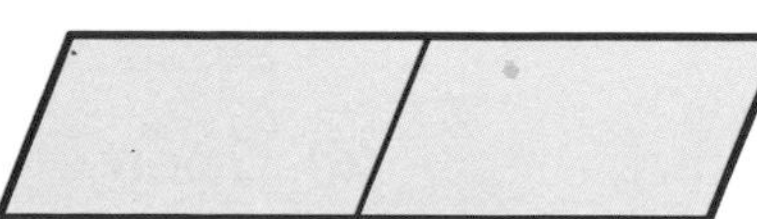

(b) What shape do two of these make:
• rectangles • squares • rhombuses • kites?

Triangles

1 Use strips to make a triangle with **3 equal sides** as shown. This is an **equilateral triangle**.

2 Use strips to make triangles as shown each with **2 equal sides**. These are called **isosceles triangles**.

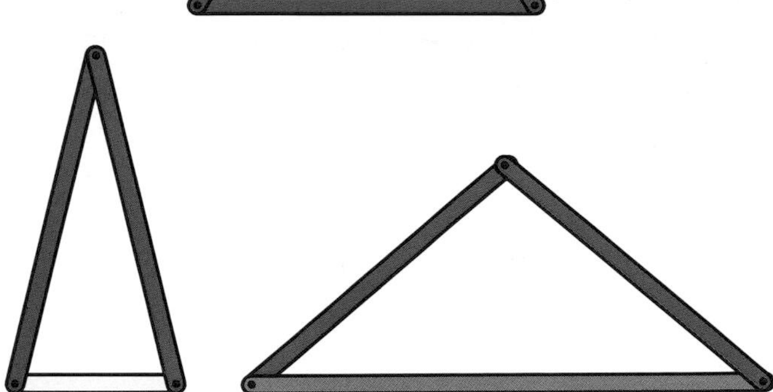

3 Use the orange triangles on **Workbook page 20**.

(a) Measure the sides of each triangle.

(b) Draw along equal sides with the same colour.

(c) Write the type of triangle.

4 (a) Cut out each orange triangle.

(b) Fold each shape to find any lines of symmetry. Draw these lines.

(c) Stick the triangles in your jotter.

5 Cut out the four red triangles from **Workbook page 20**.
Which four-sided shapes can you make with

(a) the 2 equilateral triangles

(b) the 2 isosceles triangles

(c) 1 isosceles triangle and 1 equilateral triangle?

6 **You need a paper rectangle.**

(a) Fold the rectangle in half.

(b) Draw a line like this.

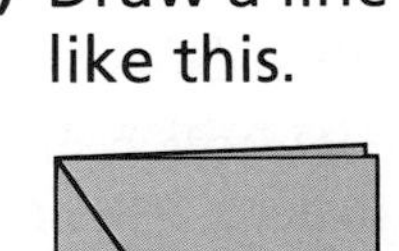

(c) Cut along your line.

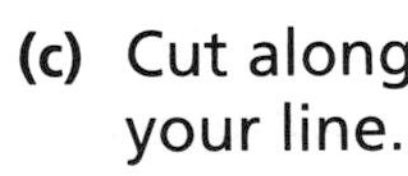

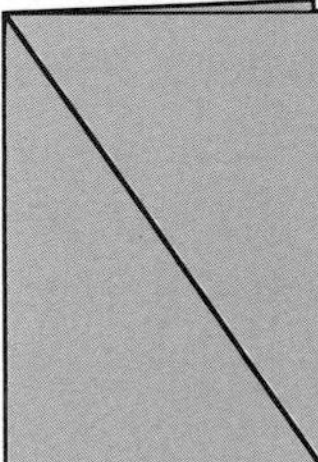

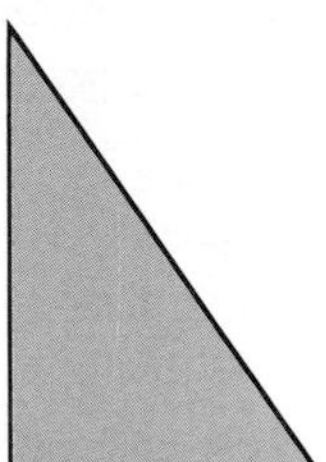

(d) Open out your triangle. Stick it in your jotter and name it.

Go to Workbook page 33.

1 Cut out the tangram from **Workbook page 18**.
Stick it on card and cut out the 5 pieces.

2 **(a)** Use **two pieces** to make this shape.
Draw round the pieces **or** sketch them to show how you did this.

(b) Use the **other three pieces** to make the same shape again. Show how you did this.

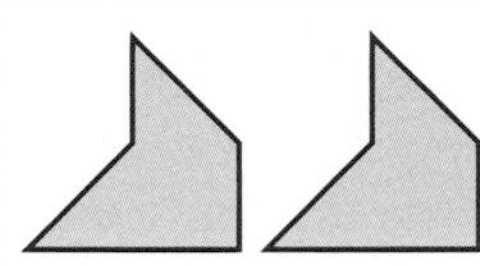

The two shapes you made are identical. They are **congruent shapes**.

3 Repeat question 2 to make shapes congruent to these.

(a)

(b)

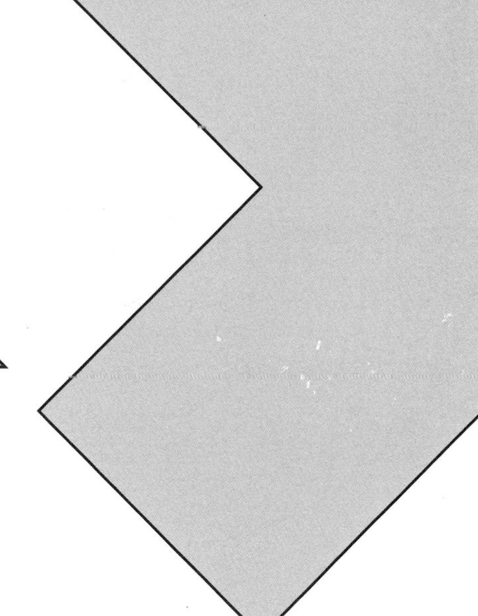

4 Use the **two small triangles** to make a shape congruent to

(a) the large triangle **(b)** the square

(c) the parallelogram.

Show how you did this.

5 Use **all five pieces** to make **(a)** a square

(b) a parallelogram **(c)** a right-angled isosceles triangle.

Problem solving

6 **(a)** Draw axes on **centimetre** squared paper.

(b) Mark the points (2, 5), (4, 8) and (2, 11).

(c) Join them to make a triangle. Colour it red.

(d) Mark the point (4, 14). Join it to (4, 8) and (2, 11) to make a triangle. Colour it yellow.

(e) Draw more congruent triangles to make a tiling.

Ask your teacher what to do next.

Circle designs

The red line shows the **circumference** of this circle.

The black line from the **centre** to the circumference of a circle is a **radius** of the circle.

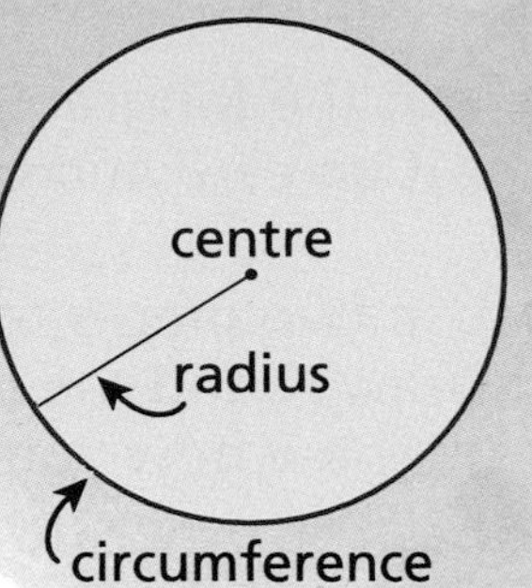

You need a pair of compasses.

1 Draw then colour a design like this.

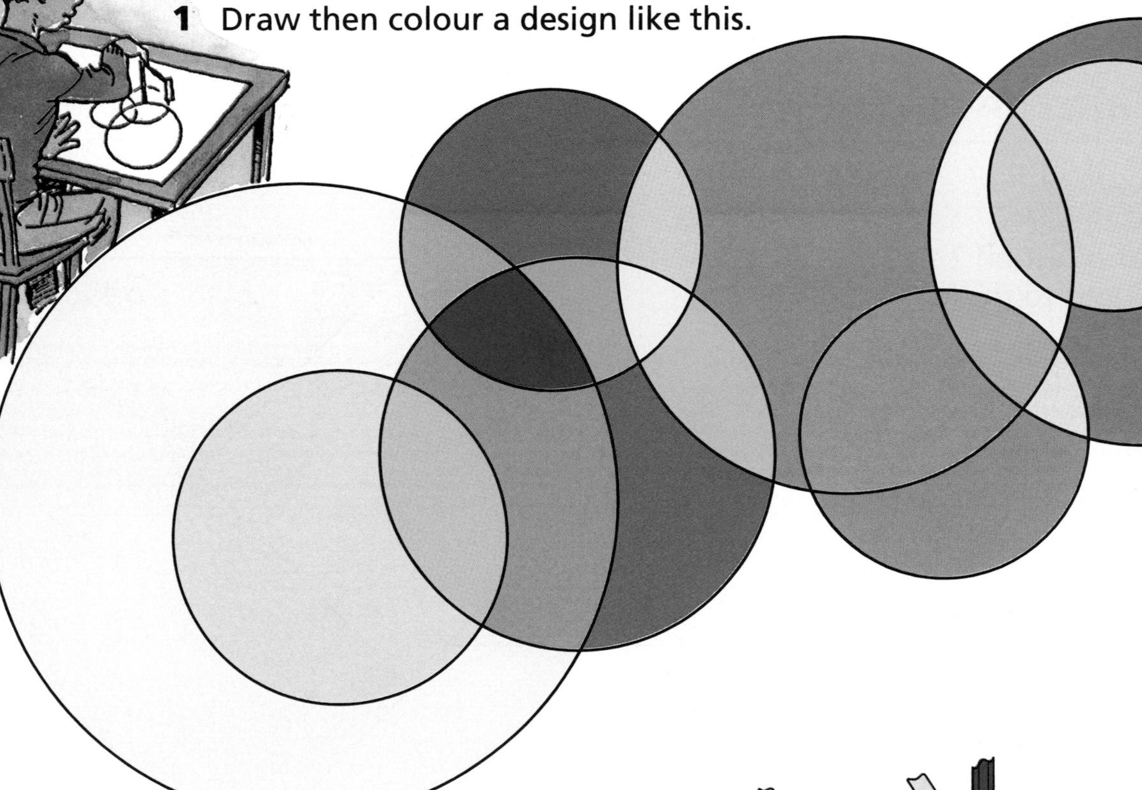

These compasses have been set to draw a circle of radius 3 cm.

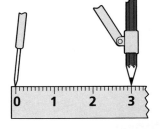

2 Draw a circle with radius
(a) 3 cm **(b)** 5 cm

3 **(a)** Draw a circle with radius 6 cm.
(b) Use the **same centre** and draw circles with radius 5 cm, 4 cm and 3 cm.
(c) Draw straight lines as shown.
(d) Colour your design.

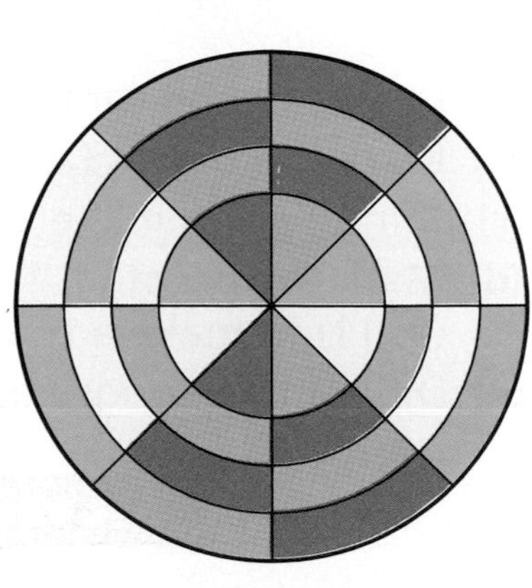

4 **(a)** Mark 2 dots 6 centimetres apart.
(b) Draw circles with radius 4 cm and radius 6 cm to make a design like this.
(c) Colour your design.

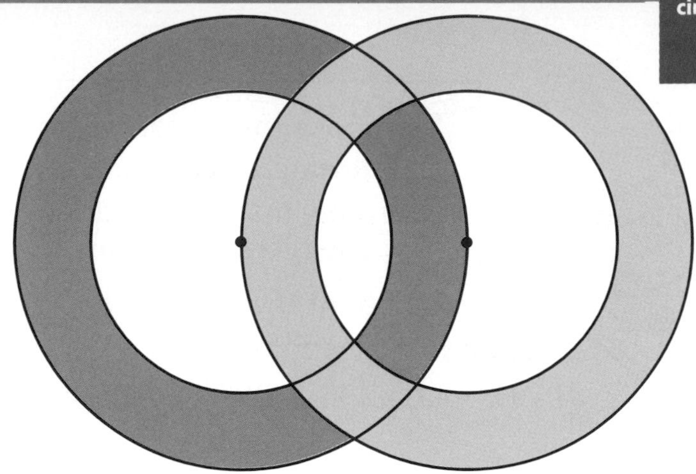

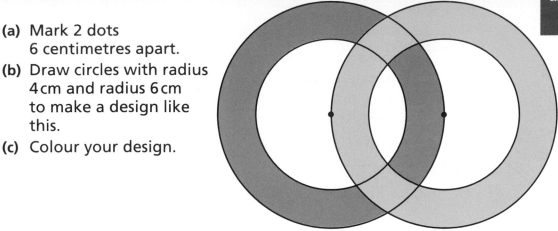

5 **(a)** Draw a square of side 3 cm on centimetre squared paper.
(b) At each corner draw a circle of radius 3 cm.
(c) Colour your design.

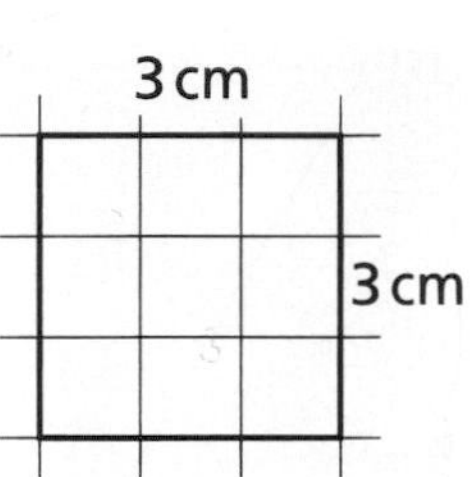

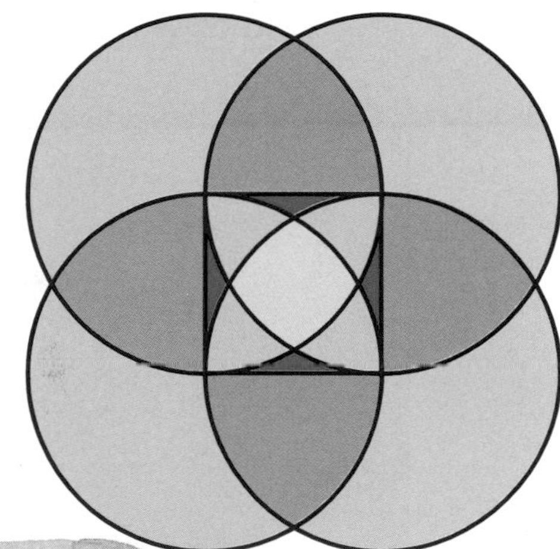

The blue line is a **diameter** of the circle.
It
- passes through the centre
- is a line of symmetry
- is twice as long as the radius
- divides the circle into 2 semi-circles.

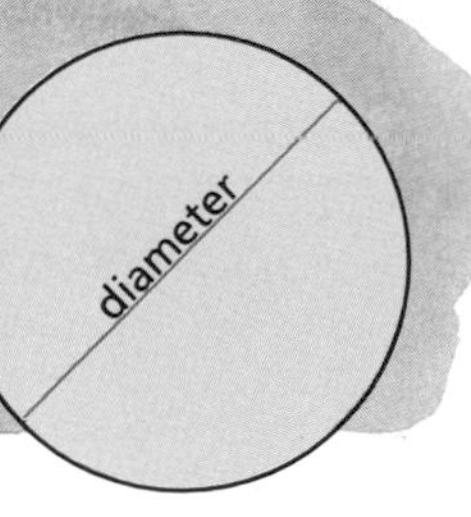

6 Draw semi-circles of **diameter** 8 cm and 6 cm to make a design like this.

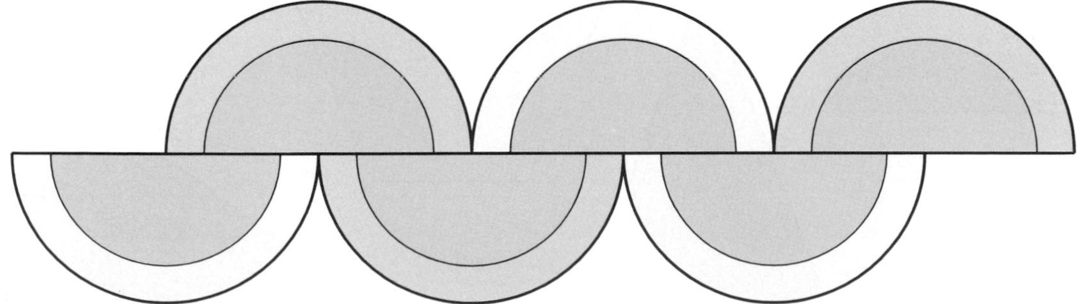

7 Design and draw your own circle patterns.

Ask your teacher what to do next

101 Rotational symmetry

2D shape: rotational symmetry

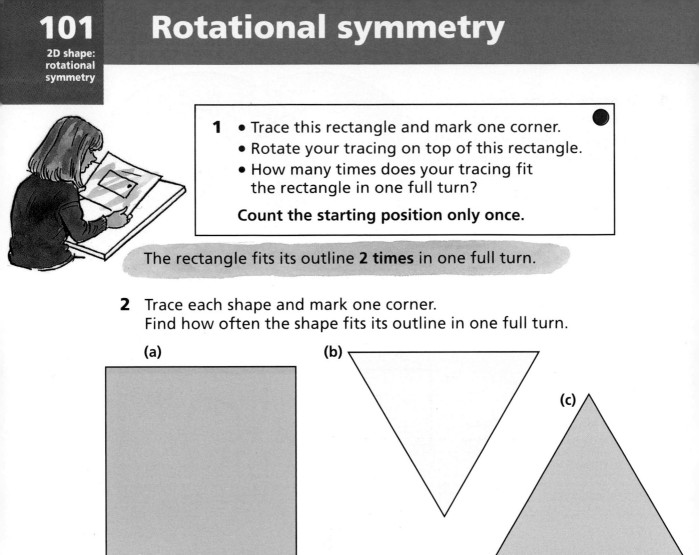

1 • Trace this rectangle and mark one corner.
• Rotate your tracing on top of this rectangle.
• How many times does your tracing fit the rectangle in one full turn?

Count the starting position only once.

The rectangle fits its outline **2 times** in one full turn.

2 Trace each shape and mark one corner.
Find how often the shape fits its outline in one full turn.

(a)

(b)

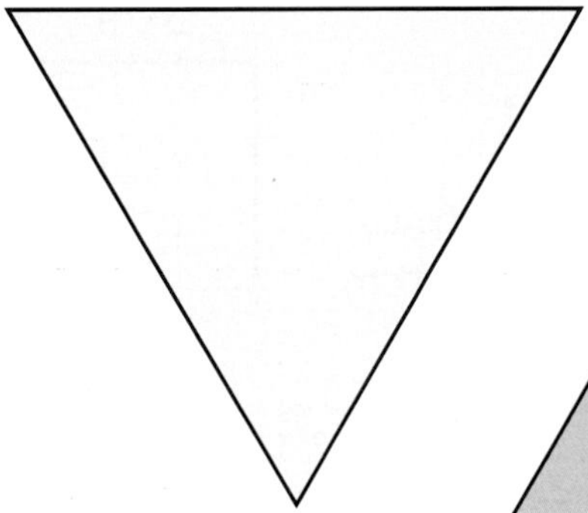

(c)

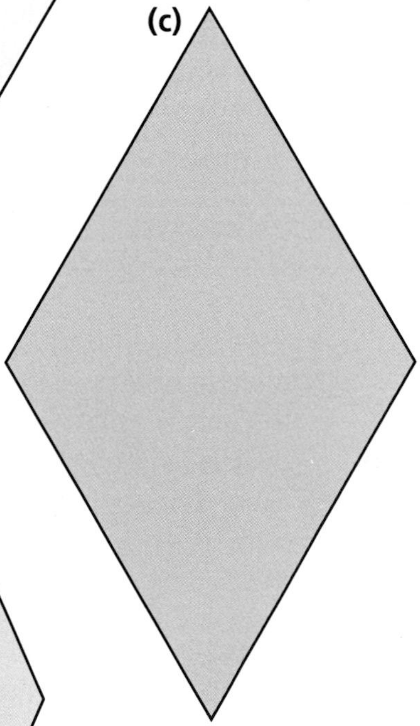

(d)

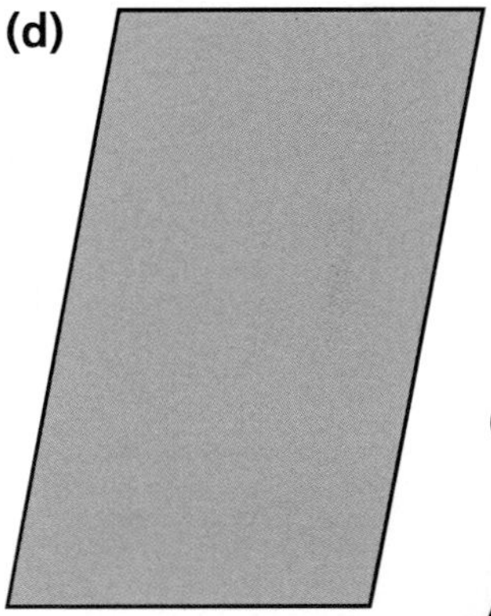

(e)

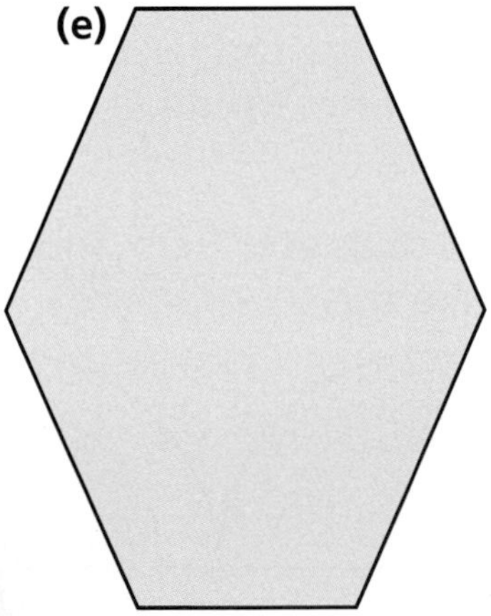

(f)

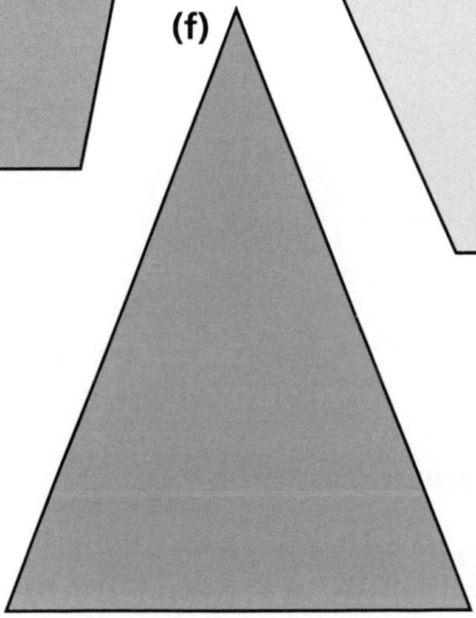

(g)

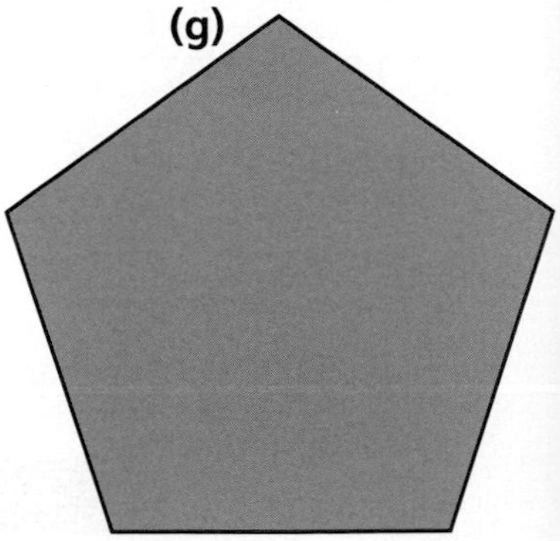

1 Trace this design and colour it as shown.
Check that the design fits its outline **4 times** in one full turn.

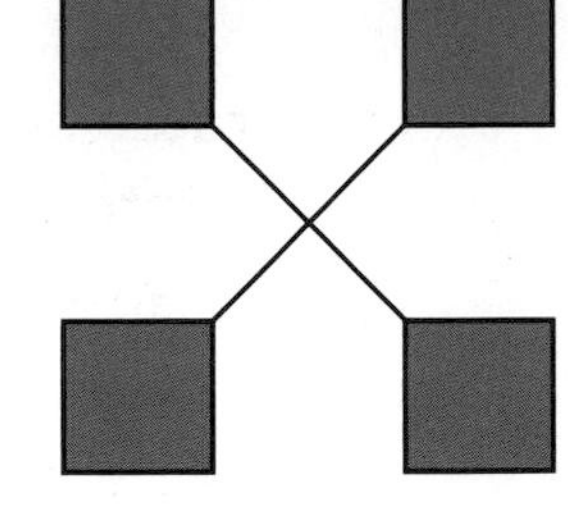

2 Trace each design and find how often it fits its outline in one full turn.

(a)

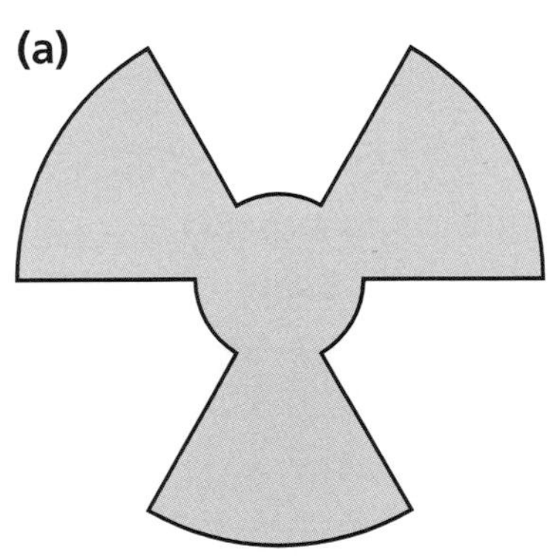

(b)

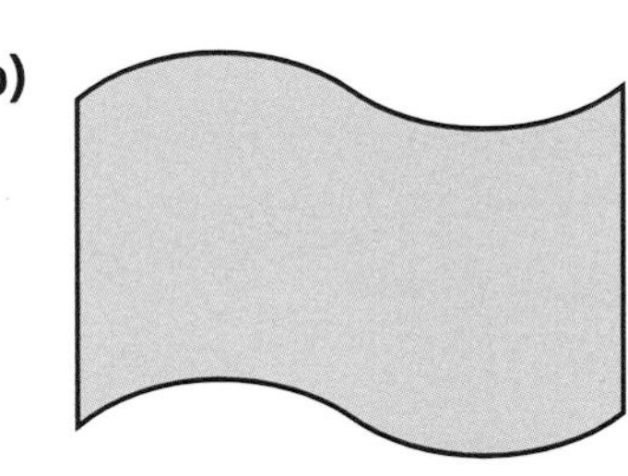

(c)

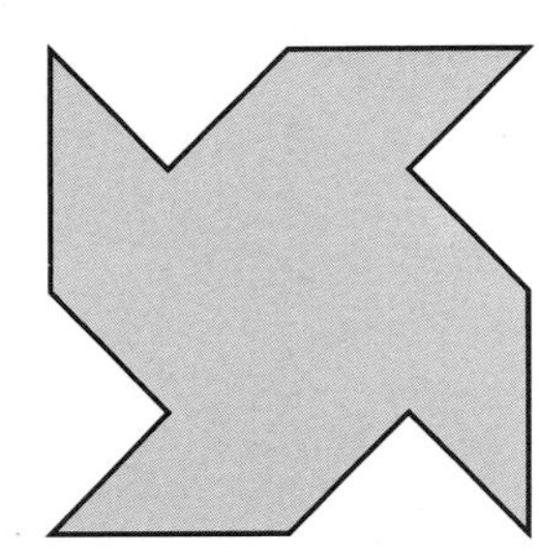

3 Trace this design and colour it as shown.
Check that the coloured design fits **2 times** in one full turn.

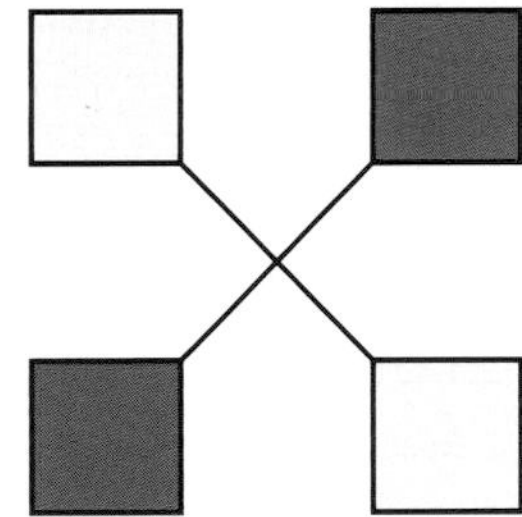

4 Trace each design and colour it as shown.
Find how often the coloured design fits in one full turn.

(a)

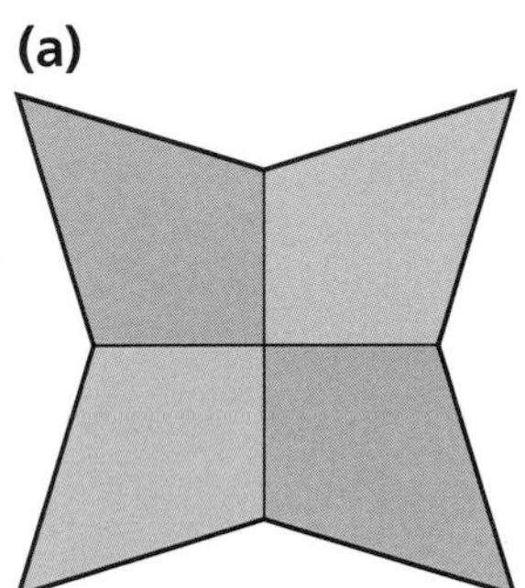

(b)

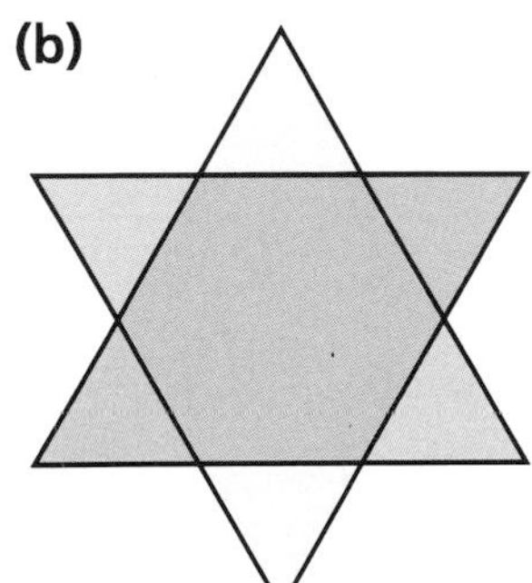

(c)

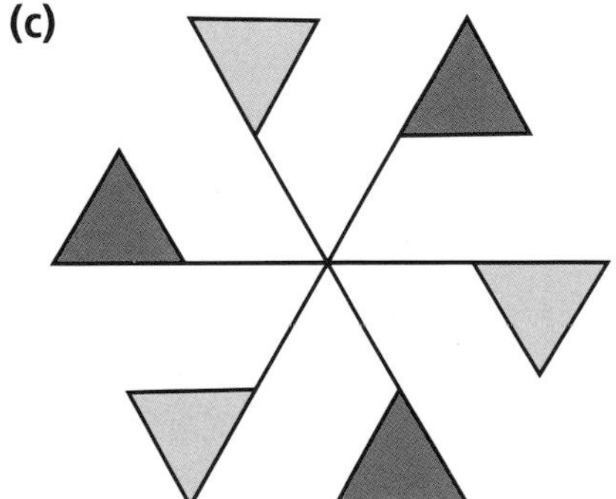

5 Make a collection of designs with rotational symmetry.

Ask your teacher what to do next

Shape talk

Other activity: shape properties, problem solving

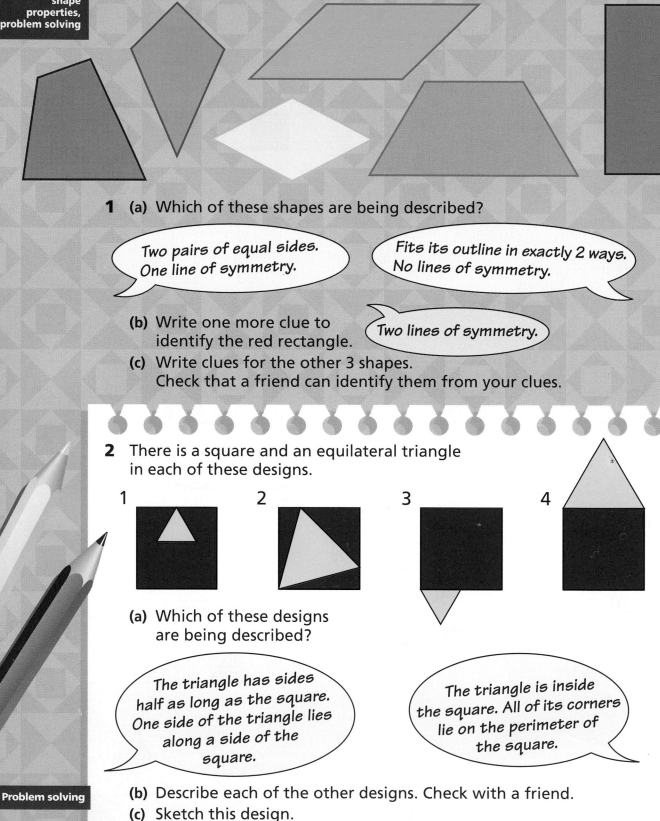

1 **(a)** Which of these shapes are being described?

*Two pairs of equal sides.
One line of symmetry.*

*Fits its outline in exactly 2 ways.
No lines of symmetry.*

(b) Write one more clue to identify the red rectangle.

Two lines of symmetry.

(c) Write clues for the other 3 shapes.
Check that a friend can identify them from your clues.

2 There is a square and an equilateral triangle in each of these designs.

1

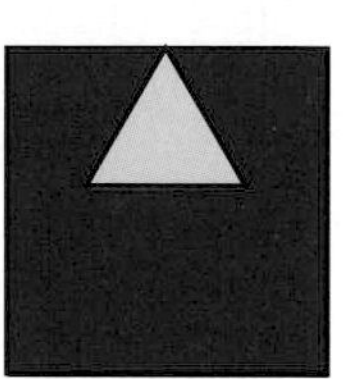

2

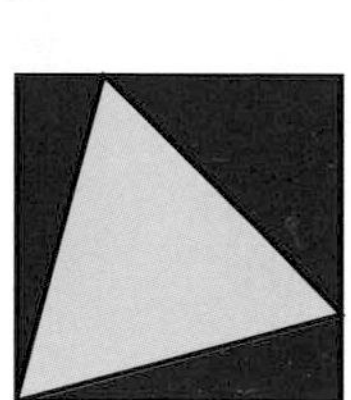

3

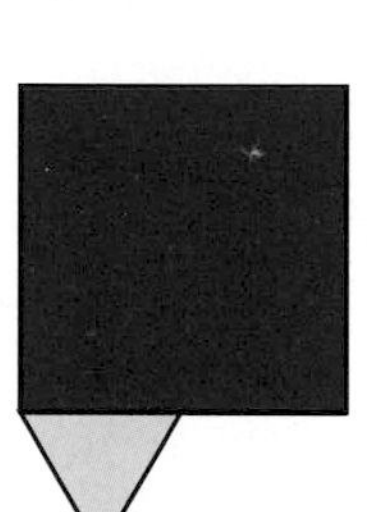

4

(a) Which of these designs are being described?

The triangle has sides half as long as the square. One side of the triangle lies along a side of the square.

The triangle is inside the square. All of its corners lie on the perimeter of the square.

Problem solving

(b) Describe each of the other designs. Check with a friend.

(c) Sketch this design.

- The equilateral triangle is outside the square.
- One corner of the square lies on the middle of one side of the triangle.
- The whole design has 1 line of symmetry.

The junk box

3D shape: cube, cuboid, nets

This carton is from the class junk box.

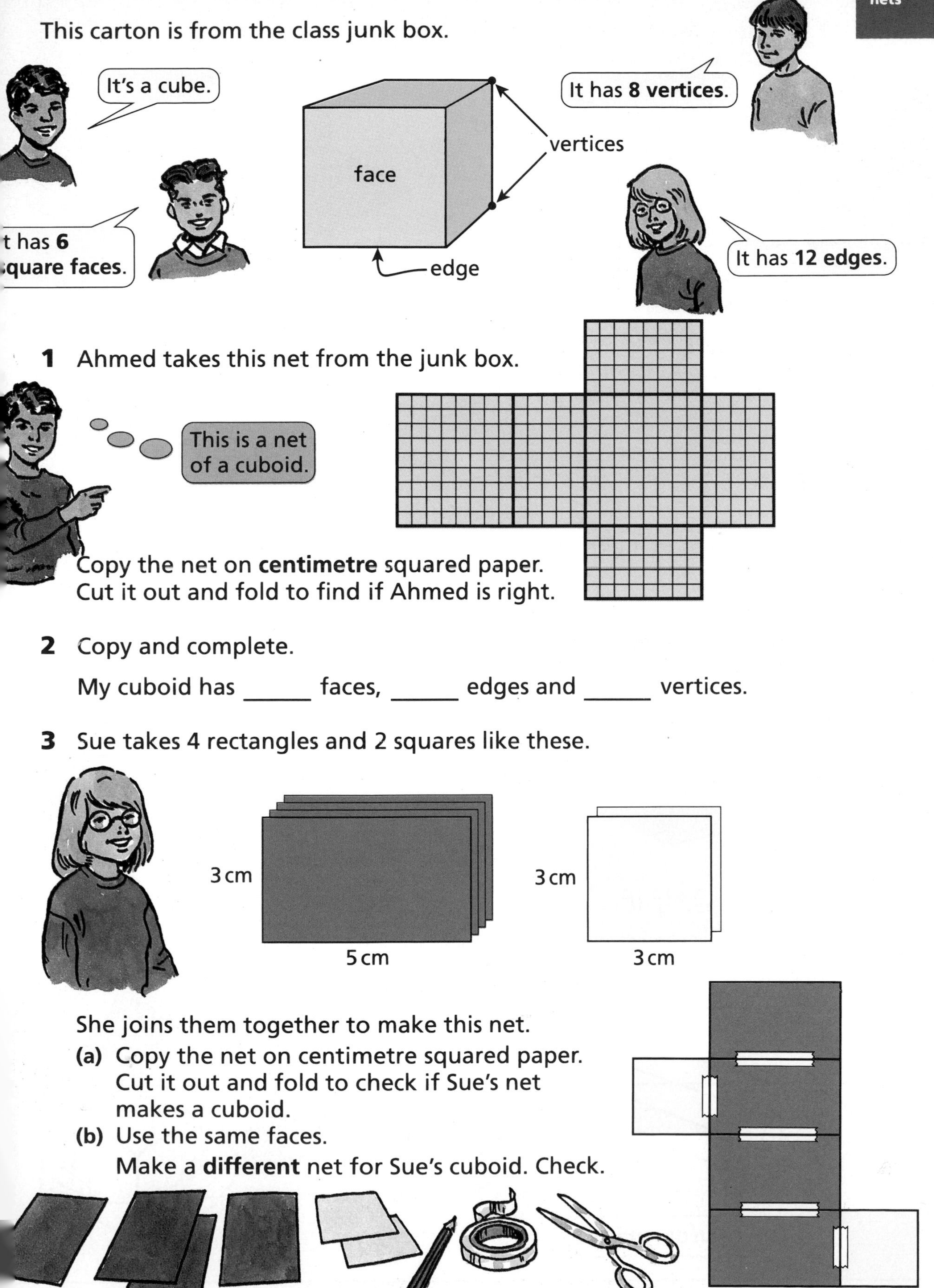

1 Ahmed takes this net from the junk box.

Copy the net on **centimetre** squared paper.
Cut it out and fold to find if Ahmed is right.

2 Copy and complete.

My cuboid has _____ faces, _____ edges and _____ vertices.

3 Sue takes 4 rectangles and 2 squares like these.

She joins them together to make this net.

(a) Copy the net on centimetre squared paper. Cut it out and fold to check if Sue's net makes a cuboid.

(b) Use the same faces. Make a **different** net for Sue's cuboid. Check.

105 Triangular prisms

3D shape: triangular prisms, nets, skeleton models

1 Marie takes this **triangular prism** from the junk box.
She opens it out to see its net.

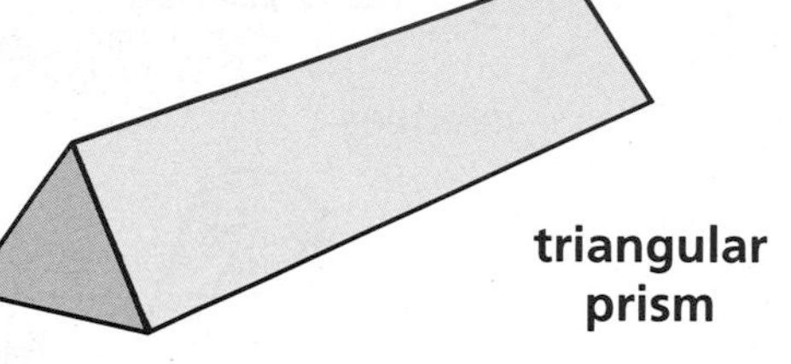

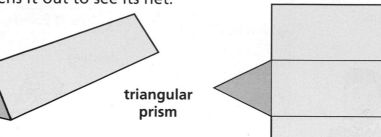

triangular prism

net

(a) Use shapes to make this net.

(b) Fold to make a triangular prism.

(c) Copy and complete.
Marie's triangular prism has ____ faces, ____ edges and ____ vertic

I can make a triangular prism from a different net.

2 Use shapes to make Leela's net.

(a) Check that it makes a triangular prism.

(b) Use the same faces.
Make a different net for a triangular prism.
Check.

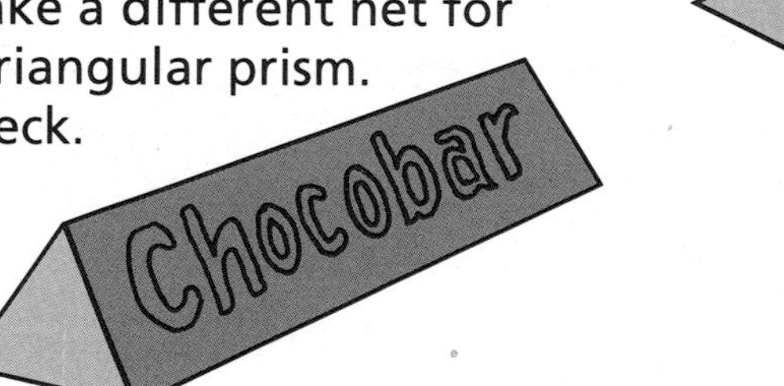

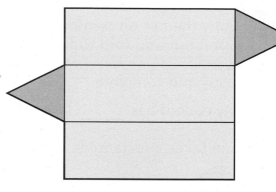

3 **Work as a group.**

I used straws and plasticine to make skeleton triangular prisms.

Make triangular prisms like Len's.

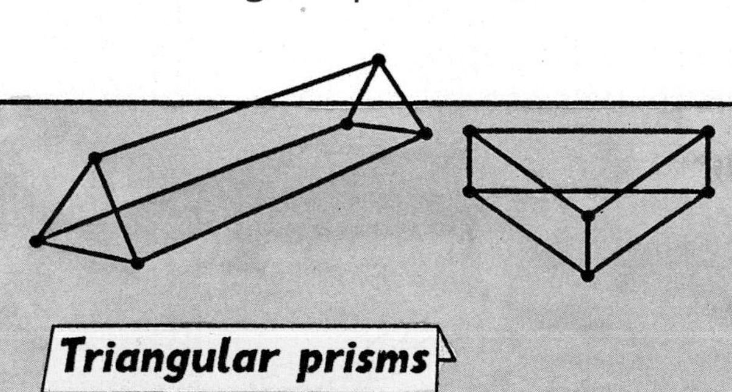

Pyramids

1 Marvin finds a **triangular pyramid** in the junk box.
He opens it out to see its net.

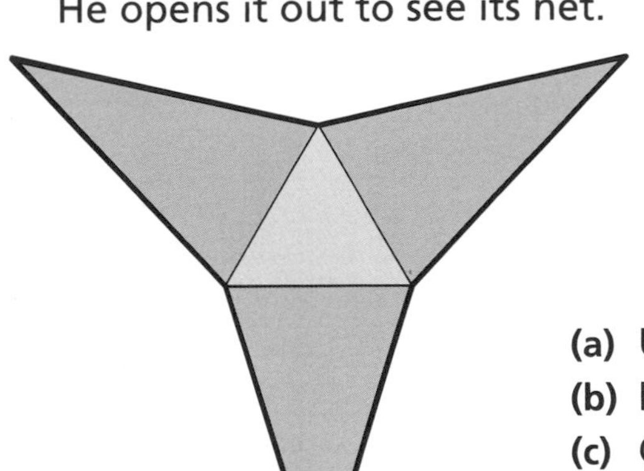

(a) Use shapes to make this net.

(b) Fold to make a triangular pyramid.

(c) Copy and complete.
Marvin's triangular pyramid has

_____ faces, _____ edges and _____ vertices.

2 Make a different net for a triangular pyramid. Check.

I think this is a net of a **square pyramid**.

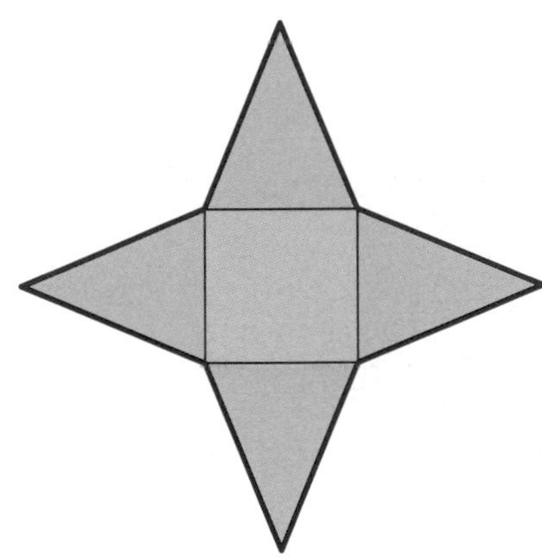

3 (a) Use shapes to make Tracey's net.
Check that it makes a square pyramid.

(b) Use the same faces.
Make a different net for a square pyramid.
Check.

(c) Copy and complete.
A square pyramid has _____ faces,

_____ edges and _____ vertices.

4 Work as a group.

I used straws and plasticine to make skeleton pyramids.

Make pyramids like Jan's.

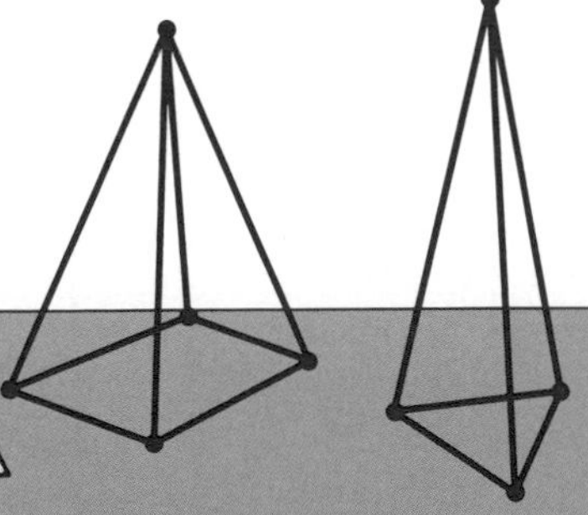

Pyramids

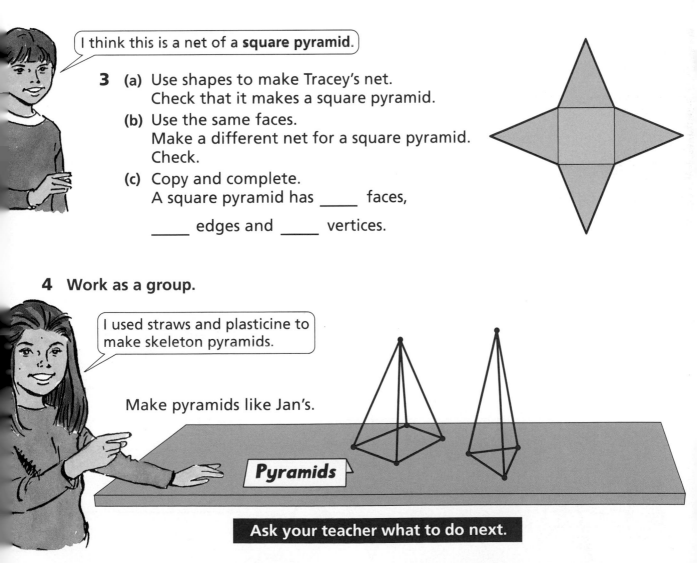

Ask your teacher what to do next.

Pentominoes

Pentominoes are made from 5 squares joined together edge to edge. Here are the 12 possible pentominoes.

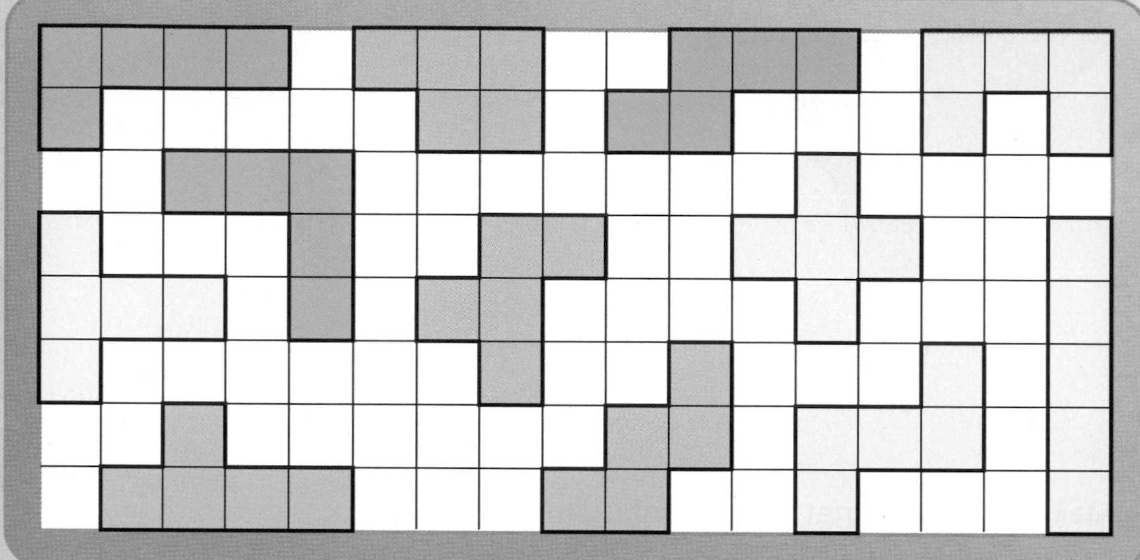

Draw each pentomino. Write
(a) its number of lines of symmetry
(b) the number of times it fits its outline in one full turn.

(a) Copy the blue pentominoes on squared paper and cut them out.
(b) Arrange them to make a rectangle like this.
(c) Make a sketch to show how the pieces fit together.

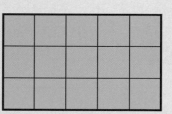

Do this again to make shapes like these with
(a) the green pentominoes
(b) the yellow pentominoes.

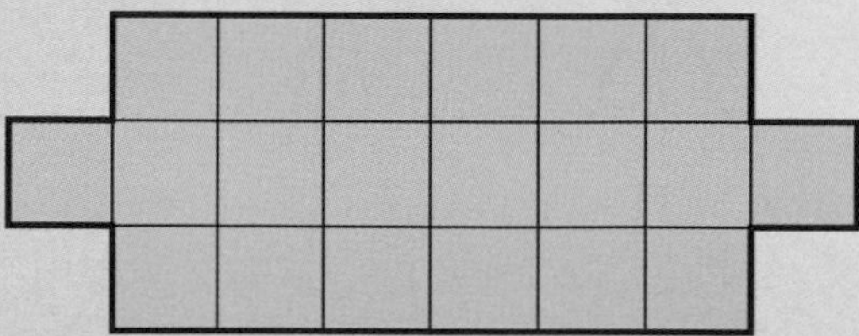

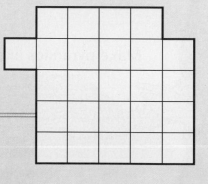

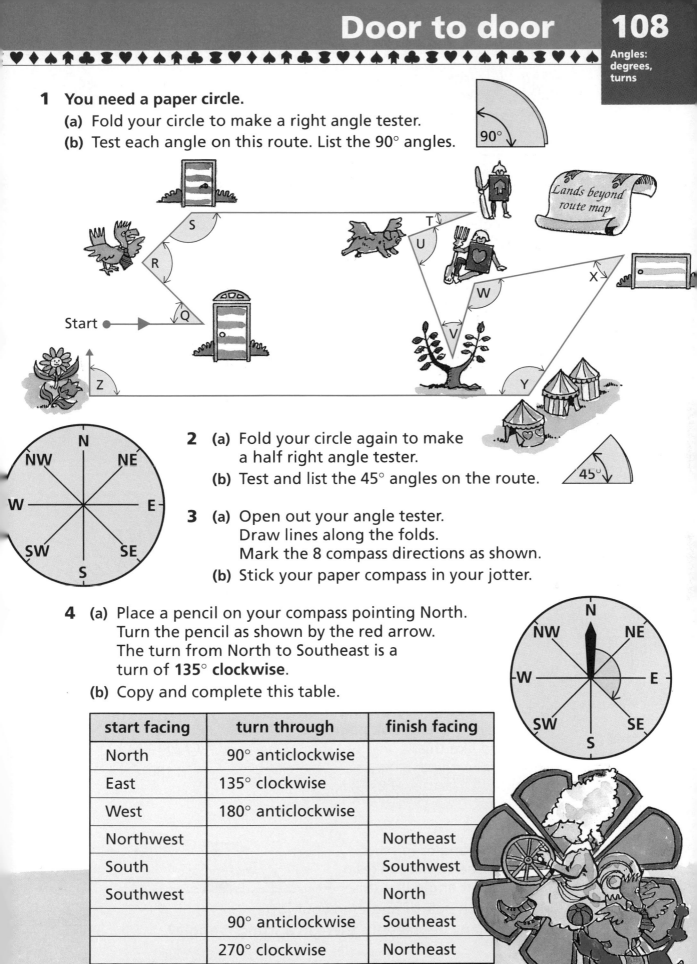

1 You need a paper circle.

(a) Fold your circle to make a right angle tester.

(b) Test each angle on this route. List the 90° angles.

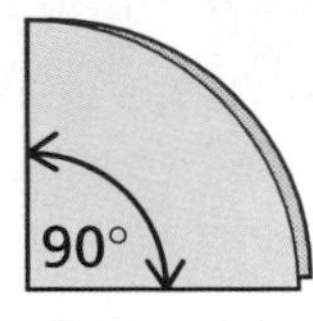

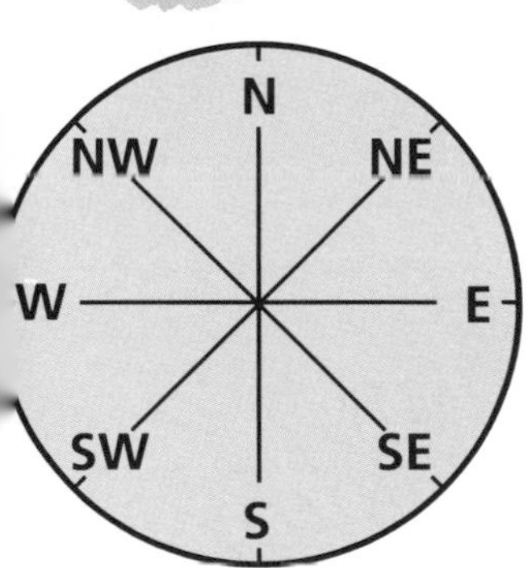

2 **(a)** Fold your circle again to make a half right angle tester.

(b) Test and list the 45° angles on the route.

45°

3 **(a)** Open out your angle tester.
Draw lines along the folds.
Mark the 8 compass directions as shown.

(b) Stick your paper compass in your jotter.

4 **(a)** Place a pencil on your compass pointing North.
Turn the pencil as shown by the red arrow.
The turn from North to Southeast is a turn of **135° clockwise**.

(b) Copy and complete this table.

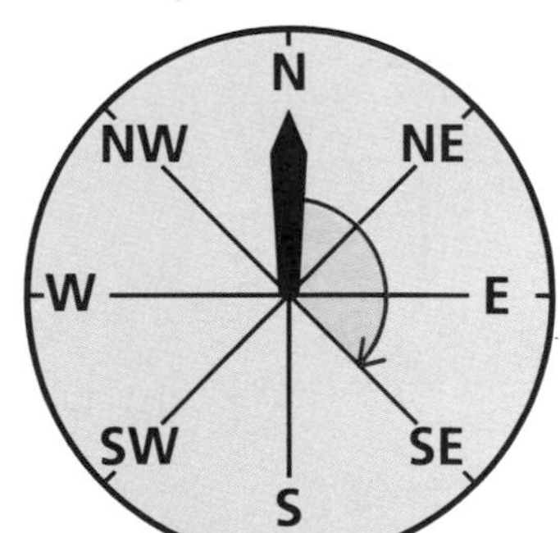

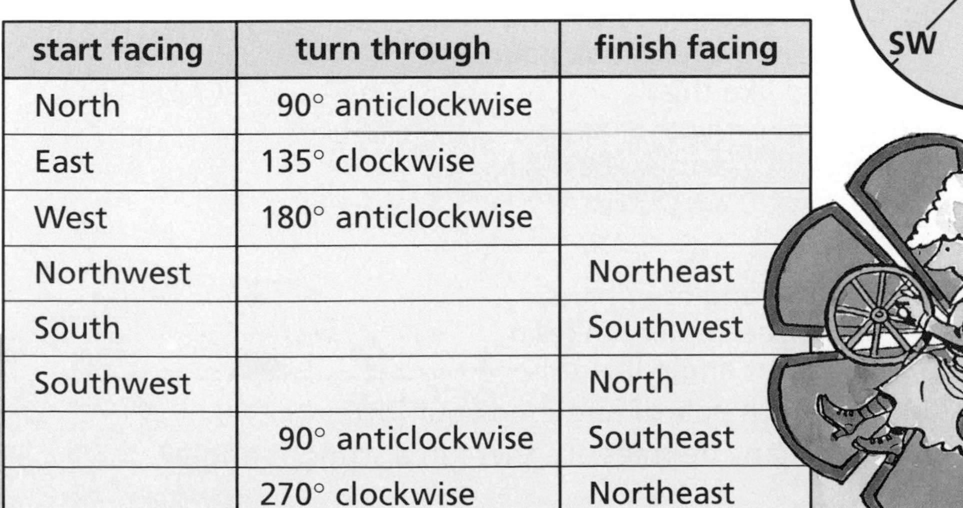

start facing	turn through	finish facing
North	90° anticlockwise	
East	135° clockwise	
West	180° anticlockwise	
Northwest		Northeast
South		Southwest
Southwest		North
	90° anticlockwise	Southeast
	270° clockwise	Northeast

The angle wall

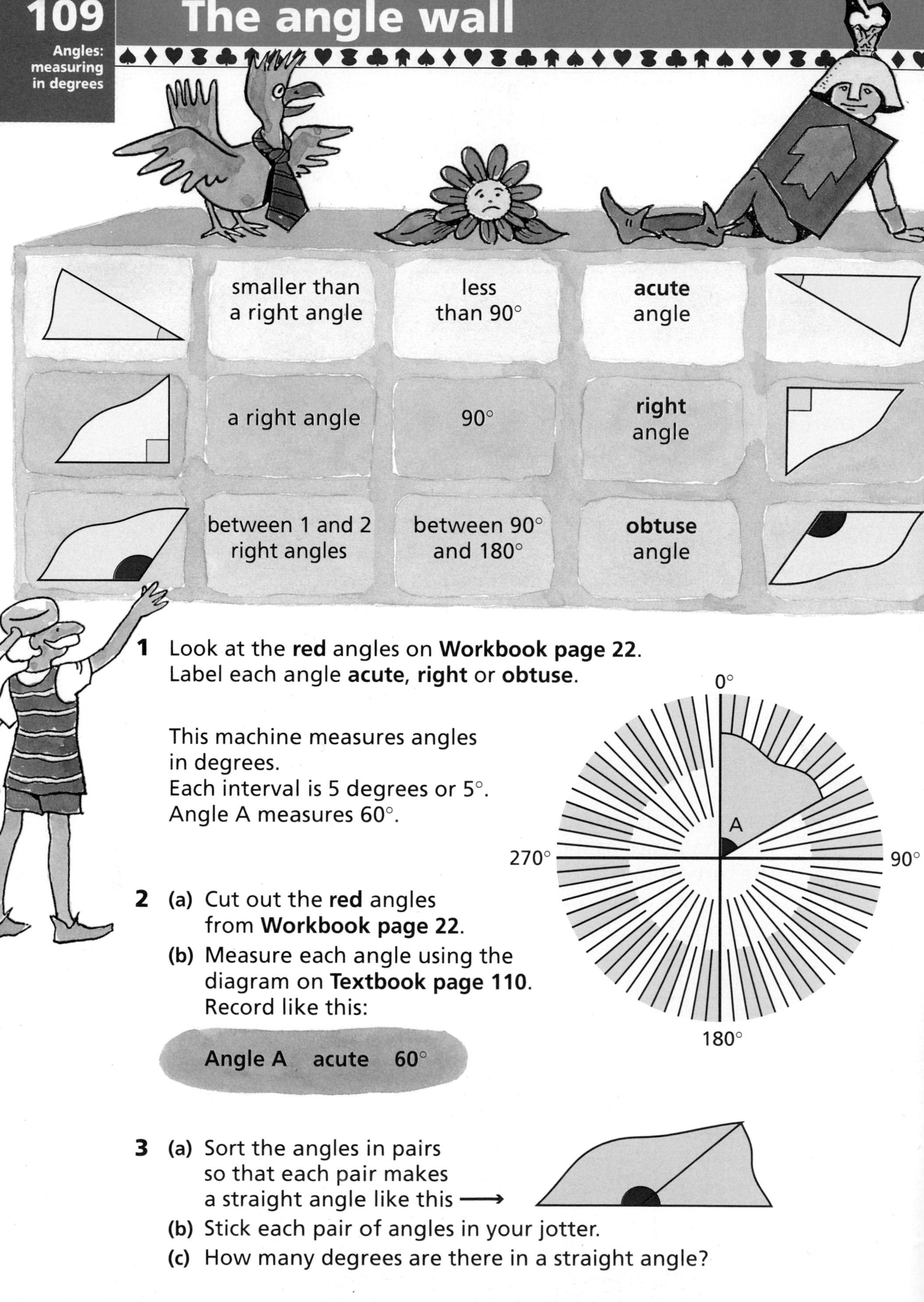

1 Look at the **red** angles on **Workbook page 22**.
Label each angle **acute**, **right** or **obtuse**.

This machine measures angles in degrees.
Each interval is 5 degrees or 5°.
Angle A measures 60°.

2 (a) Cut out the **red** angles from **Workbook page 22**.

(b) Measure each angle using the diagram on **Textbook page 110**.
Record like this:

Angle A acute 60°

3 (a) Sort the angles in pairs so that each pair makes a straight angle like this ⟶

(b) Stick each pair of angles in your jotter.

(c) How many degrees are there in a straight angle?

0°
45°
90°
135°
180°
270°

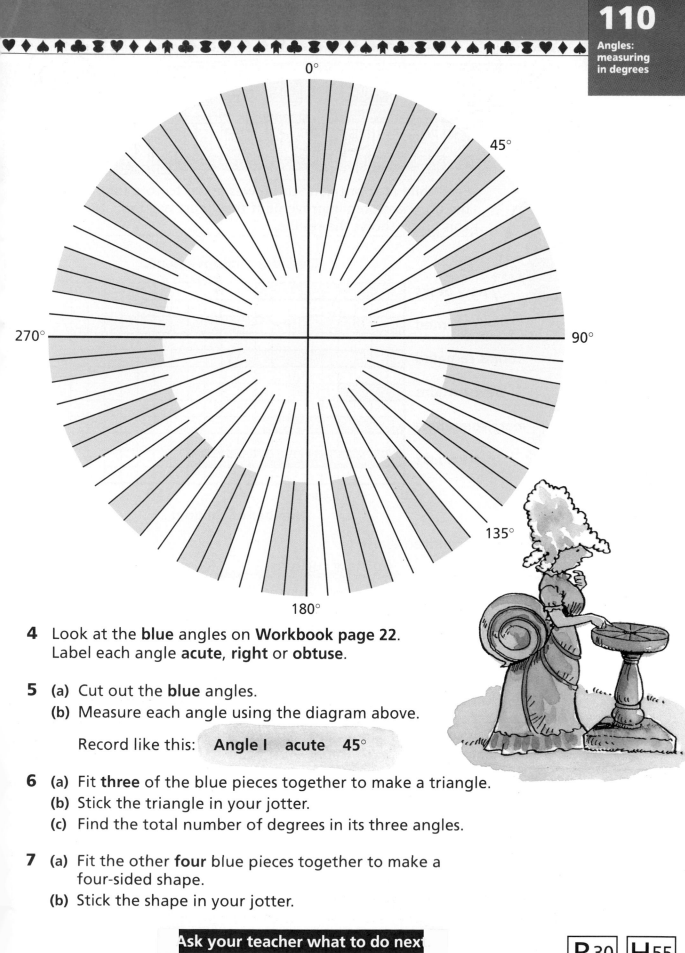

4 Look at the **blue** angles on **Workbook page 22**.
Label each angle **acute**, **right** or **obtuse**.

5 **(a)** Cut out the **blue** angles.
(b) Measure each angle using the diagram above.

Record like this: **Angle I acute 45°**

6 **(a)** Fit **three** of the blue pieces together to make a triangle.
(b) Stick the triangle in your jotter.
(c) Find the total number of degrees in its three angles.

7 **(a)** Fit the other **four** blue pieces together to make a four-sided shape.
(b) Stick the shape in your jotter.

Ask your teacher what to do next

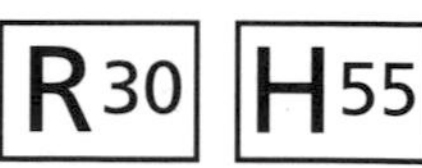

Room for improvement

Each child at Topperton School was asked to vote for the one classroom improvement they most wanted. This graph shows the results.

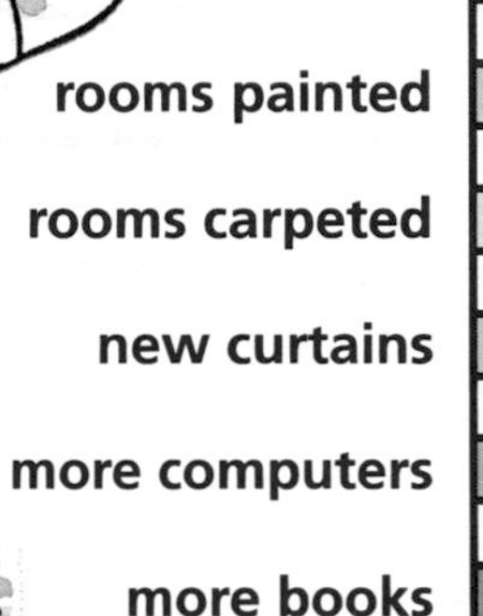

Classroom improvements

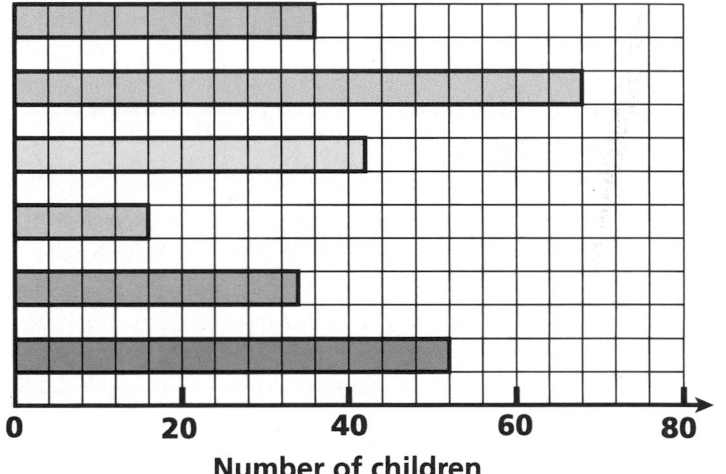

1 How many children want

(a) new desks **(b)** new curtains **(c)** more computers?

2 How many more children want the rooms painted than want

(a) more books **(b)** the rooms carpeted **(c)** new curtains?

3 **(a)** How many children voted in the survey?

(b) Do more than one quarter of the children want the rooms painted? Explain.

Choice of colours	Number of children
white and blue	44
lime and white	34
beige and brown	26
yellow and cream	52
cream and blue	64
pink and yellow	28

This table shows the children's choices of colours for their classroon

4 **(a)** How many children want **on** of the colours to be

- white
- yellow
- blue?

(b) Draw a bar graph like the on above using the information in the table.

Go to Workbook page 34.

Class 6 helps to improve the school grounds.
The **bar-line** graph shows the number of plants they order.

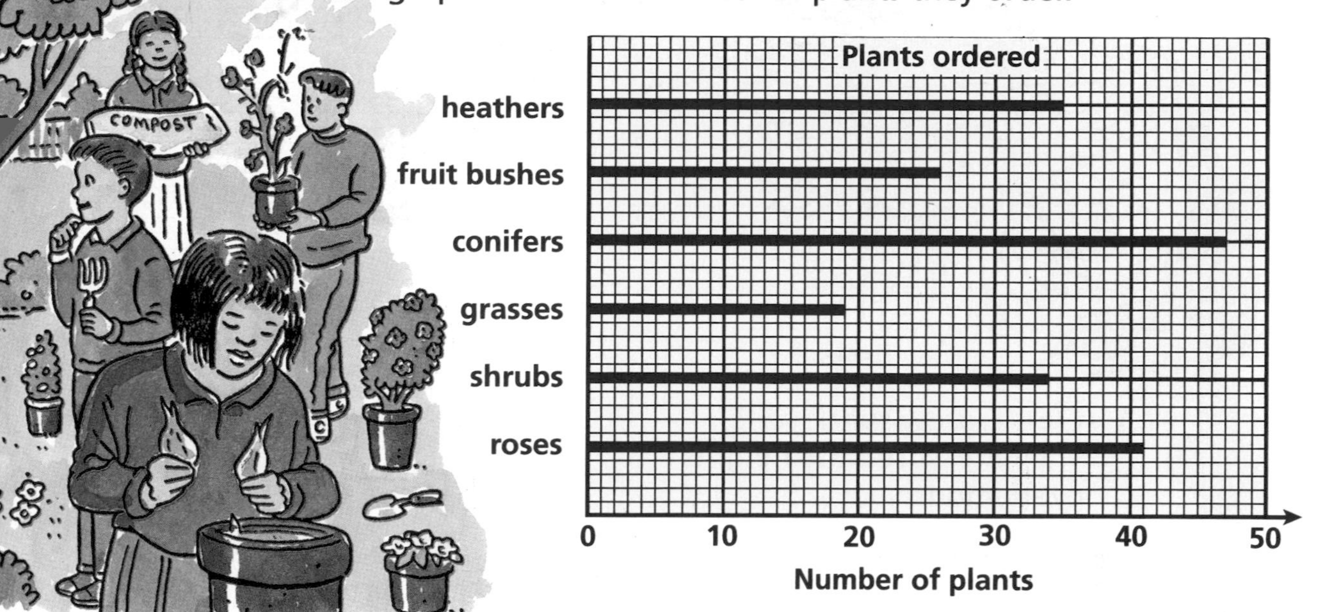

1 **(a)** Which plant do the children order • most of • least of?
(b) How many of each plant are ordered?

2 Topperton Garden Centre donates these bulbs to the school.

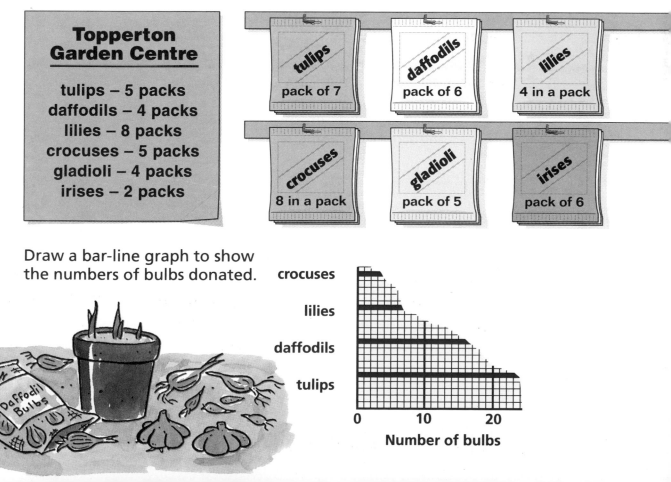

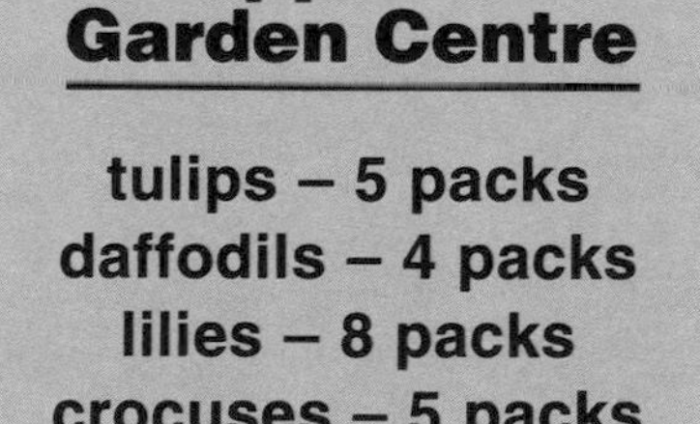

Topperton Garden Centre

tulips – 5 packs
daffodils – 4 packs
lilies – 8 packs
crocuses – 5 packs
gladioli – 4 packs
irises – 2 packs

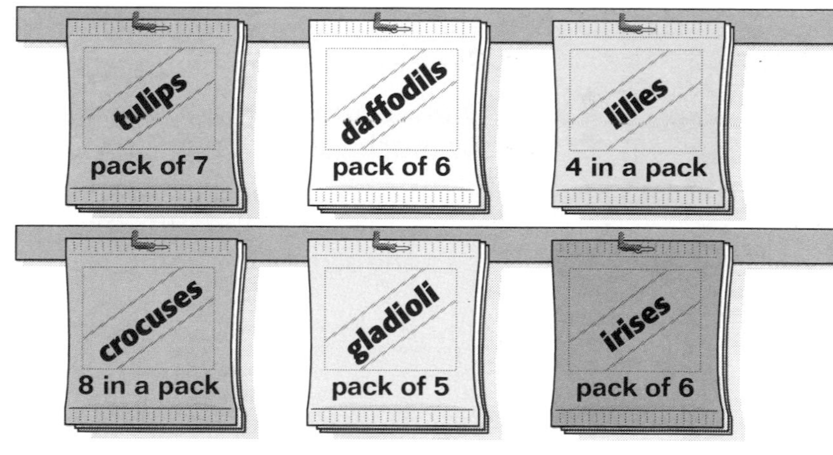

Draw a bar-line graph to show the numbers of bulbs donated.

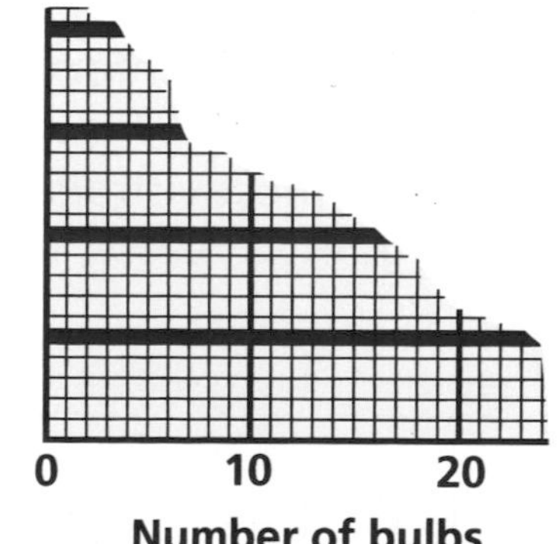

Topperton School Open Week

Greenwatch Campaign Greenwatch Campaign Greenwatch Campaign Greenwatch Campaign Greenwatch C

Competition!
Grow the tallest sunflower

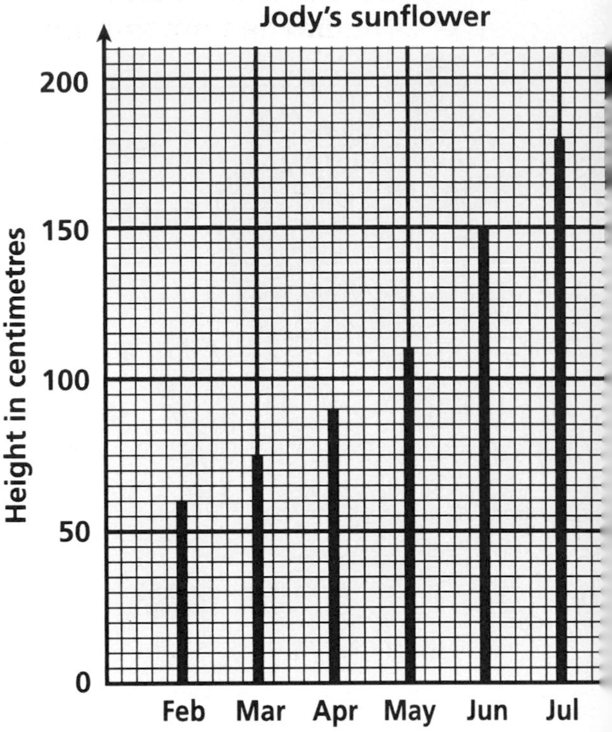
Jody's sunflower
Height in centimetres
200
150
100
50
0
Feb
Mar
Apr
May
Jun
Jul

1 Class 6 grew sunflowers. They measured the heights every month.

Use the graph.

(a) How tall did Jody's sunflower grow?

(b) During which months was its height less than 1 metre?

(c) What was the increase in height between February and March?

(d) Between which two months did the greatest increase in height take place?

(e) The prize-winning sunflower grew to a height of 2 m. How much taller than Jody's was this?

2 The table shows the numbers of visitors to the school garden.

Topperton Schoo
Open Week

Day	Mon	Tue	Wed	Thu	Fri	Sat	Sun
Number of visitors	66	42	36	38	52	84	98

(a) Draw a bar-line graph to show this information.

(b) On which two days were there most visitors? Suggest a reason for this.

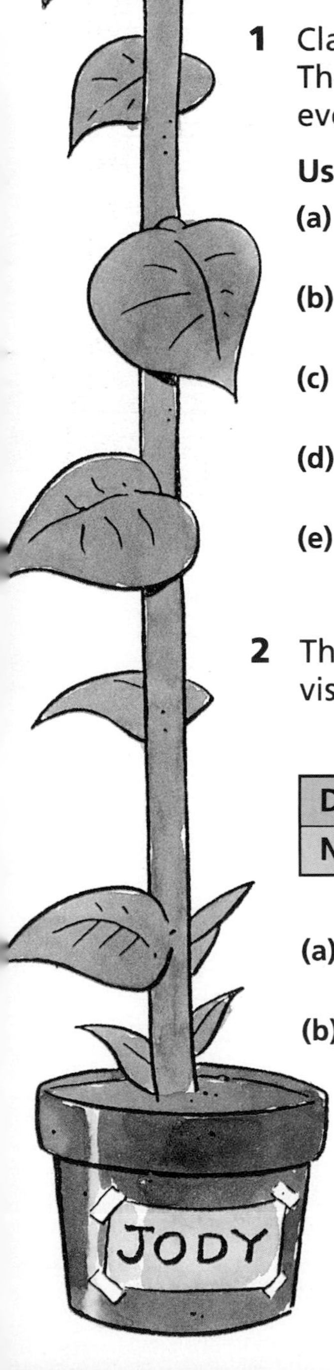
JODY

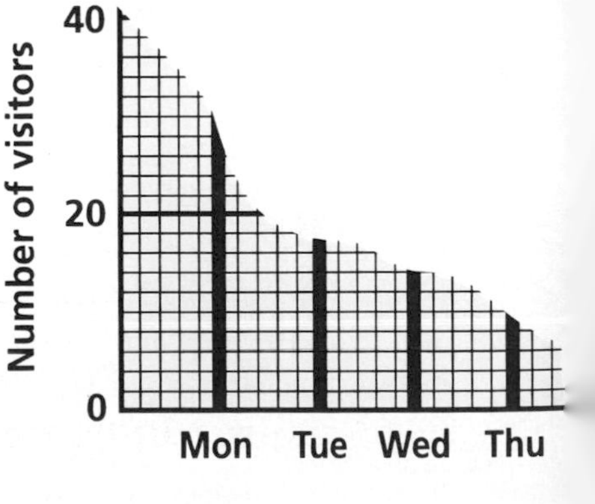
Number of visitors
40
20
0
Mon
Tue
Wed
Thu

H56

On Monday Class 6 measured the temperature in the school greenhouse every half hour. The temperatures are shown in this **trend** graph.

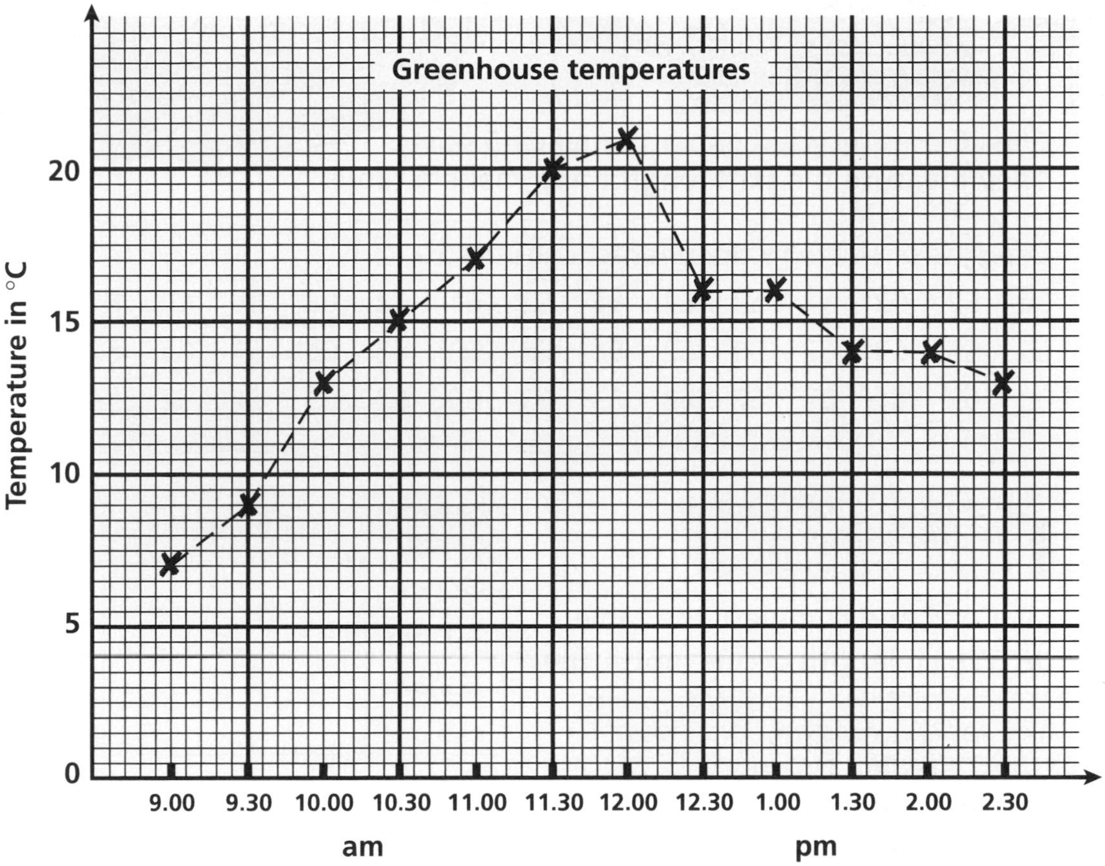

Greenhouse temperatures

Temperature in °C: 0, 5, 10, 15, 20

9.00 9.30 10.00 10.30 11.00 11.30 12.00 12.30 1.00 1.30 2.00 2.30

am pm

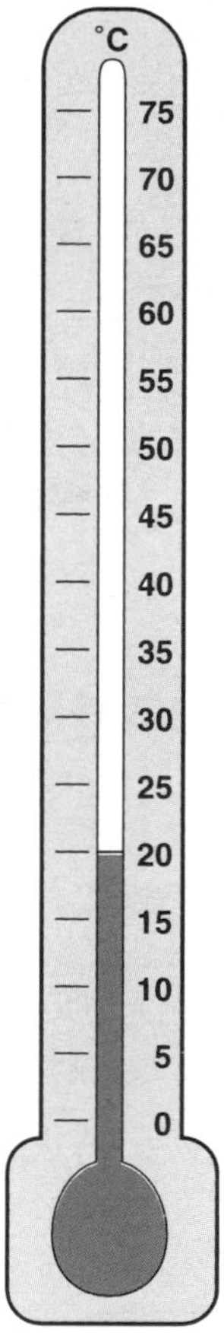

°C 75 70 65 60 55 50 45 40 35 30 25 20 15 10 5 0

1 What was the temperature at

(a) 10.30 am **(b)** 12.30 pm **(c)** 2.00 pm?

2 **(a)** Give the times when the temperature was measured as

- 7°C
- 9°C
- 13°C

(b) What was the highest temperature recorded? When was it measured?

3 **(a)** What was the rise in temperature between 9 am and 11 am?

(b) What do you think might have caused the drop in temperature between noon and 12.30 pm?

4

Garden Log Book												
Month	Jan	Feb	Mar	Apr	May	Jun	Jul	Aug	Sep	Oct	Nov	Dec
Number of rainy days	18	13	14	9	7	4	6	6	5	8	16	19

(a) Draw a trend graph using this information.

(b) Write about the trend your graph shows.

H57

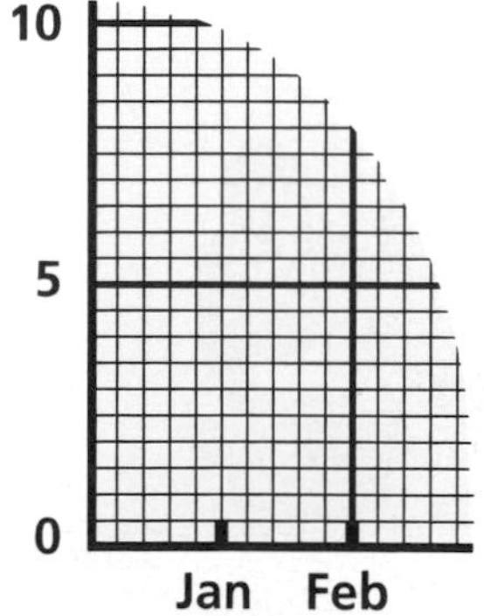

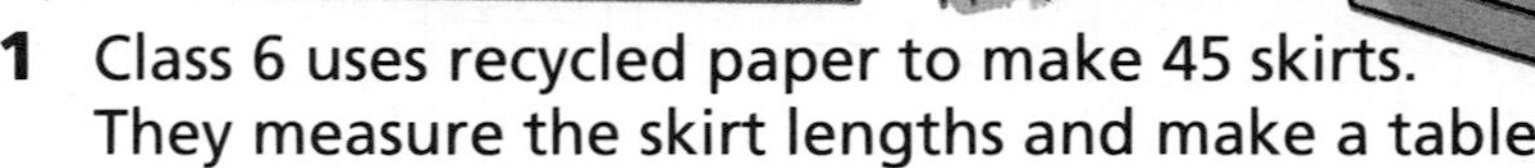

1 Class 6 uses recycled paper to make 45 skirts.
They measure the skirt lengths and make a table.

Lengths of skirts to the nearest centimetre

60	62	63	64	63	63	64	62	61	64	63	63	62	61	62
63	65	63	62	60	62	61	64	63	63	65	61	63	62	63
63	62	61	63	62	63	63	63	60	62	63	64	62	64	63

The skirt lengths **range** from 60 cm to 65 cm.

(a) Copy and complete the table.
(b) Which length occurs most often?

The length which occurs most often is called the **mode**.

Length of skirt	Tally marks	Total
60 cm		
61 cm		
62 cm		
63 cm		
64 cm		
65 cm		

2 Class 6 also make sandals for 60 children.

Lengths of feet to the nearest centimetre

21	19	23	24	22	23	24	20	24	23	21	24	23	23	22
23	24	21	23	20	24	22	23	23	22	25	23	22	26	23
22	24	23	22	25	22	21	23	24	19	23	20	24	22	24
21	20	25	24	19	23	25	23	21	23	26	22	24	25	23

(a) Copy and complete.
The lengths range from
________ cm to ________ cm.
(b) Copy and complete the table.
(c) Which length is the mode?

Length of feet	Tally marks	Total
19 cm		

(d) How many of the 60 children have foot lengths
- shorter than the mode
- longer than the mode?

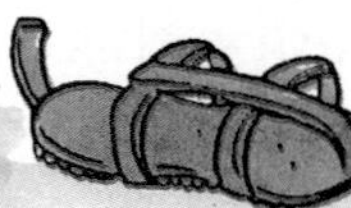

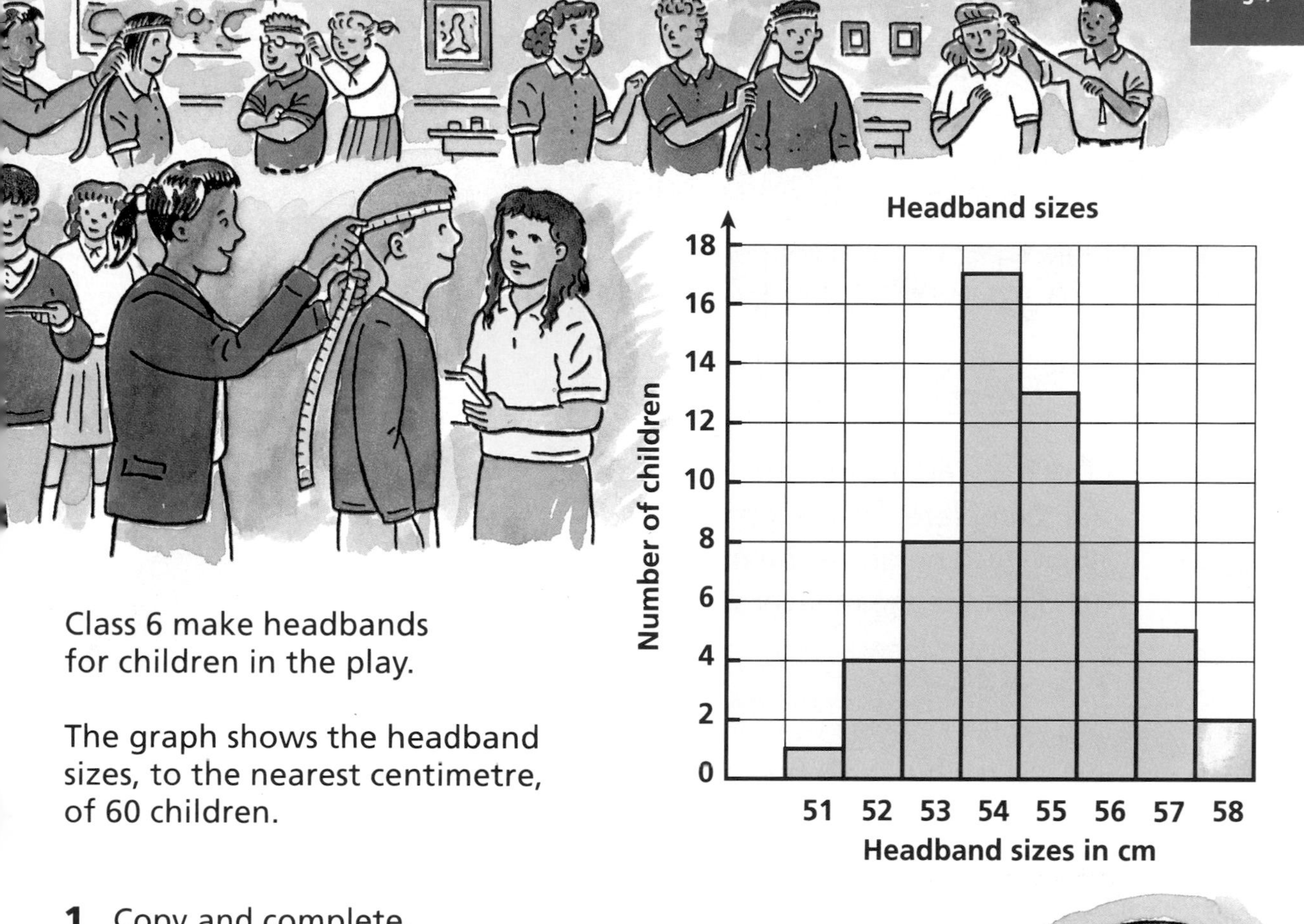

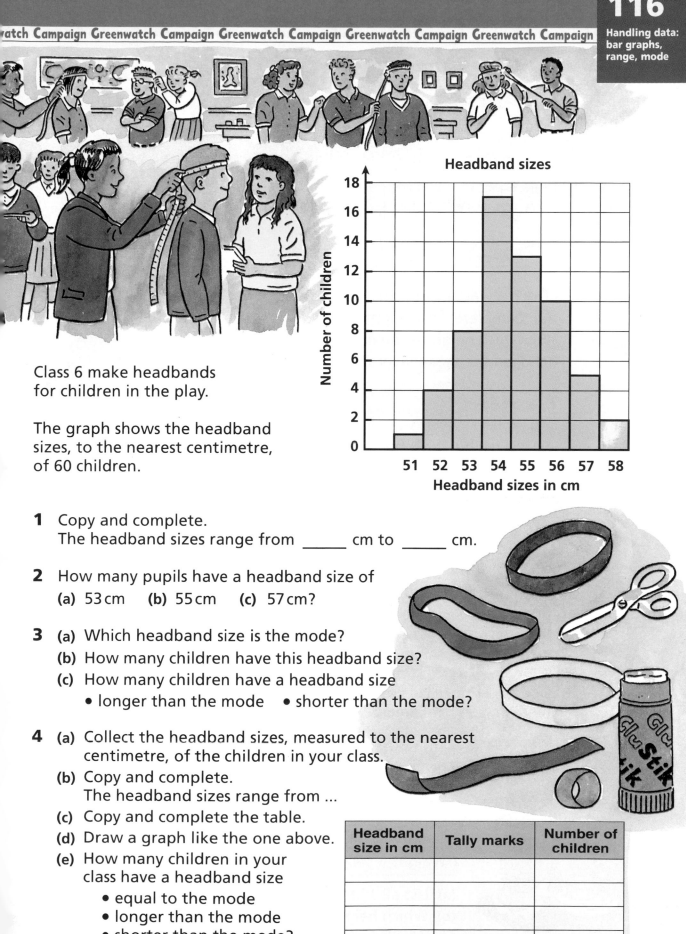

Class 6 make headbands for children in the play.

The graph shows the headband sizes, to the nearest centimetre, of 60 children.

1 Copy and complete.
The headband sizes range from _____ cm to _____ cm.

2 How many pupils have a headband size of
(a) 53 cm **(b)** 55 cm **(c)** 57 cm?

3 **(a)** Which headband size is the mode?
(b) How many children have this headband size?
(c) How many children have a headband size
- longer than the mode
- shorter than the mode?

4 **(a)** Collect the headband sizes, measured to the nearest centimetre, of the children in your class.
(b) Copy and complete.
The headband sizes range from ...
(c) Copy and complete the table.
(d) Draw a graph like the one above.
(e) How many children in your class have a headband size
- equal to the mode
- longer than the mode
- shorter than the mode?

Headband size in cm	Tally marks	Number of children

117 Greenwatch stars

Handling data: mean, median, mode

Greenwatch Campaign Greenwatch Campaign Greenwatch Campaign Greenwatch Campaign Greenwatch Ca

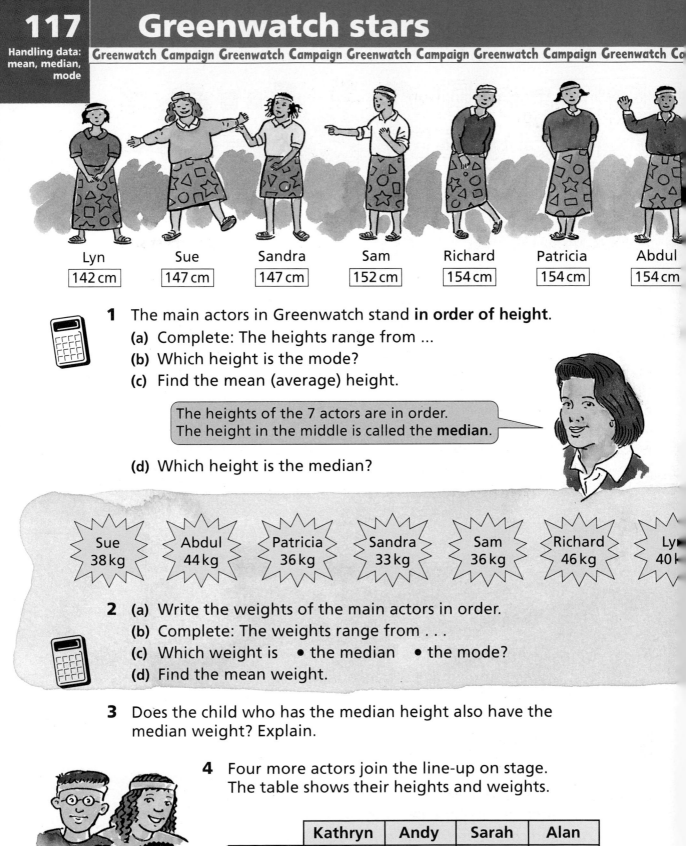

Lyn	Sue	Sandra	Sam	Richard	Patricia	Abdul
142 cm	147 cm	147 cm	152 cm	154 cm	154 cm	154 cm

1 The main actors in Greenwatch stand **in order of height**.

(a) Complete: The heights range from ...

(b) Which height is the mode?

(c) Find the mean (average) height.

The heights of the 7 actors are in order.
The height in the middle is called the **median**.

(d) Which height is the median?

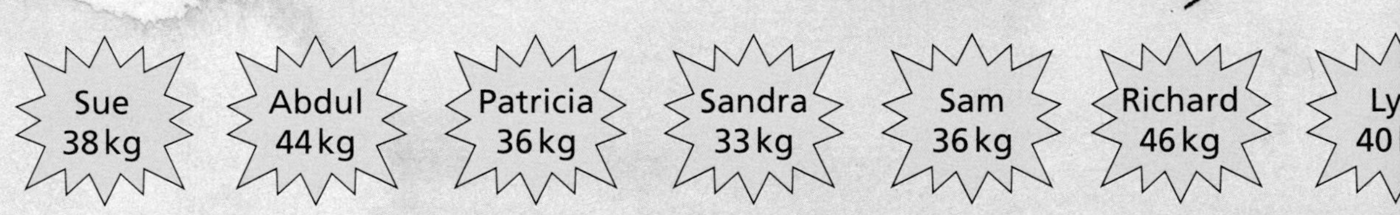

2 (a) Write the weights of the main actors in order.

(b) Complete: The weights range from . . .

(c) Which weight is • the median • the mode?

(d) Find the mean weight.

3 Does the child who has the median height also have the median weight? Explain.

4 Four more actors join the line-up on stage. The table shows their heights and weights.

	Kathryn	Andy	Sarah	Alan
Height	142 cm	143 cm	148 cm	156 cm
Weight	42 kg	34 kg	47 kg	44 kg

(a) List all 11 heights and weights in order.

(b) Which **height** is now the median?

(c) Which **weight** is now the median?

Protective clothing must be worn when cleaning rubbish from the ground beside the school.

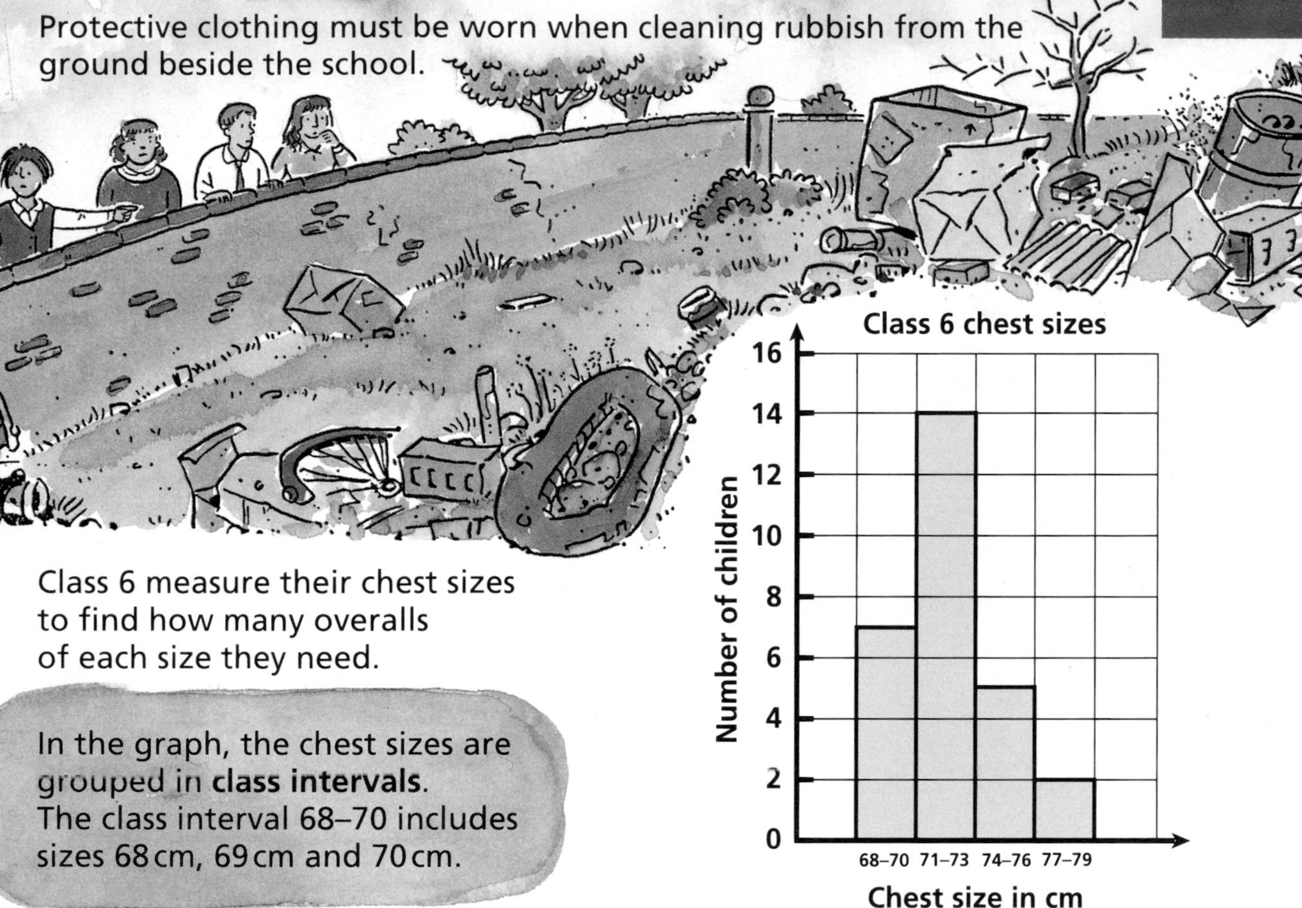

Class 6 measure their chest sizes to find how many overalls of each size they need.

In the graph, the chest sizes are grouped in **class intervals**.
The class interval 68–70 includes sizes 68 cm, 69 cm and 70 cm.

1 (a) How many class intervals are there in the graph?

(b) In which class interval is
- the largest chest size
- the smallest chest size?

(c) How many children need overalls in these sizes:
- 68–70 cm
- 71–73cm
- 74–76 cm
- 77–79 cm?

(d) How many children have a chest size
- smaller than 71 cm
- larger than 73 cm?

Do Workbook pages 35 and 36.

2 (a) Collect the chest sizes, measured to the nearest centimetre, of the children in your class.

(b) Organize the chest sizes in a table like this.

(c) Draw a bar graph using the information in your table.

Chest size in cm	Tally marks	Total
65–67		
68–70		
71–73		
74–76		
77–79		

119 Overgrown

Handling data: interpretation, database

In the corner of the waste ground there is an overgrown garden.
Class 6 uses these cards to find out about the bushes.

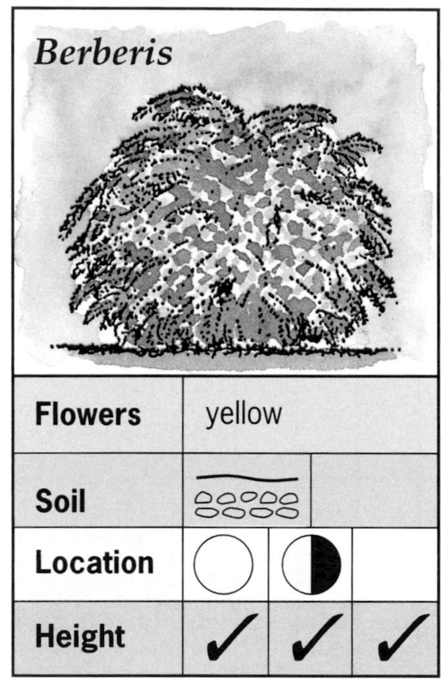

Berberis

Flowers	yellow		
Soil			
Location			
Height	✓	✓	✓

Lilac

Flowers	lilac, white		
Soil			
Location			
Height	✓	✓	

Fuchsia

Flowers	scarlet, purple		
Soil			
Location			
Height	✓	✓	

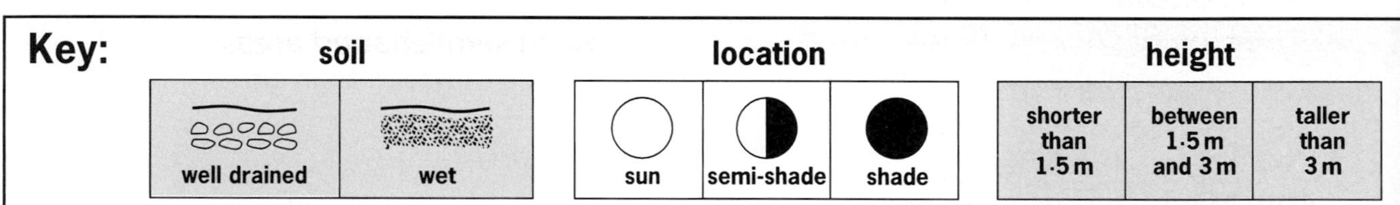

Key:

soil		location			height		
well drained	wet	sun	semi-shade	shade	shorter than 1·5 m	between 1·5 m and 3 m	taller than 3 m

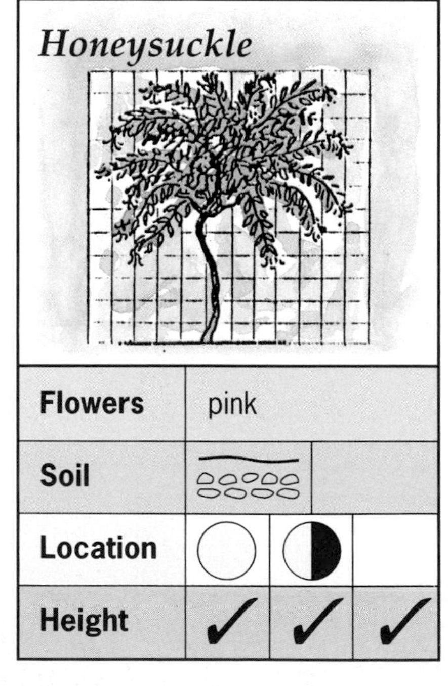

Honeysuckle

Flowers	pink		
Soil			
Location			
Height	✓	✓	✓

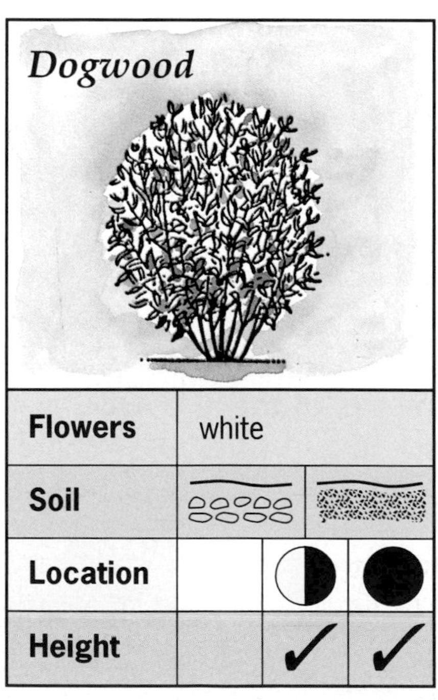

Dogwood

Flowers	white		
Soil			
Location			
Height		✓	✓

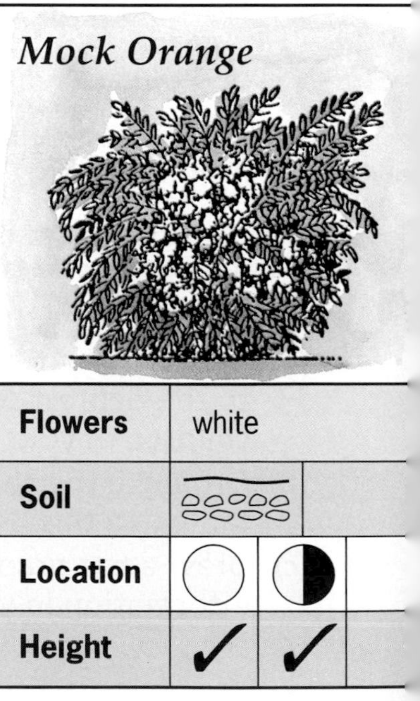

Mock Orange

Flowers	white		
Soil			
Location			
Height	✓	✓	

Lavender

Flowers	blue, purple		
Soil			
Location	○		
Height	✓		

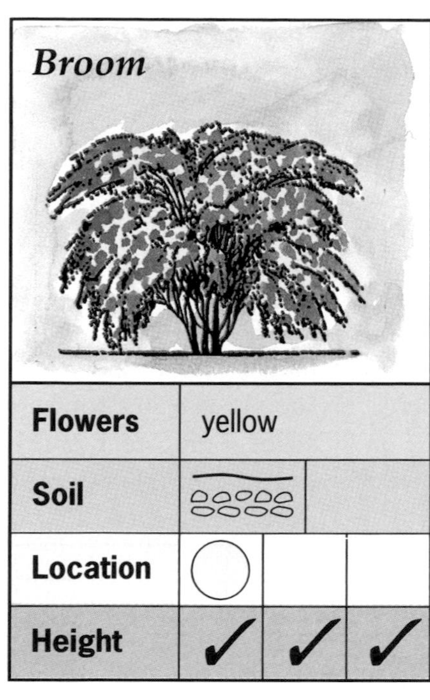

Broom

Flowers	yellow		
Soil			
Location	○		
Height	✓	✓	✓

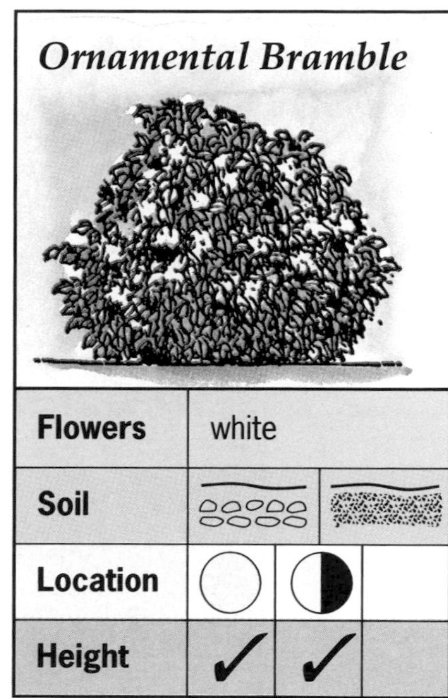

Ornamental Bramble

Flowers	white		
Soil			
Location	○	◐	
Height	✓	✓	

1 Which of the nine bushes

(a) can have white flowers **(b)** can grow in semi-shaded areas

(c) can grow between 1·5 m and 3 m tall

(d) grow in wet soil **and** in the sun

(e) have white flowers and do **not** grow in the sun?

2 Name each bush which

(a)
- needs well-drained soil
- has yellow flowers
- can grow in semi-shaded areas

(b)
- can grow in the sun
- grows between 1·5 m and 3 m tall
- can have purple flowers

3 Choose five of the bushes. Use their **pictures** to describe something interesting about each bush.

4 Make up cards for **three** other bushes.

5 Ask your teacher if you can enter all the information into a computer database.

Clean-up squad

Two groups work out how much money they must raise to restore the overgrown garden.

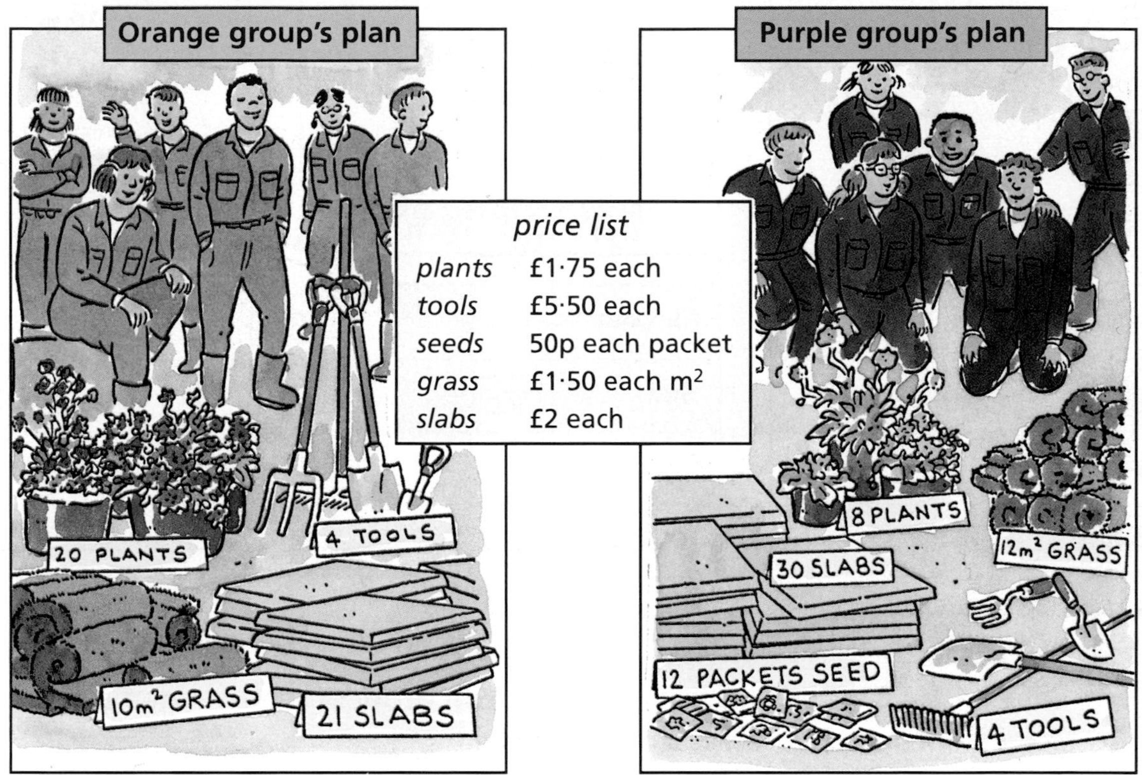

price list

plants	£1·75 each
tools	£5·50 each
seeds	50p each packet
grass	£1·50 each m²
slabs	£2 each

1 Copy and complete a table like this for **each** group.

group	**plants**	**tools**	**seeds**	**grass (m²)**	**slabs**	
Number						
Cost each						**Total**
Total cost						

2 **(a)** How much altogether does each group plan to spend?
(b) Which group plans to spend more? How much more?

3 There are 6 children in each group. Find the average amount of money that has to be raised by each child in
(a) the orange group **(b)** the purple group.

Problem solving

4 The orange group wants 3 packets of seeds.
The purple group wants 2 extra plants.
The price of slabs has increased by 50p each.
Change your tables to include this data.

Waste savers

tch Campaign Greenwatch Campaign Greenwatch Campaign Greenwatch Campaign Greenwatch Campaign

How could your school cut down on waste?

Work as a group.

1 List different types of waste you might find in your school which
(a) can be collected **(b)** cannot be collected.

2 Draw a rough sketch of
(a) your classroom **(b)** your school **(c)** the school grounds.

3 **(a)** Mark on each sketch the places where you might find waste.
(b) **In twos or threes**, collect information from one of these places.
Complete a table like this.

Place	Waste
can be collected	
cannot be collected	

(c) List possible ways of saving this waste.

4 **(a)** As a whole group, discuss the results of all the places surveyed.
(b) Write a report about the types of waste your group noticed.
Suggest how to save waste
• in your classroom • in your school • around your school.

Ask your teacher what to do next

123 A likely story

Handling data: probability

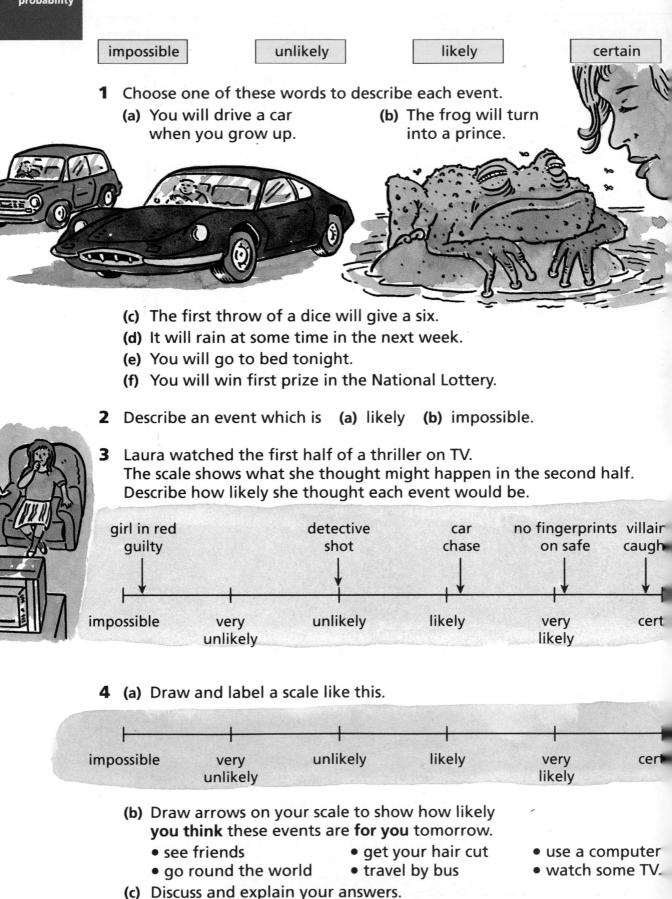

impossible | unlikely | likely | certain

1 Choose one of these words to describe each event.

(a) You will drive a car when you grow up.

(b) The frog will turn into a prince.

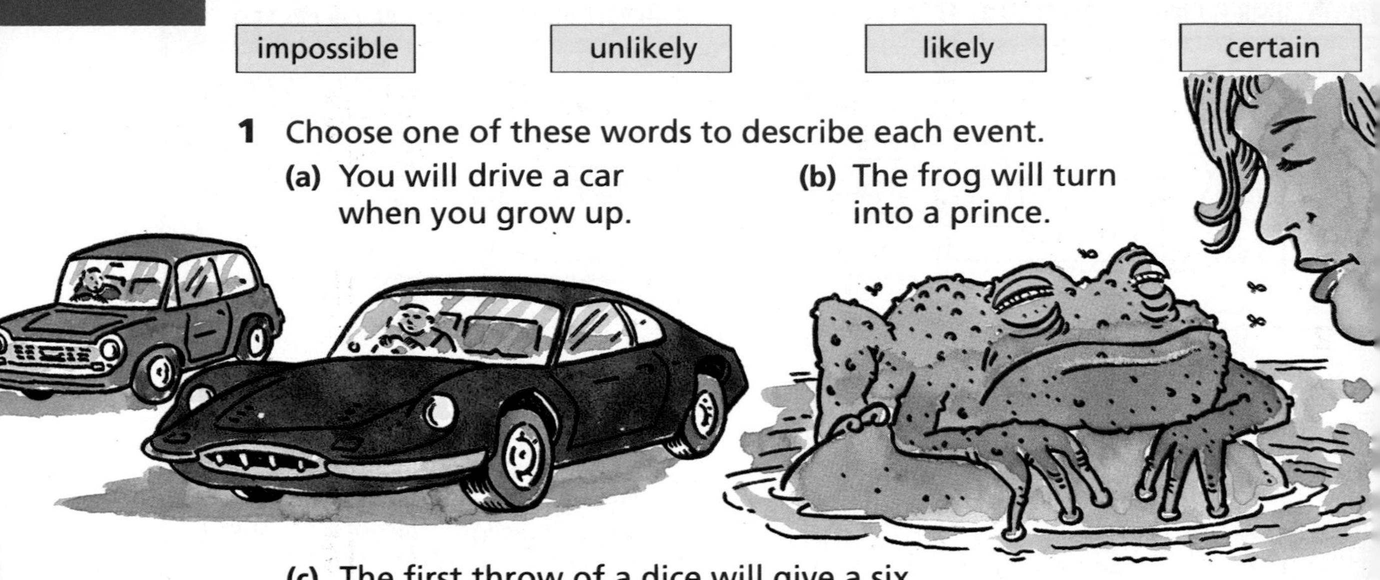

(c) The first throw of a dice will give a six.

(d) It will rain at some time in the next week.

(e) You will go to bed tonight.

(f) You will win first prize in the National Lottery.

2 Describe an event which is **(a)** likely **(b)** impossible.

3 Laura watched the first half of a thriller on TV.
The scale shows what she thought might happen in the second half.
Describe how likely she thought each event would be.

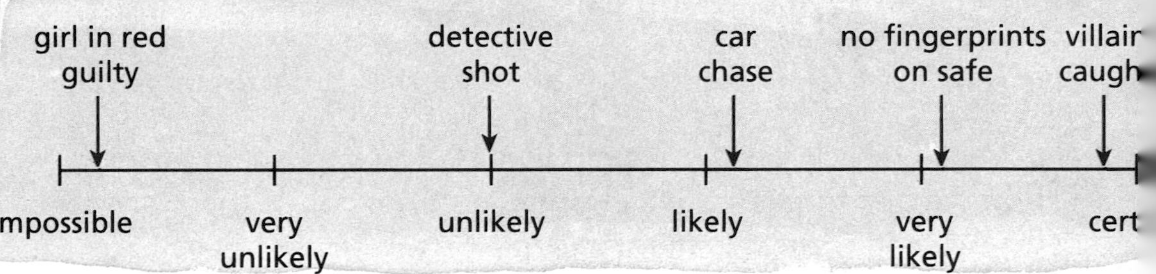

4 **(a)** Draw and label a scale like this.

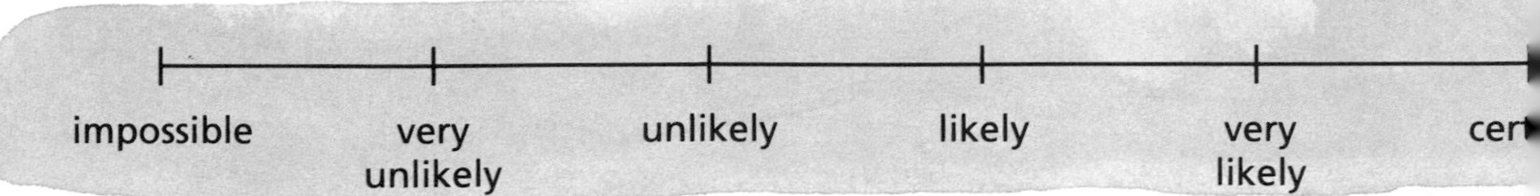

(b) Draw arrows on your scale to show how likely **you think** these events are **for you** tomorrow.

- see friends
- go round the world
- get your hair cut
- travel by bus
- use a computer
- watch some TV.

(c) Discuss and explain your answers.

1 Laura and Jamie play games with **one** dice.
Is each game fair or unfair? Explain.

	Laura wins if dice shows	Jamie wins if dice shows
Game A	1 or 2	3, 4, 5 or 6
Game B	an **even** number	an **odd** number
Game C	a factor of 6	a number **not** a factor of 6

2 **Play the Planets Game several times.** Record where you finish each time.

- Put 1 red and 4 yellow cubes in a bag.
- Put a counter on the Start.
- Shake the bag. Without looking, pick one cube. Move the counter along a path of the same colour as the cube.
- Do **not** put the cube back in the bag. Pick and move once more.

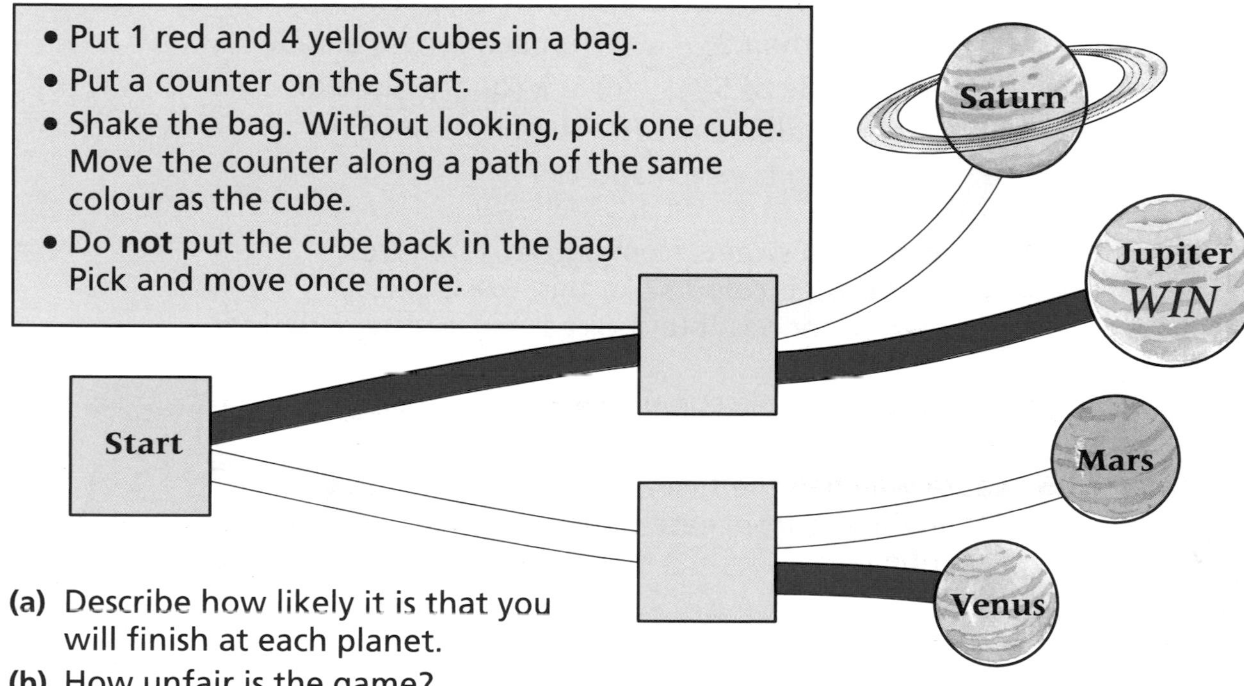

(a) Describe how likely it is that you will finish at each planet.

(b) How unfair is the game? How would you improve it?

Problem solving

3 The rules for this Prize Draw are:
- scratch **one circle only in each row** to reveal two numbers
- multiply the numbers together
- an **odd number** product wins.

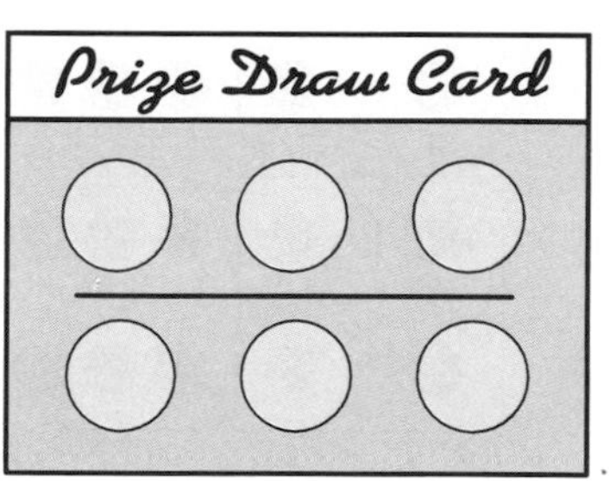

Investigate how likely you are to win if these are the numbers under the circles:

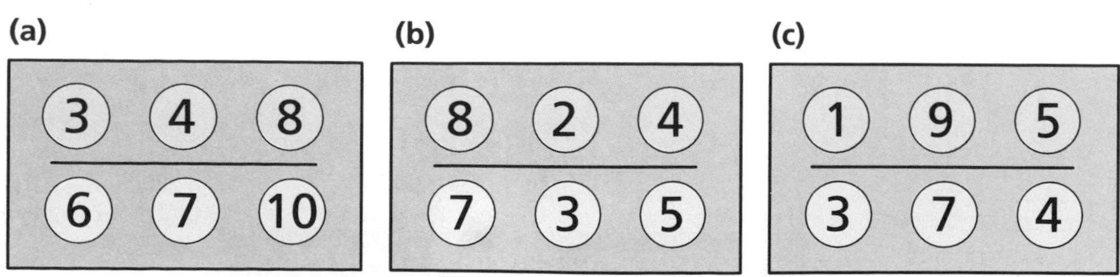

125 Choices

Handling data: probability

1 List **all** the numbers this spinner can show if it lands on

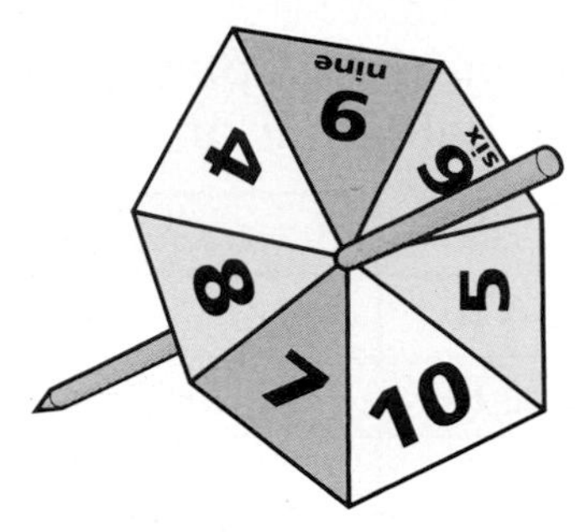

(a) an odd number
(b) a number less than 8
(c) a multiple of 3
(d) a square number
(e) a factor of 30.

2 One ticket is picked from a hundred raffle tickets, numbered 1 to 100. List **all** the numbers which can win if the winning number

(a) is greater than 95 **(b)** is between 40 and 50
(c) is a multiple of 5 **(d)** is a square number
(e) has a tens digit 2 greater than its units digit
(f) has two digits which add to 7.

3 Nick picks two sweets from bag A.
He records their colours like this ⟶ 2 yellow
The only other possible choice is ⟶ 1 blue, 1 yellow

List **all** the possible colour choices if Nick picks
(a) two sweets from bag B
(b) one sweet from each bag.

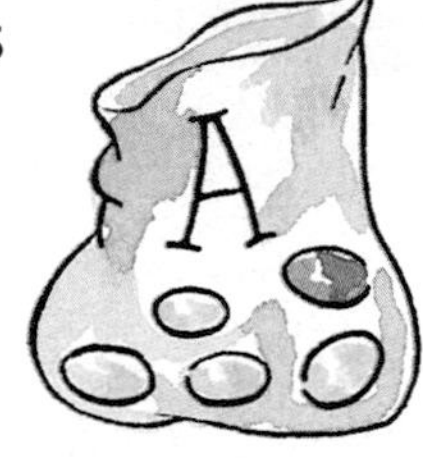

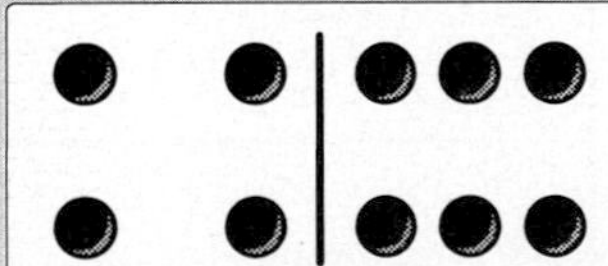

The total number of spots on this domino is 10.

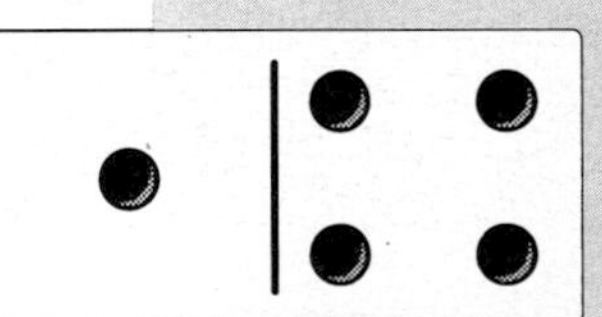

The total number of spots on these **two** dominoes is 15.

4 Find **all** the possible totals for the dominoes below when **one or two or three** of them are chosen at a time.

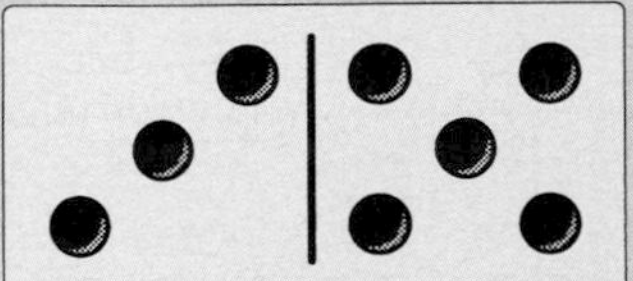

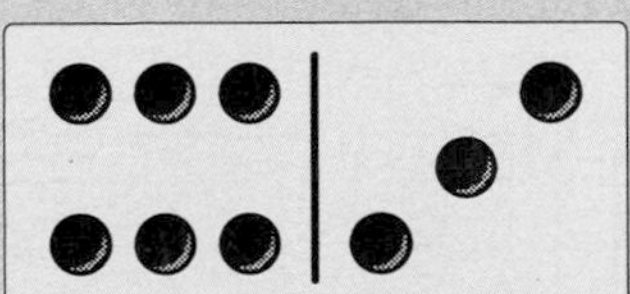

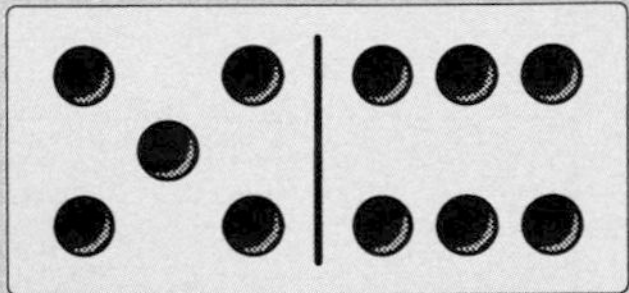

Ask your teacher what to do next